DOING THINGS TOGETHER

DOING THINGS TOGETHER: SELECTED PAPERS

Howard S. Becker

Northwestern University Press
Evanston, Illinois

Published by Northwestern University Press
Evanston Illinois 60201
Printed in the United States of America

Library of Congress Cataloging-in-Publication Data

Becker, Howard Saul, 1928–
  Doing things together.

  Bibliography: p.
  Includes index.
  1. Sociology. 2. Social groups. 3. Social
interaction. I. Title.
HM51.B387 1986   301   86-2575
ISBN 0-8101-0723-6
ISBN 0-8101-0724-4 (pbk.)

Contents

List of Illustrations

Preface

This volume reprints most of what I have written since about 1970, when an earlier collection (*Sociological Work* [Transaction, Inc.]) appeared. I have resisted the temptation to rewrite these pieces to take account of things I have learned since, and have largely left them as they originally appeared, except for minor editorial matters. The introduction tries to make clear the connectedness and underlying coherence of what may look to be a dismayingly varied body of stuff. I hope it succeeds.

In addition to the many debts acknowledged in the notes to the specific essays, I'd like to thank some other people in a more general way. Nathan Lyons, Director of the Visual Studies Workshop, has continually encouraged my interest in photography by listening to me seriously and letting me teach from time to time in his institution. Gerald Graff, Co-Director of the Northwestern University Press, saw a unity in these essays before I did and encouraged me to make them into a book. He also nagged me until the little four-page preface I thought sufficient turned into the present introduction, and I'm glad he did. Finally, my colleagues at Northwestern University, especially those in the Sociology Department but also others throughout the university, have nourished the scattered interests reflected in the table of contents.

Most of these essays first appeared in somewhat different form in the following journals and books and are reprinted here with the permission of the original publishers:

"Culture: A Sociological View," reprinted from *Yale Review* (© Yale University) 71 (Summer 1982): 513–28, with their permission.

"Dialogue with Howard S. Becker," reprinted from *Issues in Criminology* 5 (Summer 1970): 159–79, with their permission and the permission of Julius Debro.

"Consciousness, Power and Drug Effects," published by permission of Transaction, Inc. from *Society* 10 (May–June 1973): 67–76, copyright © 1973 by Transaction, Inc.

INTRODUCTION

Louis Wirth used to tell my cohort of graduate students at the University of Chicago that sociology studied what was true by virtue of the fact that people everywhere lived in groups. That definition seemed trivial and still would, if its implications were not so persistently ignored. We soon learned that it was not trivial because, taken seriously, it meant that you could not take seriously a lot of other commonly accepted ideas. Seeing things as the product of people doing things together makes a lot of other views less plausible and less interesting.

In the 1980s people often use commonsense sociological explanations for things, explaining many things by their embeddedness in groups of people acting together. We understand drug use as a product of a "subculture," worry about the "bureaucratization" of organizations and the "gentrification" of urban neighborhoods, and see the workings of "systems" everywhere from the ecosystem to the family. The understanding of phenomena in the context of relations between people and groups which Wirth recommended has not replaced the psychological explanations so prevalent when he was talking to us. We still want to know "why he did it" and still look for explanations of behavior in internalized values or inner compulsions. But we simultaneously use explanations based in society.

The papers in this book were written over the last fifteen years and have not been collected before. Prepared for special occasions, they deal with a variety of topics, but share a common point of view. They consistently, even single-mindedly, deal with their subjects by seeing them as part of what groups of people are doing together. Applying any such point of view consistently leads you to unexpected conclusions, because even people who think they accept it typically make all sorts of exceptions. "Of course what people do is conditioned by their participation in social groups, but you don't really mean to apply that idea to great works of art, do you?" Or "Naturally people act in ways suggested to them by cultural understandings they pick up in the course of social interaction, but surely you don't mean to explain drug-induced hallucinations that way?"

Why not? I'm prepared to give up even my most cherished ideas if someone shows me I'm wrong, but social science has never worked that way. My graduate-school mentors reminded us that not even the most foolish ideas about society had ever been disproved but, rather, had just fallen out of fashion and been forgotten. (Never having been disproved, they can return, the way biological explanations of social behavior have recently come back into vogue, with no more warrant than they ever had.) So no one has proved to me that I can't explain everything by an appeal to its place in social organization.

Not being wrong is not the same thing as being right. But since, despite the social science talk of "crucial tests of theories," we don't prove things right or wrong, the real test has always been how useful or interesting that way of looking at things is to an audience. If you look at things from a sociological perspective, what can you see that used to be invisible? What questions can you answer that previously had to be ignored? What operations can you undertake with a clearer conscience?

Does that mean (this view has become quite fashionable) that you can never tell if a statement is right or wrong, that all such judgments are merely subjective or determined by group interest? Some versions of phenomenological sociology (the ones that preface every noun with the "The Social Construction of . . . ") seem to suggest that there is no reality, only interpretations, whose only warrant is that a lot of people accept them. In such a situation no one could ever be wrong; at worst they would simply have failed to persuade others that they were right. In such a situation there could be no science or scholarship, no logical proof or empirical confirmation of ideas and propositions.

Witchcraft, studied by many anthropologists and historians, provides a nice example of these problems. Do witches exist just because whole societies accept that belief and act on it? Can't we prove what we all know, that witches are not "really real"? If we can't even falsify propositions any "reasonable" member of our society knows are blatantly false, how can we ever know if anything is true or right or correct? But, in fact, both social scientists and lay people frequently prove themselves and each other wrong. They also know that they are sometimes right, or at least righter than some other people or than they were at some other time.

Philosophers of science may not find the way we prove our rightness systematically defensible, nor will those who think the mechanical application of scientific methods can replace human judgment be satisfied. The influences of culture and power may make what we find out one-sided and incomplete, even biased. But we still think we know something. Are the phenomenologists wrong? Isn't reality socially constructed?

The papers in this collection don't so much argue as exemplify a position that accepts what seems to be a contradiction: that reality is socially constructed but that knowledge, while thus relative, is not wholly up for grabs. I'll oversimplify considerably and refer readers to the papers themselves for the details.

Briefly, yes, knowledge *is* relative and depends on consensus to exist. It *is* what I can get other people to accept. It *does* reflect my interests, prejudices, and biases. But it does those regrettable things mainly at certain stages of the game of acquiring knowledge. When I ask the questions whose answers will constitute my knowledge, I don't ask all the questions I might about all possible objects of inquiry. I take some things as worthy of or suitable for investigation and ignore others. The basis of that selection can never be justified logically or scientifically, only by the common practice of those who make such inquiries. Similarly, we can agree, through our common practice, on how to find an answer and on what constitutes an answer good enough for our purposes, whatever those might be.

Once we have chosen the questions to be asked and the ways of getting an answer, it is not so hard to get reasonable people to agree on when an answer is right or not. The analogy to a game, so beloved by philosophers, may be useful here. We can play chess with more or less than the standard sixteen pieces per side. We can imagine that the board is cylindrical, rather than flat, so that a piece can move off the right-hand edge of the board and end up on the left-hand edge. The rules of football, basketball, and baseball have in fact changed many times, and the variations in chess I mentioned are just a few of the hundreds that players have experimented with. Under any set of rules, players can agree on whether a move or play is legal, whether it counts toward a score, and who won. In the same way, having agreed on the rules of evaluating knowledge, we can agree reliably, in a way as near to "objective" as makes no difference for practical purposes, whether we have a valid experimental result or a reasonable interpretation of a literary text, a convincing anthropological description of a society or of a set of survey results. We can't find witches with the rules most of us now live with because our procedures don't allow for the existence of witches at all. But if we lived in the Zapotec society Henry Selby (1976) described, we would know that the disease we had had been caused by a witch, since our culture would allow no other explanation for illness, and we would, further, have ways any reasonable member of our society would accept for finding out which witch was responsible.

That doesn't mean that we can't decide between our way and the Zapotec way of knowing and that reality is therefore up for grabs. But it does mean that we choose and justify our ways of finding things out and proving them to each other in the context of all the other actions we undertake as members of our society. Acting together in that capacity, not as Zapotecs, we can agree that witches don't cause disease, germs do, and can produce convincing arguments for other members of our society who want to believe otherwise. But we won't convince a Zapotec, who lives and acts with people for whom the witch explanation of disease makes sense as the germ explanation does for us. When we begin to participate with Zapotecs in some sort of joint activity (building a new water-supply system, perhaps), we may convince them to accept our theory, but their acceptance probably won't be based on logic, since our medical theories have enough exceptions and leave enough unexplained to give a skeptic plenty of room.

The anthropologist Lloyd Warner used to tell of visiting a tribe of Australian aborigines who, the literature alleged, did not understand the physiological basis of paternity. They believed that when a woman dreamed about the clan spirit-well, where the babies waited for such dreams to take place, a baby went into her stomach. When Warner finally asked them directly if the fact that a man and woman had intercourse didn't have something to do with it, they looked at him as though he were an idiot and said that, of course, that was what made the baby but didn't he realize that men and women did *that* all the time but women only got pregnant once in a while?

Those are epistemological problems of the ultimate justification of knowledge. I'm more concerned with practical epistemology, which doesn't involve such radical differences of interpretation as separate us from Zapotecs. Some practical difficulties arise because participants in a situation don't agree on what constitute the rules of finding out who is a witch or, to get closer to home, who is mentally ill. But the bigger disagreements come about because people ask different questions about different aspects of reality, thinking that they have asked the same questions about the same things. When the results, inevitably, disagree, it may look like no knowledge is possible, but it should be no surprise that different questions have different answers.

This analysis provides the basis for a critical, though relativistic, approach to knowledge and methods of getting it. We can improve our knowledge and get more people to accept it by broadening the range of what we ask about and of the kinds of acceptable answers. We can apply available methods evenhandedly and systematically, allowing them to achieve the limited victories they are capable of. We can criticize allegedly true statements, even find them wrong, judging them by the rules on whose basis they were produced or in some slightly larger terms that clearly apply. (I've recently learned that a lot of people outside sociology share, in one way or another, the position I've taken here. For example, Richard Rorty [1979 and 1982] has explored it philosophically, in a position that has come to be known as the "new pragmatism.")

So the real problems are those of asking the right questions and of actually following the systematic procedures for finding correct answers we claim to be using. Power, culture, and the rest blind us to important features of the social world by pushing us to ask one-sided questions, to ignore what our methods and theories would tell us if we took them seriously. Specifically, students of society (sociologists and others) ask questions that powerful or highly placed or institutionally responsible people want answers to or, more generally, questions that assume what any reasonable person would assume. That usually means that we accept, implicitly or openly, the way people who are in a position to find fault conventionally, and on the basis of common sense, assign blame for conditions they don't like, for phenomena they define as "problems," often as "social problems." When students don't learn, we social scientists usually accept the view of teachers and ask what's wrong with the students, not what's wrong with teachers. We investigate the psychological or social problems of students, not those of teachers, and we do not look into the relations between teachers and students in which students' failures to learn arise. We observe in a way that leaves teachers out and so can't find out that students don't learn because no one teaches them or because teachers and schools reward them for not learning. Since most scholars are teachers, the example reminds us that we ourselves are not immune to taking offense when our own commonsense understandings are so challenged.

It's not that incomplete studies get "wrong" answers. Rather, they, and the people who do them, don't ask the right questions. They leave out the features of group life whose importance their own theories and methods insist on. They ignore variables, interactions, and social contexts that affect the relationships they want to explain. Since those researchers in fact accept, as I do, the importance of everything they leave out, they provide a philosophical basis for a relativist like me to criticize them. We need not argue the incommensurability of our paradigms to explain why our answers disagree. Given agreement on a perspective, we can argue about whether a study or argument lets the phenomena that perspective makes important show their importance empirically. Whether students cause their own failures cannot be discussed empirically unless we also examine such possible, even likely, causes as the way they were taught. An evenhanded, skeptical social science asks about and observes everybody.

The chief reason we ignore our own rules and don't do what our theories and methods suggest we ought to is that, after all, we do participate in our own society and, being reasonable people, mostly accept the version of common sense everyone else does. We may be skeptical about this or that, but we are not the complete Humean skeptics about everything good sociologists ought to be. Accepting our own culture leads us to accept ideas and assumptions rooted in the operation of powerful institutions, as though they were as self-evident as the fictional nature of witches. But applying methods evenhandedly, being widely skeptical—not believing descriptions or analyses of social facts just because they come from highly placed, knowledgeable people—leads us to ask more kinds of questions about more of the phenomena of group life than we otherwise would. Asking more, we learn more, and our chance of not being wrong surely goes up. I discussed this point in the interview of 1970 reprinted here, and many of the papers show what it leads to in such areas as education, drugs, the arts, and social science itself.

So the perspective I have taken in these papers leads a confirmed relativist like me, sometimes unexpectedly, to serious criticism of ideas sanctioned by major social institutions. Institutions and organizations—schools, professions, scientific, artistic, and scholarly disciplines—tell stories about what they do and how it turns out. They tell those stories to get support, financial and otherwise, to find allies (in Bruno Latour's [1984] phrase); to buck themselves up when things are tough; to persuade people to cooperate with them in enterprises that need a little help; to make a little sense of the world. The stories never ask all the questions and therefore never contain all the reality, and what has been left out pops up, sometimes unexpectedly, always inconveniently. But well-established organizations save face, with the collaboration of others, just as Erving Goffman (1952) described individuals doing. Sociology, done well, thus inevitably goes around describing naked emperors (on the left and right impartially), as Irving Louis Horowitz and I argue in the paper on radical politics and good sociology.

Some of these papers apply the idea that you can explain anything people do, including the methods of social research themselves, as a consequence of group life. Social scientists tell their own stories, the chief of which is foreshadowed in the title of their discipline, namely, that what they (I include myself) do is *science*. I suppose it is, if you don't insist on a strict definition. But making the claim leaves you open to being shown up as a fraud judged by a stricter definition, the kind which invokes physics as its embodiment. Until the late 1970s few people studied what scientists actually did. Although philosophers of science sometimes described their analyses of scientific practice as non-prescriptive, as simply straightening up and making more logical scientists' routine operations, they invariably operated as moral entrepreneurs dedicated to rooting out bad practice. The papers in this book dealing with social-science practice try not to do that, but rather really to see what people have been doing, how it works, and in what ways the results have turned out to be persuasive. They do occasionally get a little prescriptive, mainly by suggesting how we might ask more questions, accept a broader range of answers, and use available methods as they are meant to be used, thus getting the good that is claimed for them.

I have pushed that approach farther than most would by including genres and media ordinarily thought artistic as potential social science methods. The general justification for doing that is contained in "Telling about Society," which reports on some work, done with a number of colleagues, designed to look comparatively at ways of representing knowledge about society. I am especially interested in photography, as teacher, writer, and practitioner, and that is reflected in the several papers devoted to picture making. I think photographers (like other artists) know some tricks social scientists could make use of just as social scientists know some answers to questions that bother photographers. That view bothers photographers who believe the story that photography is art (and *only* art) just as it bothers social scientists who think that because we have always gotten along with words and numbers we needn't add anything else now. Artists do social investigation too, sometimes in inventive ways social scientists could learn from, as John Walton and I argue in our analysis of Hans Haacke's work.

Much of what I have written may be of interest to a wider audience than it would have been twenty years ago. Many new approaches in the humanistic disciplines share the interests of much of social science. Analyzing texts, when the text is taken (as it now often is) to be any common social practice, may be called literary theory, but it is getting to look more and more like sociology or anthropology. Clifford Geertz (1983) has referred to the "blurred genres" that result from this and from the increasing use of humanistic frameworks (generally trendy ones like structuralism or deconstructionism) by some social scientists. Several of these papers go a little way toward blurring the lines some more, which seems to be a good thing to do.

PART 1

SOCIAL ORGANIZATION

1

CULTURE:
A Sociological View

I was for some years what is called a Saturday night musician, making myself available to whoever called and hired me to play for dances and parties in groups of varying sizes, playing everything from polkas through mambos, jazz, and imitations of Wayne King. Whoever called would tell me where the job was, what time it began, and usually would tell me to wear a dark suit and a bow tie, thus ensuring that the collection of strangers he was hiring would at least look like a band because they would all be dressed more or less alike. When we arrived at work we would introduce ourselves— the chances were, in a city the size of Chicago (where I did much of my playing), that we were in fact strangers—and see whom we knew in common and whether our paths had ever crossed before. The drummer would assemble his drums, the others would put together their instruments and tune up, and when it was time to start the leader would announce the name of a song and a key— "Exactly Like You" in B-flat, for instance—and we would begin to play. We not only began at the same time, but also played background figures that fit the melody someone else was playing and, perhaps most miraculously, ended together. No one in the audience ever guessed that we had never met until twenty minutes earlier. And we kept that up all night, as though we had rehearsed often and played together for years. In a place like Chicago, that scene might be repeated hundreds of times during a weekend.

What I have just described embodies the phenomenon that sociologists have made the core problem of their discipline. The social sciences are such a contentious bunch of disciplines that it makes trouble to say what I think is true, that they all in fact concern themselves with one or another version of this issue—the problem of collective action, of how people manage to act together. I will not attempt a rigorous definition of collective action here, but the story of the Saturday night musicians can serve as an example of it. The example might have concerned a larger group—the employees of a factory who turn out several hundred automobiles in the course of a day, say. Or it might have been about so small a group as a family. It needn't have dealt with a casual collection of strangers, though the ability of strangers to perform together that way makes clear the nature of the problem. How do they do it? How do people act together so as to get anything done without a great deal of trouble, without missteps and conflict?

We can approach the meaning of a concept by seeing how it is used, what work it is called on to do. Sociologists use the concept of *culture* as one of a family of explanations for the phenomenon of concerted activity; I will consider some of the others below, in order to differentiate culture from them. Robert Redfield defined culture as "conventional understandings made manifest in act and artifact"(1941:132). The notion is that the people involved have a similar idea of things, understand them in the same way, as having the same character and the same potential, capable of being dealt with in the same way; they also know that this idea is shared, that the people they are dealing with know, just as they do, what these things are and how they can be used. Because all of them have roughly the same idea, they can all act in ways that are roughly the same, and their activities will, as a result, mesh and be coordinated. Thus, because all those musicians understood what a Saturday night job at a country club consisted of and acted accordingly, because they all knew the melody and harmony of "Exactly Like You" and hundreds of similar songs, because they knew that the others knew this as they knew it, they could play that job successfully. The concept of culture, in short, has its use for sociologists as an explanation of those musicians and all the other forms of concerted action for which they stand.

I said that culture was not the only way sociologists explain concerted action. It often happens, for example, even in the most stable groups and traditional situations, that things happen which are not fully or even partly covered by already shared understandings. That may be because the situation is unprecedented—a disaster of a kind that has never occurred before—or because the people in the group come from such a variety of backgrounds that, though they all have some idea about the matter at hand and all speak a common language, they do not share understandings. That can easily happen in stratified societies, in ethnically differentiated societies, in situations where different occupational groups meet. Of course, people in such situations will presumably share some understandings which will form the basis of discussion and mediation as they work out what to do. If the Saturday night musicians had not shared as much knowledge as they did, they would have sat down to discuss what kind of music they would play, sketched out parts, and so on. They would have had to negotiate, a process I will consider more fully below.

Culture, however, explains how people act in concert when they *do* share understandings. It is thus a consequence (in this kind of sociological thinking) of the existence of a group of acting people. It has its meaning as one of the resources people draw on in order to coordinate their activities. In this it differs from most anthropological thinking in which the order of importance is reversed, culture leading a kind of independent existence as a system of patterns that makes the existence of larger groups possible.

Most conceptions of culture include a great deal more than the spare definition I offered above. But I think, for reasons made clear later, that it is better to begin with a minimal definition and then to add other conditions when that is helpful.

Many people would insist that, if we are to call something culture, it must be traditional, of long standing, passed on from generation to generation. That would certainly make the concept unavailable as an explanation of the Saturday night musician. While we might conceivably say that these men were engaging in a traditional cultural activity, since a tradition of musicians playing for the entertainment of others goes back centuries and the American tradition of professional musicians playing for dances and parties is decades old, they were not doing it the way people who play for peasant parties in Greece or Mexico do, playing songs their grandparents played, perhaps on the same instruments. No, they were playing songs no more than twenty or thirty years old, songs their grandfathers never knew; in fact, few of their grandfathers had been musicians in whatever countries they came from, and, by becoming musicians themselves, these men were doing something untraditional in their families (and usually something not desired by their families either). They, of course, had learned to do many of the things they were doing from others who were slightly older, as I had learned many of the tricks of being a weekend musician when I was fifteen from people as old as seventeen or eighteen, who had in turn learned them from still older people. But, still, they did not know how to do what they were doing because it was traditional.

Many other people would insist that, if we are to call something culture, it must be part of a larger *system,* in which the various parts not only cohere in the sense of being noncontradictory, but, more than that, harmonize in the sense of being different versions of the same underlying themes. Such people would not use the term "culture" to describe the patterns of cooperation of the weekend musicians unless those patterns were also reflected in the music they played, the clothing they wore, the way they spent their leisure time, and so on. But none of that was true because they were not just musicians, and much of what they did reflected understandings they had acquired by participating in other social arenas in which the musicians' culture was irrelevant and vice versa. Nor, in any event, did they play what they might have played if they had been free to express their cultural understandings, for what they played was largely what they were paid to play (polkas on Friday, mambos on Saturday).

And many people would insist that my example is misleading to begin with, for the kinds of coherence that constitute "real" culture occur only at the level of the whole society. But if we connect culture to activities people carry on with one another, then we have to ask what all the members of a whole society do, or what they all do together, that requires them to share these general understandings. There are such things, but I think they tend to be rather banal and not at the level usually meant in discussions of general cultural themes. Thus, we all use the money of our society and know how many of the smaller units make one of the larger ones. Less trivially, we probably share understandings about how to behave in public, the things Edward T. Hall and Erving Goffman (1971) have written about—how close to stand to someone when we talk or how much space someone is entitled to in a public place, for example. But, even if for the sake of the argument we imagine that some substantial body of such materials exists, as it might in a relatively undifferentiated or rural society, that would not help us understand how the weekend musicians did their trick, and we would need some other term for what they were able to do and the web of shared understandings they used to do it.

Other people have other requirements for what can be called culture, all of which can be subjected to similar criticisms. Some think that culture, to be "really" culture, must be built in some deep way into the personalities of the people who carry it; others require that culture consist of "basic values," whatever might be meant by that. In neither case would the activities of the Saturday night musicians qualify as culture, however, if those definitional requirements were observed.

Normally, of course, we can define terms any way we want, but in the case of culture, several things seem to limit our freedom. The two most important are the quasi ownership of the term by anthropologists and the ambiguity of the word with respect to the problem of "high culture," to which I will return later. Anthropologists, and most other people, regard culture as anthropology's key concept and assume that the discipline is therefore entitled to make the definition. But anthropologists do not agree on a definition of culture; indeed, they differ spectacularly among themselves, as a famous compendium by Alfred Kroeber and Clyde Kluckhohn (1963) demonstrates. That did not dissuade Kroeber and Talcott Parsons (1958) from signing a jurisdictional agreement (like those by which the building trades decide how much of the work carpenters can do and where electricians must take over) giving "culture" to anthropology and "society" to sociology. But the social sciences, unlike the building trades, have not respected the deal their leaders made.

Which of these additional criteria, if any, should be incorporated into the definition of culture I have already given? Do we need any of them? Do we lose anything by using the most minimal definition of culture, as the shared understandings that people use to coordinate their activities? I think not. We have an inclusive term which describes not only the Saturday night musicians and the way they accomplish their feat of coordination, but all the other combinations of attributes that turn up in real life, raising questions about when they go together and when they do not.

Much depends on what kind of archetypal case you want the definition to cover, since a small Stone Age tribe living at the headwaters of the Amazon, which has never been in contact with European civilization, is obviously quite different from such typical products of twentieth-century urban America as the weekend musicians. The kinds of collective action required in the two situations differ enormously, and, consequently, the kinds of shared understandings participants can rely on vary concomitantly. Many anthropologists have a kind of temperamental preference for the simplicity, order, and predictability of less complicated societies, in which everyone knows what everyone else is supposed to do, and in which there is a "design for living." If you share that preference, then you can turn culture into an honorific term by denying it to those social arrangements which do not "deserve" it, thereby making a disguised moral judgment about those ways of life. But that leaves a good part of modern life, not just the Saturday night musicians, out of the cultural sphere altogether.

The Cultural Process

How does culture—shared understanding—help people to act collectively? People have ideas about how a certain kind of activity might be carried on. They believe others share these ideas and will act on them if they understand the situation in the same way. They believe further that the people they are interacting with believe that they share these ideas too, so everyone thinks that everyone else has the same idea about how to do things. Given such circumstances, if everyone does what seems appropriate, action will be sufficiently coordinated for practical purposes. Whatever was under way will get done—the meal served, the child dealt with, the job finished, all well enough so that life can proceed.

The cultural process, then, consists of people doing something in line with their understanding of what one might best do under the given circumstances. Others, recognizing what was done as appropriate, will then consult their notions of what might be done and do something that seems right to them, to which others in return will respond similarly, and so on. If everyone has the same general ideas in mind, and does something congruent with that image or collection of ideas, then what people do will fit together. If we all know the melody and harmony of "Exactly Like You," and improvise accordingly, whatever comes out will sound reasonable to the players and listeners, and a group of perfect strangers will sound like they know what they are doing.

Consider another common situation. A man and woman meet and find each other interesting. At some stage of their relationship, they may consider any of a variety of ways of organizing their joint activities. Early on, one or the other might propose that they "have a date." Later, one or the other might, subtly or forthrightly, suggest that they spend the night together. Still later, they might try "living together." Finally, they might decide to "get married." They might skip some of these stages and they might not follow that progression, which in contemporary America is a progression of increasingly formal commitment. In other societies and at other times, of course, the stages and the relationships would differ. But, whatever their variety, insofar as there are names for those relationships and stages, and insofar as most or all of the people in a society know those names and have an idea of what they imply as far as continuing patterns of joint activity are concerned, then the man and woman involved will be able to organize what they do by referring to those guideposts. When one or the other suggests one of these possibilities, the partner will know, more or less, what is being suggested without requiring that every item be spelled out in detail, and the pair can then organize their daily lives, more or less, around the patterns suggested by these cultural images.

What they do from day to day will of course not be completely covered by the details of that imagery, although they will be able to decide many details by consulting it together and adapting what it suggests to the problem at hand. None of these images, for instance, really establishes who takes the garbage out or what the details of their sexual activity may be, but the images do, in general, suggest the kind of commitments and obligations involved on both sides in a wide range of practical matters.

That is not the end of the matter, though. Consider a likely contemporary complication: the woman, divorced, has small children who live with her. In this case, the couple's freedom of action is constrained, and no cultural model suggests what they ought to do about the resulting difficulties. The models for pairing and for rearing children suggest incompatible solutions, and the partners have to invent something. They have to improvise.

This raises a major problem in the theory of culture I am propounding. Where does culture come from? The typical cultural explanation of behavior takes the culture as given, as preexisting the particular encounter in which it comes into play. That makes sense. Most of the cultural understandings we use to organize our daily behavior are there before we get there, and we do not propose to change them or negotiate their details with the people we encounter. We do not propose a new economic system every time we go to the grocery store. But those understandings and ways of doing things have not always been there. Most of us buy our food in supermarkets today, and that requires a different way of shopping from the corner grocery stores of a generation ago. How did the new culture of supermarkets arise?

One answer is that the new culture was imposed by the inventors of the concept, the owners of the new stores which embodied it.

They created the conditions under which change was more or less inevitable. People might have decided not to shop in supermarkets and chain stores, but changing conditions of urban life caused so many of them to use the new markets that the corner grocery, the butcher shop, the poultry and fish stores disappeared in all but a few areas. Once that happened, supermarkets became the only practical possibility left, and people had to invent new ways of serving themselves.

So, given new conditions, people invent culture. The way they do it was suggested by William Graham Sumner a century ago in *Folkways* (1907). We can paraphrase him this way. A group finds itself sharing a common situation and common problems. Various members of the group experiment with possible solutions to those problems and report their experiences to their fellows. In the course of their collective discussion, the members of the group arrive at a definition of the situation, its problems and possibilities, and develop a consensus as to the most appropriate and efficient ways of behaving. This consensus thenceforth constrains the activities of individual members of the group, who will probably act on it, given the opportunity. In other words, new situations provoke new behavior. But people generally find themselves in company when dealing with these new situations, and since they arrive at their solutions collectively, each assumes that the others share them. The beginnings of a new shared understanding thus come into play quickly and easily.

The ease with which new cultural understandings arise and persist varies. It makes a difference, for one thing, how large a group is involved in making the new understandings. At one extreme, as I have noted, every mating couple, every new family, has to devise its own culture to cover the contingencies of daily interaction. At the other, consider what happens during industrialization when hundreds of thousands—perhaps millions—of people are brought from elsewhere to work in the new factories. They have to come from elsewhere because the area could not support that many people before industrialization. As a result, the newcomers differ in culture from the people already there, and they differ as well in the role they play in the new industries, usually coming in at the bottom. When industrialization takes place on a large scale, not only does a new culture of the workplace have to be devised but also a new culture of the cities in which they all end up living—a new experience for everyone involved.

The range of examples suggests, as I mean it to, that people create culture continuously. Since no two situations are alike, the cultural solutions available to them are only approximate. Even in the simplest societies, no two people learn quite the same cultural material; the chance encounters of daily life provide sufficient variation to ensure that. No set of cultural understandings, then, provides a perfectly applicable solution to any problem people have to solve in the course of their day, and they therefore must remake those solutions, adapt their understandings to the new situation in the light of what is different about it. Even the most conscious and determined effort to keep things as they are would necessarily involve strenuous efforts to remake and reinforce understandings so as to keep them intact in the face of what was changing.

There is an apparent paradox here. On the one hand, culture persists and antedates the participation of particular people in it: indeed, culture can be said to shape the outlooks of people who participate in it. But cultural understandings, on the other hand, have to be reviewed and remade continually, and in the remaking they change.

This is not a true paradox, however: the understandings last *because* they change to deal with new situations. People continually refine them, changing some here and some there but never changing all of them at once. The emphasis on basic values and coherence in the definition of culture arises because of this process. In making the new versions of the old understandings, people naturally rely on what they already have available, so that consciously planned innovations and revolutions seem, in historical perspective, only small variations on what came before.

To summarize, how culture works as a guide in organizing collective action and how it comes into being are really the same process. In both cases, people pay attention to what other people are doing and, in an attempt to mesh what they do with those others, refer to what they know (or think they know) in common. So culture is always being made, changing more or less, acting as a point of reference for people engaged in interaction.

Culture and Cooperation

What difference does it make that people continually make culture in the way I have described? The most important consequence is that they can, as a result, cooperate easily and efficiently in the daily business of life, without necessarily knowing each other very well.

Most occupations, for example, operate on the premise that the people who work in them all know certain procedures and certain ways of thinking about and responding to typical situations and problems, and on the premise that such knowledge will make it possible to assemble them to work on a common project without prior team training. Most professional schools operate on the theory that the education they offer provides a basis for work cooperation among people properly trained anywhere. In fact, people probably learn the culture which makes occupational cooperation possible in the workplace itself. It presents them with problems to solve that are common to people in their line of work, and provides a group of more experienced workers who can suggest solutions. In some occupations, workers change jobs often and move from workplace to workplace often (as do the weekend musicians), and they carry what they have learned elsewhere with them. That makes it easy for them to refine and update their solutions frequently, and thus to develop and maintain an occupational culture. Workers who do not move but spend their work lives in one place may develop a more idiosyncratic work culture, peculiar to that place and its local problems—a culture of IBM or Texas Instruments or (because the process is not limited to large firms) Joe's Diner.

At a different level of cooperative action, Goffman (1971) has described cultural understandings which characterize people's behavior in public. For instance, people obey a norm of "civil inattention," allowing each other a privacy which the material circumstances of, say, waiting for a bus do not provide. Since this kind of privacy is what Americans and many others find necessary before they can feel comfortable and safe in public (Hall [1958] has shown how these rules differ in other cultures), these understandings make it possible for urban Americans to occupy crowded public spaces without making each other uneasy. The point is not trivial, because violations of these rules are at least in part responsible for the currently common fear that some public areas are "not safe," quite apart from whatever assaults have taken place in them. Most people have no personal knowledge of the alleged assaults, but they experience violation of what might be called the "Goffman rules" of public order as the prelude to danger and do not go to places which make them feel that way.

Cultural understandings, if they are to be effective in the organization of public behavior, must be very widely held. That means that people of otherwise varying class, ethnic, and regional cultures must learn them routinely, and must learn them quite young, because even small children can disrupt public order very effectively. That requires, in turn, substantial agreement among people of all segments of the society on how children should be brought up. If no such agreement exists or if some of the people who agree in principle do not manage to teach their children the necessary things, public order breaks down, as it often does.

In another direction, cultural understandings affect and "socialize" the internal experiences people have. By applying understandings they know to be widely accepted to their own perhaps inchoate private experiences, people learn to define those internal experiences in ways which allow them to mesh their activities relevant to those topics with those of others with whom they are involved. Consider the familiar example of falling in love. It is remarkable that one of the experiences we usually consider private and unique—falling in love—actually has the same character for most people who experience it. That is not to say that the experience is superficial, but rather that when people try to understand their emotional responses to others, one available explanation of what they feel is the idea, common in Western culture, of romantic love. They learn that idea from a variety of sources, ranging from the mass media to discussion with their peers, and they learn to see their own experiences as embodiments of it. Because most people within a given culture learn to experience love in the same way from the same sources, two people can become acquainted and successfully fall in love with each other—not an easy trick.

Because shared cultural understandings make it easy to do things in certain ways, moreover, their existence favors those ways of doing things and makes other ways of achieving the same end, which might be just as satisfactory to everyone involved, correspondingly less likely. Random events which might produce innovations desirable to participants occur infrequently. In fact, even when the familiar line of activity is not exactly to anyone's liking, people continue it simply because it is what everyone knows and knows that everyone else knows, and thus is what offers the greatest likelihood of successful collective action. Everyone knows, for instance, that it would be better to standardize the enormous variety of screw

22

threads in this country, or to convert the United States to the metric system. But the old ways are the ones we know, and, of course, in this instance, they are built into tools and machines which would be difficult and costly to change. Many activities exhibit that inertia, and they pose a problem that sociologists have been interested in for many years: which elements of a society or culture are most likely to change? William Fielding Ogburn (1922), for instance, proposed sixty years ago that material culture (screw threads) changed more quickly than social organization, and that the resultant "lag" could be problematic for human society.

A final consequence: the existence of culture makes it possible for people to plan their own lives. We can plan most easily for a known future, in which the major organizational features of society turn out to be what we expected them to be and what we made allowances for in our planning. We need, most importantly, to predict the actions of other people and of the organizations which consist of their collective actions. Culture makes those actions, individual and collective, more predictable than they would otherwise be. People in traditional societies may not obey in every detail the complex marriage rules held out to them, but those rules supply a sufficiently clear guide for men and women to envision more or less accurately when they will marry, what resources will be available to them when they do, and how the course of their married life will proceed.

In modern industrial societies, workers can plan their careers better when they know what kinds of work situations they will find themselves in and what their rights and obligations at various ages and career stages will be. Few people can make those predictions successfully in this country any more, which indicates that cultural understandings do not always last the twenty or thirty years necessary for such predictability to be possible. When that happens, people do not know how to prepare themselves for their work lives and do not receive the benefits of their earlier investments in hard work. People who seemed to be goofing off or acting irrationally, for example, sometimes make windfall profits as the work world comes to need just those combinations of skills and experiences that they acquired while not following a "sensible" career path. As technical and organizational innovations make new skills more desirable, new career lines open up which were not and could not have been predicted ten years earlier. The first generation of computer programmers benefited from that kind of good luck, as did the first generation of drug researchers, among others.

High Culture

In every society, some of the understandings we have been talking about are thought to be more important, more noble, more imbued with the highest aspirations or achievements of that society. For hundreds of years, Western societies have given that kind of privileged position to what some regard as "high culture" and what others regard as "culture" without a qualifying adjective—art, reflective thought, philosophy. These pursuits are generally opposed to more manual occupations and to those connected with industry and commerce, although the growth of science and the commercialization of art in more recent times have created substantial areas of ambiguity. It seems obvious, without Thorstein Veblen to point it out, that these judgments reflect the relative prestige of those segments of society which more often engage in or patronize those pursuits. They are the hobbies, the playthings of political and religious leaders as well as of people of power and privilege in general, and it is a good sociological question whether they receive their *mana* from the power of those interested in them or whether they lend some portion of that *mana* to those supporters.

How do these areas of cultural understanding differ from the more mundane examples I addressed earlier? They have a better reputation, of course, but is the basis for that reputation discernible in them or could any set of concerns and activities achieve that special estate? That is an enormously complicated question which I am not going to answer in a few words. It is enough to ask, from the point of view assumed here, what kinds of activities, pursued by whom, follow from the existence of these understandings. Who can do what together as a result of their existence?

One answer is that, in Western societies originally at least, culturally reputable activities are carried on by specialists who make a profession of them. Those professions gather around them a special world—a network of people who collaborate in the production, distribution, and celebration of "high" culture—and that collaboration is made possible by the kinds of cultural understandings I have been discussing throughout this paper.

In addition, the people who cooperate in these ventures regard the work they do as having special value. "Art" is an honorific category, a word applied to productions that a society decides to treat as especially valuable. A great deal of work that seems to share the observable qualities of what comes to be called high art never earns that distinction, and that suggests that the difference does not lie in the *work* so honored but rather in the process of *honoring*. We can easily observe, furthermore, that the same objects and events earn the label of "art" on some occasions and not others, often migrating back and forth across the dividing line as fashions change. (I have discussed these matters at length in *Art Worlds* [1982].)

High culture, then, consists of work recognized as belonging to an honored category of cultural understandings by the people who have the power to make that determination and to have it accepted by others. We may be able to devise systematic criteria that will identify work of superior quality, but it is unlikely that the work we can distinguish in that way will be the same as the work legitimated as high culture by the institutions that make that decision for any society.

Thinking of high culture this way suggests the leveling impulse contained in most systematic sociological analysis. Basic social processes, such as the development of common ways of looking at things, usually cross the honorific lines drawn in a society. Discussing culture in this fashion may seem awkward or impudent, but the warrant for doing it comes from the increased understanding the procedure gives us of the processes that lie under all our activities, honorable and otherwise.

2

DIALOGUE WITH HOWARD S. BECKER (1970)
An Interview Conducted by Julius Debro

The now defunct School of Criminology of the University of California at Berkeley used to publish a student-edited journal called Issues in Criminology. *It ran a series of interviews with people known in the field of criminology, and included me because I had written* Outsiders, *considered an important statement of the "labeling theory" of deviance. Julius Debro, then a student at the school, interviewed me in my home in San Francisco in the spring of 1970 (I was, during that year, a fellow at the Center for Advanced Studies in Behavioral Science in nearby Palo Alto). When undergraduates who "have to write a term paper" about me write or call for biographical materials (one desperate student simply said "Please send all information!") I send them this. It only gives partial help, since it stops abruptly in 1970. I have amplified and revised many of the ideas contained here in later work and have updated the story somewhat in Becker 1985, pp. 90–107.*

Debro: Dr. Becker, how did you become a sociologist?

Becker: I entered sociology by accident. I was going to the University of Chicago College. You graduated from that college at the end of the second year of conventional college, then you had a bachelor's degree, and if you wanted a master's degree you went three more years. Actually, I was playing the piano; I intended to be a musician. I was quite young and my father thought I should continue school. The question was, what should I study? I thought about going into English literature because I enjoyed reading stories. But that spring I read *Black Metropolis* (Cayton and Drake 1945) and that really turned me on. One of the things that turned me on was the ethnographic detail. If you know that book, you know that it gives you a feel for things in that area which no one person in that area could know. That was one thing. The other was a kind of vision of a comparative science of communities. That idea really came from Lloyd Warner and it turned me on too. I think I probably had it more in mind to be an anthropologist than a sociologist, not that I had made much distinction between the two. So I signed up in sociology, without knowing what I was getting into.

I went through the first year of graduate work in some sort of daze; I guess most people do. At the end of the first year I was required to take a class in advanced field studies with Ernest Burgess. We had a choice of either getting twelve questionnaires filled out for Mr. Burgess's old-age study, or writing a master's thesis. I was working in a tavern on Sixty-third Street that summer playing the piano. I had learned that if you took notes on what you were doing, that was considered fieldwork. So I started keeping a diary, the way I had learned from Everett Hughes, thus avoiding the twelve old-age questionnaires. At the end of the summer I showed Mr. Burgess the field notes. He read them, thought they were very nice, said that I was really in the field of occupations and professions, and advised me to see Mr. Hughes on the fifth floor of the social science building because that was his field. So off I went to the fifth floor to deposit the notes with Mr. Hughes.

Well, Everett read them and when I came back to see him he treated me very royally. It was great. Here I was a first-year student, and ordinarily he wasn't that gracious to beginning students. It turned out that he had had a lot of students who had studied various professions, medicine and law in particular, but he found it very difficult to get people to study lowly kinds of occupations. Here was somebody who was doing it without being urged. He had gone over my notes—there were only about twenty-five pages of field notes for that whole summer and they weren't very good. He had made the most elaborate annotations saying, "Look, this suggests that problem and that suggests this problem, and you ought to explore this." "When people use language like this, it probably means so and so. You ought to find out about that." I guess I didn't expect to be taken so seriously. Besides, what he said was very interesting.

So I started writing my master's thesis on dance musicians. I eventually published pieces of it in the journals (Becker 1951 and 1953a) and later in *Outsiders* (Becker 1963). So there I was. And I liked it. Sociology was fun. I finished my master's degree and got married, and I was going to quit right there . . . time to go out and earn a living like an honest man. This was about 1949. When Everett heard about my plans to quit he asked if I had applied for a fellowship. I said no, because I had just gotten married and I was going to work. He suggested that I apply, so I did and I got one. I figured I might as well go to school. Everett had gotten a bit of research money for a project to study the public schools, and hired me for a dollar an hour to interview Chicago schoolteachers. I started doing that and got into what turned out to be my Ph.D. thesis.

I went through graduate school very rapidly. I attribute that to having been in the music business, in the following way: since I really didn't care about a career in sociology, I wasn't very serious about it. I studied sociology like a hobby, and had very little anxiety. I had plenty of anxieties about playing the piano, because that was serious, that was my life's work. I used to practice a lot and work very hard at it. But I never worried about examinations. Then I became very interested in my Ph.D. thesis. For the first time I became interested in my research as a theoretical problem. The people I studied weren't interesting; schoolteachers aren't really interesting people. But the theoretical problem about different kinds of careers that they exemplified *was* interesting. That was an eye-opener to me; that a piece of research could be interesting even though, superficially, the subject matter wasn't terribly interesting.

I got through school and graduated. There I was, a Ph.D. and playing in joints on Sixty-third Street. The question was, was I going to be the most educated piano player on Sixty-third Street or go to work as a sociologist? I decided to be a sociologist.

I should say something about the University of Chicago. I started in sociology in 1946, graduated in 1951, and stayed on two more years teaching as an instructor; so I was seven years in that department. It was a very exciting place. There were an awful lot of good sociologists in my age group. It was right after World War II and many of the students had been in the army, had come out, and were using the GI Bill. There were about two hundred graduate students in sociology. I can't even begin to tell you all the people who were in my class—Erving Goffman, David Gold, Bill Kornhauser, Eliot Freidson, Jim Short—I could go on half a day naming them. We were all very excited about sociology, and we talked very seriously about it so that there was a lot of education going on among the students themselves. It was a very good faculty, too, some of whom made more of an impression upon me than others.

The man I worked with most closely was Everett Hughes. He taught me many things. Essentially, he taught me how to think sociologically. The anthropologist Lloyd Warner was another big influence on me, as was Herbert Blumer, who taught me my social psychology. When people talk about the "Chicago School" they tend to tie it up with Hughes and Blumer. It's true that they were a very distinctive feature of it. But there were other people there, like Ernest Burgess, William Ogburn, and Phil Hauser, who represented a quantitative side which we *didn't* regard as foreign. We fought about it a lot, but we didn't regard it as foreign—the way people now see that split. They think that if you are a symbolic interactionist, you can't be interested in demography, which is foolish. We were very interested in demography and ecology. Although I didn't propose to do that kind of work, I took it for granted that that kind of work was going to get done and that I would have it available to me as a resource. If I was going to study something in the city of Chicago, I knew that I could turn to the Local Community Fact Book Louis Wirth had put together, which had all kinds of statistics on the local areas of Chicago. I'll never forget that when I first came out to San Francisco I was surprised that there wasn't such a book for the Bay Area. I just took it for granted there would be, and I found that no one had done what I regard as basic demographic and ecological work on this city. As far as I know, it still hasn't been done. I was terribly shocked.

That interest in ecology goes back to a style of sociology I associate with the name of Robert E. Park, who isn't much in favor these days, but who ought to be because he practically founded American sociology. In Park's view, society had two sides: the symbolic kind of interaction; and nonsymbolic interaction (which included ecology), which he thought equally important. What you had was not either/or, but both of those. We grew up with that idea. What we *didn't* grow up with was any notion of what is now spoken of as the structural or functionalist approach, the kind of theory associated with Talcott Parsons. I don't know if that style can be defined in one sentence, but certainly one distinguishing feature of it is the notion of a system in equilibrium or balance, that if there is a strain in society, it will somehow right itself, and get the unbalanced balanced. We didn't have any notion that society had to do certain things so that it would go on. It was perfectly conceivable that it wouldn't go on or wouldn't go on the way it had been, that it could change in some drastic way. Things that seemed to be such terrible problems from certain theoretical points of view—like how does social change occur—didn't seem to us to be terrible theoretical problems. It was obvious that society was always changing. If anything had to be accounted for, it was stability. If anything stayed the same for any length of time, that was unusual. Although we fought a lot with one another, without quite knowing it we all shared that basic point of view, and became more aware of it as we got out in the world and met people from Columbia, Harvard, and other places who didn't seem to understand things the right way. They were talking about equilibrium and stuff like that.

When I was finishing my dissertation Everett Hughes said to me, "You know, you ought to write an article." I said, "O.K., what should I write it about?" He said, "Take something from your master's thesis." I wrote an article about musicians and their audiences, and that was published in the *American Journal of Sociology* (Becker 1951) just about the same time I got my Ph.D. I learned an important lesson from Hughes: your work isn't finished until you've had it published. Until you have put your work in such shape that you are willing to let your scientific peers look at it, you aren't finished. They need to have your research, and you aren't doing it just for yourself, unless you're on some sort of ego trip. Your work is part of the scientific enterprise. A lot of people have negative feelings about publishing. They can't conceive good reasons for doing it and think it must be to get ahead or to gain prestige. That always amused me because I published a fair amount when I first got out of school and never seemed to be getting anywhere. There must be something wrong with that theory.

I graduated and stayed on for two years at the University of Chicago as a part-time instructor. I taught social science in the undergraduate college and a few courses in the graduate department. Simultaneously, I went to work for the Institute for Juvenile Research and did the marijuana study that is reported in *Outsiders* (Becker 1963:41–78). You see, I had trouble getting a teaching job. I was twenty-three years old when I got my Ph.D., and people could hire a grown-up man for the same price. They didn't want some kid. I really had a difficult time, because jobs were quite tight. So I hung around Chicago where I knew I could make a living playing the piano.

I started the marijuana study more or less as a technical experiment. I had read Alfred Lindesmith's book *Opiate Addiction* (1948), in which he used the method of analytic induction. It really struck my fancy and I wanted to try it. I started the study in '51 and it was done in '53, and it was done because of Lindesmith's book.

It was years before I began to see what the marijuana study was really about; I didn't see it at the time. What it was really about was the way social interaction affected the interpretation of individual experiences. How do you know what you feel like? That's what it's all about. I didn't quite see it then, and the papers that I published suffer because they waste time arguing with people who think individual experience depends on personality. But that wasn't what it was all about. I didn't prove that it wasn't personality, though I tried. That's not even an important issue now, but I thought it was then.

After I did the marijuana research I got a postdoctoral fellowship for personality research at the University of Illinois. I was at Illinois for two years. There were five or six postdoctoral fellows in the program. It was a very interesting time for me. Some very good psychologists were involved in that program, as well as some very good sociologists. The person I worked with most closely was Jim Carper, who I did some research with. He was a psychologist who had worked with rats and was tired of doing that. He wanted to work with people. He was also interested in social problems of various kinds and had been involved in various political movements; he was a conscientious objector and had a much more radical way of looking at society than I did. He wanted to study people, so we did a study of how people got attached to their occupations. We interviewed graduate students in various fields and wrote it up (Becker and Carper 1956a, 1956b, and 1957). Eliot Freidson, another sociologist who studied occupations, was there, and some other good psychologists like Sam Messick and Joel Davitz. We had a lot of fun. That was 1953–55.

In 1955 I was looking for a job again. By that time I wasn't even sure I wanted to teach. When I graduated from school in 1951, everyone knew that you went out and taught, that's what sociologists do. So I spent two years teaching part time and playing the piano, and two years not teaching at all and doing a lot of research and enjoying it thoroughly. I wasn't really as interested in getting a teaching job as I might have been. About that time Everett Hughes called and said, "How would you like to study a medical school?" He explained that he had been talking to some people about studying the University of Kansas Medical School, and the people who ran the school were very interested. An organization called Community Studies Incorporated was going to sponsor it and help us raise money. It sounded pretty good. I did go out and get interviewed for a few academic jobs, none of which I got, and finally I went to Kansas City by default and began what became a long, involved, and elaborate study.

Community Studies Incorporated was a locally based, nonprofit research organization. Nobody really knew what it was supposed to do, but that was good, because it meant you could do anything, as long as you were doing something. W. D. Bryant, who ran it, was an economist and a good social scientist. He had excellent connections in the community and had built up a good reputation for the organization, so that if you wanted to study something or some organization and you needed permission or access to files, all you had to say was that you were from Community Studies. That was a big help, because everybody in the town knew about Community Studies.

I went in and began studying the medical school. I spent a year in the field. The next year we hired Blanche Geer, who became one of the coauthors of the book we published. She affected my thinking in a number of ways, but in one way especially. She had been trained in experimental statistical work at Johns Hopkins, and when she started to do fieldwork, she said, "You people have a lot better evidence to base your conclusions on than you let people know. Now that I'm doing fieldwork myself I can see why you are so sure of what you say." But having come from an experimental background, she knew why people didn't quite trust the conclusions reached in ethnographic fieldwork. She gave us an impetus to try to work out ways of presenting evidence more completely than was customary in qualitative research. The book we wrote with Everett Hughes and Anselm Strauss, *Boys in White* (Becker et al. 1961), shows the marks of that attempt all over. We were constantly looking for ways to make clear to people why they should accept our results instead of, in effect, saying, "Look, we were there. You have to believe what we say."

While we were doing the research, Everett Hughes was very much involved in it but he also spent some time with the dean of the University of Kansas undergraduate school, a very interesting man named George Waggoner. Between them they decided that it would be wonderful if we went in and studied the undergraduate school. We had already thought about doing that, and soon, there we were studying this undergraduate school. I know that sounds like a put-on, that all these things happened by accident, but it is true.

Debro: You were still playing the piano in Kansas City?

Becker: Oh, sure! In fact, I was one of the better piano players in Kansas City.

We went up to study the college, and one of the things that happened—I suppose it happens to most people—is that as much involved as I was in the research (I was working full time in research), it always takes longer to complete a research project than you expect. I was always finishing up one project while another one was started. Here I was writing about graduate students, and I was beginning another project.

The study of the college was a vast enterprise. We gathered so much data we haven't finished working with it yet. We published one book based on our findings: *Making the Grade* (Becker et al. 1968).

In the middle of all this I wrote *Outsiders*. That book had a very funny history. I guess it is now considered one of the important statements of what is known as "labeling theory." But I started it long before those ideas got popular. I wrote the first draft of the theoretical part of the book in 1954. I must have had fifty pages of manuscript. At that time I had not read E. M. Lemert's book (1951). I should have, but I hadn't. That probably was because I wasn't teaching; if I had taught deviance, I would have read it. But there is an interesting point in that. "Labeling theory," so called, is a way of looking at deviance which actually represents a complete continuity with the rest of sociology. In other words, if a sociologist were going to study any topic, he would probably take such an approach, unless there were reasons not to. But there have been reasons not to approach criminology and the study of crime in the same way we might approach some more neutral topic. In studying most kinds of social organization, we will more likely understand that we have to study the actions of all the people involved in that organization. If we study a hospital, for instance, we study doctors, patients, nurses, aides, and so on. We may focus on one category of people, but we know that the actions of the others are important as well. That's true in studying any occupation or organization.

But somehow when sociologists studied crime they didn't understand the problem that way. Instead, they accepted the commonsense notion that there must be something wrong with criminals, otherwise they wouldn't act that way. They asked, "Why do people go into crime? Why don't they stop? How can we stop them?" The study of crime lost its connection with the mainstream of sociological development and became a very bizarre deformation of sociology, designed to find out why people were doing bad things instead of finding out the organization of interaction in that sphere of life. I had approached the problem differently, the way I'd learned to do in studying occupations. If someone had asked me in 1954 what my specialty was, I probably would have said social psychology or, more likely, occupations and professions. So I approached deviance as the study of people whose occupation, one might say, was either crime or catching criminals.

Ed Schur (1969) makes this point, that labeling theory represents a return to a wholly sociological way of approaching the problems of deviance. In a way, I'm surprised that I had such notions in 1954. In another way, it was a natural idea for a sociologist to have who hadn't been trained in criminology.

But I wrote that draft in 1954. Then I got into other research and it just sat there for a while. Every once in a while I would show it to someone and they would say, "Gee, that's interesting," but it stayed in my files. I remember showing Irwin Deutcher the manuscript. He was at Syracuse University's Youth Development Center, and wanted me to finish the manuscript for a series of publications he put out from the Center. He said, "Why don't you write that up, whip it into shape?" That started me thinking about it again, so I began to write, and I really got interested. A lot of time had passed, and I had become a little more sophisticated, so I expanded the essay and put the musician and marijuana studies I had published earlier into the book. Some of the reviews remarked quite correctly that the two parts didn't seem too well integrated.

I wasn't the only one interested in saying things about deviance. Kai Erikson (1962) had been saying the same thing. John Kitsuse (1962) was saying the same things. Lemert had said it years before. There were a number of people whose ideas were in the air. Probably what I did was to make a very clear and simple statement as to what it was about. At least I think it's a clear and simple statement. However, I am constantly amazed at the ambiguities that people can discover and the complications that they can create with what seems to me a very simple and concise set of ideas. One of the objections some people raised was that "labeling theory" is not a theory of how people become deviant (e.g., Gibbs 1966). I don't know what to say to them because that is obviously true. No one intended it to be. The very question, when it is put that way, assumes there is such a thing as being deviant. I think what people mean is that such a theory does not tell them why someone becomes a robber of banks or one who takes dope. The theory doesn't say why they did those particular things, or why they engaged in those activities. Of course, it wasn't designed to do that. What it was designed to do was to make clear the distinction between an observable act, like robbing a bank or smoking dope, and the unobservable quality of "deviance" such an act was alleged to have. The theory, and it really was a pretty rudimentary theory, wasn't designed to explain why people robbed banks but rather how robbing banks came to have the quality of being deviant. The theory suggested that you had to answer that second question by looking at the process by which some people define some actions as "bad" and by looking at the consequences of something being defined that way. One possible consequence, and this may be where the confusion arose, is that under certain circumstances the person who was defined as "bad" or "deviant" might, by virtue of that definition, be pushed to continue his deviance. I didn't state that as a necessary and inevitable thing, but only as a possibility under some circumstances and not under others. So I have never been able to understand the kind of angry criticisms that were raised because the theory doesn't explain why people who are deviant rob banks.

Anyway, that is my involvement in the deviance field and it's minimal. I did one study about fifteen years ago, based on this idea. I've kept in touch with the field; you can't help but do that. And I have written something else about drug experiences just recently (Becker 1967b). But aside from that I have had very little to do with it. Most of my work has been in education, studying educational institutions, and also in social psychology and qualitative methodology. If somebody tried to pin me down and say what are your specialties, I might mention those.

I should mention one other big project I have been associated with. After we finished studying the undergraduate college, Geer and I decided that we didn't want to study such a large organization ever again, because it was so much work. We decided to study trade schools, apprenticeships, or kinds of training programs for people who are college age but don't go to college. I guess that we were reacting to a funny bias in educational sociology, especially in studies of colleges, which is that people want to study those schools that are classiest and have the best reputations. When we studied the University of Kansas, that was regarded as odd, because it wasn't a well-known school. Most people studied Harvard, Yale, Swarthmore, those institutions or places that were regarded as "excellent." The idea was to see how they became so excellent. It's not that the University of Kansas is not a first-rate institution; I know it is. However, it isn't regarded as a Harvard or Yale, so people regarded our study as quaint. "How could you study such a place?" That was the reaction of most people. The idea of study-ing people who didn't go to college at all, that was really considered to be bizarre.

I already had a reputation among my friends as being somewhat peculiar in the things I studied. Some of my friends used to say, "Well, he studied musicians, that wasn't so nice, but then he studied physicians, that was nice; then he studied marijuana, that wasn't so nice, but then he studied graduate students, that was nice; now here he is backsliding again studying barber colleges." A very funny thing happened a few years ago which contains a very instructive lesson. When we were getting ready to study trade schools, some people wanted to know why we were going to study barber colleges and places like that. Suddenly the War on Poverty was launched and those became very exciting subjects. It suddenly became a ques-tion of vast interest: how could you train "those people"? All of these institutions suddenly became of interest. They weren't any more interesting to me than they had been before. They were vastly more interesting to many other social scientists. So we did the study anyway. We just finished and it is being written up now. [It was eventually published as Geer 1972.]

It is the first time I haven't done any fieldwork myself. A student, a research assistant, would pick out something he or she wanted to study, as long as it was in this area. We didn't have any good ideas as to how to go about sampling this vast universe of institutions which weren't colleges, which covered a lot of ground. So we more or less left it to the circumstances of individual students, whatever they wanted to do. The study started when I was at Stanford in 1962. I was at Stanford for three years, working in Nevitt Sanford's Institute for the Study of Human Problems. That year Clyde Woods, an anthropologist, studied a barber college (Woods 1972).

Then I went to Northwestern. The first year Hannah Marshall did a study of butchers' apprentices (Marshall 1972). The next year Lewis Mennerick did a study of a school located in a big county jail (Mennerick 1972). Then Lee Weiner began a study of the Officers' Training School of the Salvation Army, with an eye to learning something about revolutionary cadre development.

I began to see from these studies some very interesting things. What they give you is a really comparative study of education. It was an eye-opener. I began to see what was characteristic of schools. If you study places that are not really schools, you begin to see the essential characteristics of a school. I began to see more and more that the problem of schools is a problem of certification. In the vocational studies we were trying to find out how educational systems work. There are seven to ten of these vocational studies, and each one gave us an opportunity to study some particular aspect of education in a detailed way. For example, in the barber college we studied there happened to be almost no formal teaching; if the students learned anything, they learned from each other. Now students always learn a lot from each other, but that process may not be seen if you focus on what the teacher is doing. When the teacher isn't doing anything you have to look at how the students teach each other. There are eight or ten of these studies, done at Northwestern, and at Syracuse and Northeastern, where Blanche was located; they're being readied for publication now.

At the present time (1969–70) I have a fellowship for one year at the Center for Advanced Studies in Behavioral Science. I'm now into a new area of interest, the sociology of art, which includes music, film, dance, and so forth. One of the many reasons I think art is an interesting area to study is because it represents a kind of social organization which operates in a much more unplanned and anarchic way than we ordinarily intend things to run in our society. For instance, I think that conventional centralized education has just about had it. We have to reorganize our education so that in some way it will be more responsive to what people want—which means that we will have to find out what people do want so that those people who are teaching will not go nuts trying to find out for themselves what people want.

It seems to me that both art and science are organized in a free-wheeling way: they are organized so as to allow a maximum of variety—or at least a great deal more than, for instance, we allow in a highly centralized thing like education. So I think I can use what I find out about the social organization of art worlds to learn what the possibilities of a more anarchic style of society might be, to see how freedom might be increased by decentralization and what prices would be entailed.

I should mention here that another big influence on me has been Irving Louis Horowitz. Irving made me see the political implications of the way I was looking at deviance. The piece he wrote with Martin Liebowitz (Horowitz and Liebowitz 1968) made me see that deviance has a political character, that what gets defined as deviant often depends upon someone's personal interest. That definition often gets formalized in a law. It is obvious, therefore, that you are studying politics when you study deviance. It is a political issue whether what you're doing is "right" or "wrong."

Debro: That raises a general question about the political implications of sociological research, a topic that's much debated today.

Becker: A general question, and a very complicated one. I hardly know where to start. For instance, some people make this mistake: they think they can find scientific reasons for the moral position they hold, that science will show that they are morally correct. My opinion is that if you want to espouse a moral point of view, then do it. You can't avoid making an ultimate commitment by saying that science requires you to say it. Know what you think is right and say it.

Sociology, as a science, is value-free in just the same sense that chemistry is. It's not that you can't use chemistry for evil ends. Nor do I mean that research in chemistry can't be perverted by the uses to which the results will be put. Still, it doesn't make any difference which political party you belong to, chemicals are chemicals. In the same way, if the effects of smoking marijuana are a consequence of how you interpret the experience, I don't care what your politics are, if you study the effects of marijuana smoking, you are going to find that out. Conversely, if it's not true, whatever your politics are, you are going to find out it's not true.

Of course, people often fail to study things that ought to be studied because of implicit and explicit prohibitions, political and otherwise. I run into this a lot. People ask me, "Why do you look at things from the point of view of medical students or people who smoke dope? What do they know about it? Why don't you ask people who know about these things? Why don't you accept what the good people or the people in the hospitals say?" It is the same criticism Erving Goffman gets. "Why does Goffman go around acting as if the people who run the mental hospitals are out to do patients in?" That's the way the criticism is put. I don't think it's valid. What he does is not take it for granted that their pious protestations are correct. If they are doing wonderful things, he will see it. If they are not doing them, he won't see it. But by not taking things for granted he is already in opposition to some people. In the same way, I'm forever being harangued by people who say I am too radical in my approach because I don't believe that schools and colleges are necessarily the best way to teach people.

Debro: Are sociologists more radical than in the past?

Becker: No, I think sociology has been subject to political fads for a long period of time. We have always had radical sociologists: Trotskyists, other Marxists, and various other people who were considered, or considered themselves, radicals. I don't believe that sociology has been basically changed in its approach or has become any more radical than it has been in the past. Good sociologists produce radical results. But I'm not sure that all the sociologists who proclaim themselves radical produce radical results. What I mean by a radical result is one that rises above current orthodoxies, whether they are political, moral, institutional, scientific or whatever. That may or may not go with political radicalism, conventionally defined. [See Becker and Horowitz, in this volume.]

Debro: What are some of the problems of doing research that produces radical results?

Becker: One big problem is that the people you have studied will not like or approve of what you say about them in your final publication. I don't mean that you have to do research that people like, but rather that when you don't you will pay a price for it and you must be ready to handle that situation. Suppose, for example, you study a police department, as Jerome H. Skolnick did in *Justice without Trial* (1966). You can do that in various ways. You might join the department and study them as a member of it. You might engage in illegal activities that would bring you in contact with them, and study them from that standpoint. You might engage in political activities, like the Panthers or the Chicago demonstrations, and do the same.

But all those strategies limit the amount of data you can get. The best way of doing studies is openly, not disguised, because you can get so much more information. At the same time, you ought not to pay a price for this in some kind of censorship by the agency or group you have studied. I have often followed the practice of letting people read what I have to say about them. They can often point out mistakes I have made in the manuscript. However, they do not have a right of censorship. I don't know whether the police Skolnick studied would say that everything he wrote is wrong. What I think they would say is that, while it may be true, they don't want it published and disseminated to the public at this time. Many organizations in our society are really not prepared to have such information made public. You can't limit your research report to what is inoffensive, because if the only kind of research you can do is the kind that prevents you from telling what you found out, the research serves no purpose. I made a very formal argument on this topic in "Whose Side Are We On?" (1967). I connected the problems of doing research that produced unconventional (radical in the sense of being less constrained by conventional wisdom) results with a theory of the structure of hierarchical systems. The key idea is that of the *hierarchy of credibility,* which suggests that the superiors of any hierarchical setup will be conceived of by everybody who accepts the legitimacy of that setup as knowing more about it than anyone else. Their questions, their proposed answers, their notion of what constitutes the area being looked at, all of that will be taken as obviously correct and sensible. In the areas of deviance sociologists usually study, it's the views of legislators, police inspectors, prison wardens, and so on that are regarded as the "proper views." And I mean "proper" in the sense of "obviously correct," in the sense of "how else could it be?" or in the sense that it would be foolish to ask any other kind of question. It's been criminals and deviants who have been the subordinates in the systems we ordinarily look at, and thus these are the people whose views we've slighted. It doesn't follow that they're the only subordinates involved.

If you study a prison system and look at it not just as prisoners and guards, but as prisoners, guards, and a warden, then it would be necessary to look at who the warden reports to, to look at the warden and guards, for example, as subordinates in some larger system. You can imagine, perhaps, research which studies the prison from the point of view of the prisoners and causes the guards and the warden to be very upset. They say you're giving credence to all that nonsense the prisoners told you. Okay, so now you undertake a study from the point of view of the guards and the warden. Only when this reaches the State Department of Corrections, they look at it and say, "Why are you listening to those guards and that warden? What do they know about it?" You see, in that system the warden becomes the subordinate, and his superiors, who represent the state agency, become the people attention must be paid to.

When I say that their views have to be taken into account, I don't mean that you have to like the prisoners or the warden or whoever. I don't mean that you have to get inside their skins, but that you have to be aware that another kind of question could be asked if you take their point of view, and that question is as much subject to scientific study and analysis as the question you raise from a management point of view. Taking an instrumental view of scientific knowledge, it's just as easy to raise the question "How can we make the guards allow for more freedom for inmates?" as it is to raise the question "How can we get the inmates to behave better so the guards won't have so much trouble?" It's just as easy to raise the question from the point of view of the guards, "How can we get the Department of Corrections off our backs?" as it is to raise it from the point of view of the Department, "How can we get those guards and that warden to run the prison in the way we think best?" What usually happens is that the questions are raised from the point of view of the superiors in whatever system is being discussed. You don't necessarily have to take the point of view *at all times* of the lowest man in the system. But it is crucial to consider his viewpoint. It is a useful way to proceed because ordinarily you are not likely to be able to forget or ignore the positions taken by people who are the superiors in the system. They will remind you. They have plenty of power to make their voices heard. It's more useful to take the position of the people who are subordinate in the system because they are not as likely to be heard and that will direct your attention toward different kinds of variables, causes, and so on.

Debro: If you take the position of the superordinates, people will say you're being objective. But if you take the position of the subordinates, then they will say you are being biased. How can you deal with that problem?

Becker: One way is to make certain you ask your questions in such a way that you will get the same answer no matter what your emotional disposition is, no matter where your sympathies lie. That's an important requisite which I think every scientist has to take into account. Another is to make sure you've raised all the appropriate questions. That's also an important point. But there's a third criterion some people use, which is the criterion of seeing things in the "right way," in the way any "sensible person" would see it, namely, the way that people who run things see it. You have to be careful not to mix up the second and third. It's perfectly possible to be objective in the second sense, that is, to take account of the questions that might be raised both from the subordinate's point of view and the superior's point of view. But if you do that (and this is really the argument in that paper) you're going to be accused of not being objective by the superiors, because they will judge anything that takes the subordinate's point of view into account as nonobjective—even though you take both points of view equally, or take some larger point of view that encompasses both. It's nonobjective from that "commonsense" point of view to pay any attention to subordinates. If you do that, you will be called nonobjective. I don't see any way out of that and don't think it's worth worrying about.

Debro: I'm very interested in this distinction you draw between how you ask questions and how you go about answering them. In other words, you're saying that we must be conscious of whose side we are on when we frame the questions and that we must be objective in answering the questions,which is quite independent of whose position you take in asking the question. Have I put your position correctly? What criticisms would be removed if you asked questions which were strictly specified, instead of from the deviant point of view?

Becker: None because, for example, if you say that in a particular prison prisoners gamble, take drugs, and engage in homosexual activity, this statement will be regarded as a criticism of the people who run the prison and they will complain that you aren't objective. However objectively you have answered the question, if it turns out that such activities are going on, the implication, obviously, is that they wouldn't be going on if those people were doing their job. In that sense, they will say to you, "You're giving us a bad name." It won't be a question of fact but a question of interpretation. They will agree on the facts if you count it up and show that so much dope was confiscated and so much could be found, and so on. But they will say, "That isn't very much. You make it look like that was a lot." I think these points are important, but they don't solve the problem you raised: is it possible to do your research in such a way that the people who might be offended by it will have to keep quiet? Is it possible to do it so cleanly and so objectively that they won't be able to complain about it? I don't think you can because the problem doesn't lie in the realm of logical discourse. It's political. You're making trouble for them, you're a troublemaker, and that's how you'll be treated. You may be a powerful trouble-maker; it may be difficult for them to deal with you. They may be called on to try to answer you in the language of scientific discourse, which will make it hard for them. In fact, they often do. They will say you didn't have a good sample and your methods are inaccurate, that you didn't tell the truth; that's the way it comes out.

Debro: When you are doing research, is it possible to get "the whole story"?

Becker: Obviously, you don't take every factor into account because you don't consider every factor equally important. The symbolic interactionist point of view requires you to take into account more things than almost any other perspective. At least, it disposes you to do your research in such a way that if anything is obviously (or not so obviously) affecting the phenomenon you want to under-stand, you'll be free to take advantage of finding that out. This distinguishes it from other kinds of research which, for either the-oretical or technical reasons, limit your view of what's relevant, so that you just don't see those other factors which might be important. There's something in between strictly designed research and re-search based on the notion of including everything which is practical and workable. It's not practical to talk about including every factor. I doubt that anybody means that when they speak of telling "the whole story." What's clear is that you do want to take into account the perspectives, the ideas, and the actions of people at each level of a hierarchy.

However, in a given piece of research it may not be possible to study all of those people. If you look at the prison warden and the

State Department of Corrections, you soon find out that they don't consider themselves bosses either. There is another set of bosses, which might be the governor or the legislature. And if you study them, they will tell you they have another boss, the voters. Maybe there's not an infinite regress, but it points to the fact that you can't study it all. But you have to get the reactions and perspectives of the people who are relevant to the phenomenon that you've been looking at. Now "relevant" is, of course, a weasel word. If you take, for example, J. Edgar Hoover's point of view, "the whole story" might include the actions and ideas of communist leaders who are sending dope to this country in enormous amounts in order to mislead our youth. From another point of view, you'd have to take into account the interests of the big-money people in Zurich.

Debro: Have you used the method of participant observation in all your research?

Becker: Either that or intensive interviewing.

Debro: Then you proceed to classify or interpret the meanings. How do you show that your interpretations of what people say are correct?

Becker: That's a problem in doing social research of any variety. It's the same problem if you use a questionnaire, for example. What you do there is to assume that the meaning of the question you formulated will be understood by the respondent in exactly the way you meant it. There is quite a bit of evidence that sometimes they do and sometimes they don't. It's variable even with regard to census kinds of questions. What we did was to try and settle that question more directly, by an appeal to evidence. We try to establish the meanings of various activities, objects, or words by looking at them as they occurred, as they were used, or as they were engaged in a great variety of settings. We abstracted from a great mass of materials the common meanings that seem to be involved, then tested those meanings by using those notions in our own interactions with the students we were studying. If you pick up a slang word that's used in a certain group in a distinct way, one way to see if you understand it is to use it. If you don't use it correctly, either people will not understand you or they will correct you. They won't let you use it incorrectly; they won't respond in the way you anticipated. When you find that you can act in appropriate ways, talk in an appropriate way, do the right thing at the right time, it's evident that you do understand what they mean. That's the criterion a lot of anthropologists now use: you understand the culture well enough to behave like a well-socialized member of it.

Debro: It seems to be much easier reading your work than that of a lot of other sociologists, and I wondered how you got the kind of style that you have. Your style of writing seems to be much different than that of most sociologists.

Becker: I had the fortune or misfortune of being nagged by many people who write well and simply would not allow me to write in a sloppy way or in a way that wasn't clear. Everett Hughes was very tough about that. I have some dreadful letters in my files he wrote me about things I had written. He said, "What's the matter? Why don't you write correctly?" There are other people, like Mark Benny, a social researcher who came here from England just about the time that I was getting out of graduate school. We taught together for a while. Mark had been a professional journalist. I'll never forget him saying to me after he read a draft of a paper I was sending to a journal, "Well, I suppose you have to write it in that funny style in order to get it published in these journals." He said it in the kindest possible way, but I found it very painful. Blanche Geer is an excellent writer and an excellent editor, and I've learned a tremendous amount from the writing we've done together.

I guess the other thing is that I rewrite a lot. I seldom publish anything I haven't rewritten five or six times, at least. That's one way of avoiding bad writing, by just working at it. A lot of people don't. Most of the tricks that I use you will find in any good style book (e.g., Gowers 1954, Read 1952, or Orwell 1967).

I'll give you an example of the importance of good style: one of the worst things sociologists do is to use passive grammatical constructions. They say, "It was found that so and so . . . ," instead of saying, "I found so and so," or "We found so and so." Since you never use any active verbs, you're allowed to get away with not being specific about what actually happened. It also means that since you don't have to say who the subject of the sentence was, you don't have to say who did what. So you can say that a person was "labeled as a deviant" without saying who labeled him. The whole point of the interactionist approach to deviance is to make it clear that *somebody* had to do the labeling. It didn't just happen.

Using the passive grammatical form allows you to get away without saying who did it. "He was labeled"—without saying the court labeled him or his parents labeled him or the people in the community or whoever. There's a lot of sloppy thinking that gets by because people have very bad writing habits. [I eventually expanded these ideas into a book (Becker 1985).]

Debro: How can we correct this?

Becker: Now we're getting into the realm of my prejudices and crank ideas. I have hundreds of them. The problem lies in the way schools are organized. Colleges and graduate schools are organized on the quarter or semester system. That leads to students writing term papers which are turned in at the end of the course, getting grades, and that's the end of it. Next quarter the students write another term paper. The only way you can learn to write well is by rewriting things. Nobody can write something perfectly the first time. At least, it's not likely. I would like to dream up some way to require students to rewrite their papers until they are well written, until they get them into some kind of readable form. When a friend of mine gives me a paper to read, I scribble all over it, I rewrite it. I rewrite sentences, I say, "This is terrible! Why did you say it this way? This idea is cockeyed, etc." I won't give him an A or a B or a C because that's irrelevant; he asked for help, not a grade. When students have some real professional obligation, such as giving a paper at a meeting, that's where it usually comes up. Suddenly, it's not done the first time. They rewrite and rewrite because it's for real now and they want it to be good. But we don't have enough occasions where students have to do that. It's difficult to require it. "Required" isn't really the right way to talk about it. It's very hard to encourage good writing with the term-paper system. You have to have students with an interest in it, who are good at it. Very often students can help each other, if they will.

Debro: Perhaps people should be judged as artists are, by their work rather than by their degrees.

Becker: That's the way people are judged in the professional and scientific worlds we work in. You get a degree and once you get it, nobody takes it to mean anything. Yes, there are certain jobs which require a master's degree. Having a master's degree doesn't mean you're competent, but you're judged on whether you have that degree.

In contrast, research people are judged by a hard audience—their scientific colleagues—on the basis of the work they do. That being the case, I don't see why graduate schools should louse up the educational situation by making an unnecessary evaluation, especially when the evaluation causes such a deflection of student effort away from useful kinds of scholarly work and training. Bernard Beck and I published an article recently [1969, reprinted in this volume] which makes this argument at great length.

These crank ideas of mine, by the way, have all been stimulated by the research I've done in educational organizations. So that research has been immediately relevant and useful, at least to me in dealing with my own work problems.

3

CONSCIOUSNESS, POWER, AND DRUG EFFECTS

Scientists no longer believe that a drug has a simple physiological action, essentially the same in all humans. Experimental, anthropological, and sociological evidence has convinced most observers that drug effects vary greatly, depending on variations in the physiology and psychology of the persons taking them, on the state the person is in when he ingests the drug, and on the social situation in which drug ingestion occurs. We can understand the social context of drug experiences better by showing how their character depends on the amount and kind of knowledge available to the person taking the drug. Since distribution of knowledge is a function of the social organization of the groups in which drugs are used, drug experiences vary with variations in social organization. I will explore that possibility in three quite different settings of drug use: the illegal use of drugs for pleasure, the use of medically prescribed drugs by doctors' patients, and the involuntary ingestion of drugs by victims of chemical warfare.

Drug effects have a protean character, varying from person to person and place to place. They can vary in that fashion because drugs almost always have more than one effect on the organism. People may conventionally focus on and recognize only one or a few of these effects, and ignore all others as irrelevant. Most people think the effect of aspirin is to control pain; some know that it also reduces fever; few think of gastric irritation as a typical effect, though it is. The example suggests that users focus on "beneficial" effects and ignore those irrelevant to the benefit they seek. Because drugs have so many effects, the effects can be interpreted variously and thus reflect extremely subtle contextual influences.

Drug Effects, Knowledge, and Social Structure

When a person ingests a drug, his subsequent experience is influenced by his ideas and beliefs about that drug (Becker 1967b).

What he knows about the drug influences the way he uses it, the way he interprets its manifold effects and responds to them, and the way he deals with the sequelae of the experience. Conversely, what he does not know affects his experience too, making certain interpretations impossible, as well as actions based on that missing knowledge. I use "knowledge" in an extended sense to refer to any ideas or beliefs about the drug that any of the actors in the drug-use network (e.g., illicit drug sellers, physicians, researchers, or lay drug users) believe have been tested against experience and thus carry more warrant than mere assertions of faith. All people are probably likely to take knowledge they believe to have been tested against experience as a guide to their own interpretations and actions. Members of contemporary Western societies, who accept the value of science and scientific knowledge so uncritically, must do so doubly.

Dosage.–Many drug effects are dose-related. The drug has one set of effects if you take x amount and quite different effects if you take $5x$. Similarly, drugs have different effects when taken orally, by inhalation, intramuscularly, or intravenously. How much of the drug you take and how you take it depend on what you understand to be the proper amount and route of use. Those understandings depend on what you have learned from sources you consider knowledgeable and trustworthy.

If I have a headache and ask how many aspirin I should take, almost anyone will tell me two; that knowledge is widely available both on the package and in lay medical folklore. It will also be understood that I should swallow the aspirin rather than dissolving them in water and injecting them. Most people, however, have no knowledge readily available about the use of a large variety of drugs, either those medically prescribed (e.g., cortisone) or those used without benefit of medical advice (e.g., LSD). To use them would-be users develop some notions about how much to take and how to take it, either by trial-and-error experimentation or by adopting the ideas suggested by sources they consider reliable (scientists, physicians, or more experienced drug users). Those sources usually have recommendations about drug use. They can tell the prospective user how much he should take and how he should take it in order to cure his cold, control his blood clotting time, have a mystical experience, get high, or whatever other effect he may desire. They can also tell him how much will be too much, producing unwanted effects of overdose. They may tell him to take four pills of the kind the druggist will sell him, one after each meal and one before retiring; they may give more elaborate instructions, such as those given diabetics about controlling their metabolic balance with food and insulin; they may informally suggest that the novice has probably smoked enough hashish and ought to stop until it takes effect; or tell him that most people find five hundred micrograms of "good acid" enough to induce an adequate amount of consciousness expansion.

Using these acquired understandings, the user takes an amount whose effect he can more or less accurately predict. He usually finds his prediction confirmed, though the accuracy of conventional knowledge (as opposed to its confirmation by a retrospective adjustment of expectations) needs to be known. In this way, his access to knowledge exerts a direct influence on his experience, allowing him to control the physiological input to that experience.

This analysis supposes that the user has complete control over the amount he takes, any variation being due to variations in his understanding of the consequences of taking different doses or taking the drug in different ways. But drug availability is often regulated by law, so that the user can take only what he can get under given conditions of supply. I might want to take large amounts of cortisone, but am restricted to what a doctor will prescribe and a pharmacist will sell. Except in hospitals, doctors ordinarily prescribe and pharmacists sell amounts larger than recommended for one-time use, so that a user can take more than he is "supposed to," as sometimes occurs with prescriptions for barbiturates. I can also purchase drugs illicitly or semi-licitly (e.g., from a friendly neighborhood pharmacist) and so evade medical control of dosage.

A user also loses control over the amount he takes when someone more powerful than him forces him to take more than he wants or, indeed, to take a drug he does not want to take at all. This occurs commonly in pediatric medicine, in mental hospitals, and in tuberculosis hospitals when patients are given drugs whose taste or effects they dislike; in chemical and biological warfare; and in the addition of chlorine or fluorides to city water supplies. In these cases, the relevant knowledge for an understanding of the drug's effects, insofar as they depend on dosage, is the knowledge held by the powerful person or organization which can force the user to ingest the drug.

Main effects.—Social scientists have shown how the definitions drug users apply to their experience affect that experience. Persons suffering opiate withdrawal will respond as "typical" addicts if they interpret their distress as opiate withdrawal, but not if they blame the pain on some other cause (e.g., recovery from surgery). Marijuana users must learn to interpret its subtle effects as being different from ordinary experience and as pleasurable before they "get high" (Becker 1953b). Indians and Caucasians interpret peyote experiences differently (Aberle 1966), and LSD "trips" have been experienced as consciousness expansion, transcendental religious experience, mock psychosis, or being high (Blum et al. 1964).

The user brings to bear, in interpreting his experience, knowledge and definitions derived from participation in particular social groups. Indian culture teaches those who acquire it a different view of the peyote experience than is available to non-Indians. Marijuana users learn to experience the drug's effects from more experienced users. LSD trips are interpreted according to the understandings available in the various settings in which it is taken.

The process has been studied largely in connection with nonmedical drug use, but presumably occurs in medical use also. Here the chief source of authoritative interpretations is the physician who prescribes the drug, and for many people the pharmacist. Patients on maintenance regimes of a drug for a chronic disease like diabetes, epilepsy, or gout might develop a user's "drug culture," trading information and generalizing from their common experiences, but this has not been extensively studied.

In both cases, the knowledge acquired from authoritative sources lets the user identify the drug's main effect, know when it is occurring, and thus decide that what is occurring, even when it seems undesirable or frightening, is really acceptable, if only because expected.

Side effects.—Side effects are not a medically or pharmacologically distinct category of reactions to drugs. Rather, they are effects not desired by either the user or the person administering the drug. Both side effects and main effects are thus socially defined categories. What is a side effect or a main effect will vary according to the perspective applied; mental disorientation might be an unwanted side effect to a physician, but a desired main effect for an illicit drug user.

A drug user's knowledge, if adequate, lets him identify unwanted side effects and deal with them in a way satisfactory to him. A user concentrating on a desired main effect (relief from a headache) may not observe an unpleasant side effect (gastric irritation) or may not connect it with his use of aspirin. He interprets his experience most adequately if those who prepare him for the drug's main effects likewise teach him the likely side effects and how to deal with them. Illicit drug users typically teach novices the side effects to look out for, give reassurance about their seriousness, and give instruction in how to avoid or overcome them; this mechanism probably prevents a great deal of potential pathology, though it can only operate when drug users are adequately connected in networks through which the information can pass. Many LSD users became expert at "talking down" people experiencing "bad trips," and marijuana users habitually teach novices what to do if they get "too high." Physicians probably vary in the degree to which they teach patients the potential side effects of the drugs they prescribe. Patients for whom physicians prescribe drugs seldom share a user culture. Since their medication may produce potent side effects, they can experience profound effects without knowing their prescribed drug is responsible, should the physician fail to inform them. The physician himself may not know, since the drug may have become available before the effects had been discovered; this seems to have happened when oral contraceptives were introduced and many women experienced edema, depression, vascular difficulties, and other undesired effects which no one, at the time, attributed to the Pill (Seaman 1969).

Research and communication.—Knowledge and the social channels through which it flows affect the interpretations and responses of a drug user to the experience the drug produces. Where does that knowledge come from? We can call its production "research," using the term in the extended way I have been speaking of knowledge. Research, so conceived, consists of the accumulation of ideas tested more or less systematically against experience of the empirical world. Researchers may use elaborate techniques and equipment or rely on simple devices and modes of analysis. At one extreme, the research pharmacologist systematically tests the effects of a drug on a wide variety of organ systems; at the other, a casual experimenter with a drug he thinks will get him high takes it over a period of weeks, noting his own reactions, and possibly comparing them with those of others experimenting with the same drug.

Research, especially that concerning subjective experiences produced by drugs, relies heavily on conventionally accepted rules of logic, inference, and common sense and scientific reasoning. Those rules help people decide when they have "experienced" something and what has produced the experience. Even when a variation from the ordinary that might be due to ingestion of a drug is identified, drug users often have to decide whether it is an ordinarily uncommon event or something special that might be due to the drug. Marijuana users, for instance, experience considerable hunger and must decide whether it is ordinary hunger or drug-induced. In deciding such questions, users make use of such commonsense notions as that antecedents produce consequences, lay versions of such scientific procedures as Mill's method of difference.

This leads to the question of whether drug effects are entirely mental constructs or whether they are in some way constrained by physiological events in the body. To what degree can people have, as research on placebo effects suggests, "drug experiences" which have no physiological base? Experimental work (Schacter and Singer 1962) suggests that there must be some physiological basis for the experience. Without arguing the matter here, I believe that there must be some physiological event to be interpreted, but that it need not be drug-caused. Human beings experience a variety of physiological events all the time; when one is properly alerted, those ordinary events can be interpreted as drug-caused, as can events that in fact are drug-caused.

In any event, anyone who wishes to demonstrate to himself and others that he is experiencing a "drug effect" is constrained by the rules of common sense and folk or professional science. He cannot convince himself of the validity of his experience unless he can manipulate some actual experience according to those rules to produce an acceptable conclusion. (To the degree that other systems of producing knowledge are employed—e.g., divination—users appeal to their rules for validation.)

The kind of research done on a drug depends on the facilities, technical skills, and motivations available to those who do it. I describe varieties of social structures producing research later, so will not go into them here. Similarly, whatever knowledge has been accumulated may or may not be available to the ultimate user of the drug, depending on the constraints on communication in the organizations in which the drug use occurs.

We can distinguish three major social structures in which drug use occurs, according to the degree of control the ultimate users of the drug exercise over their own drug taking and especially over the production and distribution of drug-relevant knowledge. In one variety users retain control; the major empirical case is illicit drug use for pleasure, though the use of patent medicines provides an interesting comparison. In a second variety, the user delegates control to an agent presumed to act in his behalf; the major empirical case is modern medical practice, though the use of drugs for religious purposes is also relevant. Finally, in some cases, chemical warfare being the most prominent, the user has no control over his ingestion of the drug or over the production and distribution of knowledge associated with use of the drug.

User Control

In a situation of user control, such as the illicit use of drugs for pleasure, the user takes as much as he wants on whatever schedule he wants; his dosage is self-initiated and self-regulated. He relies on knowledge generated in user groups to organize his drug-taking activities and interpret his drug experiences. He may feel substantial pressure from drug-using peers with whom he associates, but his use is voluntary and under his control in that no one has issued him anything as authoritative as a medical order and no one has forced the drug on him over his objections, as occurs in chemical warfare and forced medication.

Users generate knowledge about the drugs that interest them largely by their own research, though that may include consulting such scientific and medical sources as pharmacology texts or the *Physicians' Desk Reference*. They use the lay techniques available to them, largely self-experimentation and introspective observation. These methods are particularly appropriate when the effects to be investigated consist largely of subjective experiences difficult to tap by other means. While such methods are unreliable in individual cases, they are less likely to be influenced by idiosyncratic errors when a large number of users pool their observations and produce generalizations consonant with their collective experience. The reliability of generalizations so constructed depends on the efficiency of the communication channels through which information moves and the adequacy of the mechanism for collating it.

Ordinarily, information about a drug illicitly used accumulates slowly, often over many years, in the pooled experience of users, who compare notes on their own experiences and those of others they have heard about. Insofar as users are connected, even though very indirectly, over a long time a large number of experiences circulate through the connected system and produce what can be called a "drug culture" (not the mélange of political and cultural attitudes the term is often applied to, but rather a set of common understandings about the drug, its characteristics and the way it can best be used). The development of knowledge about marijuana probably best approximates this model, many years of extensive marijuana use in the United States having produced a vast body of lore which does not vary much by region or social group.

Other methods of cumulating and collating knowledge occasionally occur. The drug known as STP underwent a hip equivalent of the mass testing of polio vaccines when thousands of pills containing it were thrown from the stage at a be-in. Though no one knew what they were, many took them and within a few days most interested people had heard something about their effects. Information piled up at the Haight-Ashbury Free Medical Clinic and other places where people suffering adverse reactions were likely to go. In a short time, the major effects, appropriate dosages, likely side effects and effective antidotes were well known.

Knowledge produced this way has certain defects. It cannot discover anything not capable of being discovered by the simple techniques known to a mass population of users. If, as alleged, LSD damages chromosomes and thus produces birth defects in offspring even after drug use ceases, typical styles of user research could not discover it, for that kind of knowledge requires more sophisticated equipment and techniques of analysis than users have available. Further, any unwanted effect whose onset is delayed is likely to be missed by user research, which relies on simple and immediate cause-effect relations; if the effect occurs a year after use begins, the user population may not discover the connection. (If, however, the user population includes well-trained scientists, as was always the case with LSD and is increasingly true with respect to all psychedelic drugs, this problem can be overcome.) Finally, the effectiveness of the research is limited by the connectedness of the user network. The operation depends on redundancy for the reliability of the knowledge produced, and poorly connected networks may gather insufficient data to overcome the unreliability of the individual datum. The underground news media might help with this difficulty; insofar as they are widely read, they can provide an otherwise nonexistent link between isolated users or user groups.

But knowledge produced by user research has the great virtue of being directed precisely to the questions the user is interested in having answered. If he wants to know whether the drug will make him high, the available research, conducted by people who share his interest, will give him an answer. In this it differs from research done for medical purposes, which is typically directed to questions raised by scientists or physicians, not by the ultimate user of the drug.

Users thus have available, under optimal conditions of knowledge production, relatively reliable and accurate answers to their questions about the drug they use. They use this knowledge to maximize the benefits they desire from use of the drug, whatever those benefits might be, and to minimize side effects. Often, because they participate in user groups, when a question arises whose answer they do not know, someone who does know it is readily available. This is particularly important in dealing with potentially dangerous or disturbing side effects. Naturally, the optimal circumstances seldom obtain; when knowledge is incomplete, inaccurate, or unavailable, users will have predictable troubles. This is particularly obvious when a drug first appears and knowledge has not yet been produced and disseminated.

If we switch to another instance of user control—the use of patent medicines—we see the importance of the character of user networks. (I rely here on informal observation and speculation.) If my speculations are correct, people produce knowledge about patent medicine effects either on their own or in small family groups. Take the case of laxatives. The constipation they are used for is presumably not widely discussed among people suffering from it. Users cannot easily identify one another as fellow sufferers and thus as potential sources of information. Parents may share the results of their own experiments with their children, as may spouses with one another, but one can imagine that the knowledge would not move much beyond that. Specialized groups (e.g., fellow inmates of an old people's home) might share such information, but in general, knowledge probably would not cumulate, except in families (perhaps descending, like toilet words, in the female line); each new user or small group would have to rediscover it. My speculations may be incorrect, but they highlight the importance of communication channels in understanding the experiences of users who control their own drug use.

Control by the User's Agent

When the user delegates control to an agent, interesting variations in the production and distribution of knowledge occur, with equally interesting variations in the kinds of experiences users have. The major empirical case is that of the physician prescribing medication for his patient (though an interesting variation is provided by religious use of drugs, as in the relation between Don Juan and his pupil Carlos Castaneda [1968]). Here the user takes the drug the doctor prescribes for him, in the amounts and on the schedule the doctor recommends. The doctor's prescription reflects what the doctor wants to accomplish, rather than what the patient wants; their desires may coincide, but need not and in many cases do not.

The doctor uses at least two criteria in evaluating drugs. He wants to alleviate some dangerous or unpleasant condition the patient is suffering from, in a way clearly visible both to him and to his patient. The drug effect which most interests the doctor is one which produces demonstrable (in the best case, visible to the patient's naked eye) improvement. But the doctor also uses a second criterion: he does not want the drug to interfere with his control over the patient. The rationale for that desire is well known: since (the rationale goes) the doctor knows what will help the patient better than the patient himself, the patient must surrender himself to the physician to achieve maximum results; if the patient rejects the physician's advice his health may be impaired. While I do not believe the rationale is factually correct, it is unnecessary to demonstrate that to observe that doctors believe they have a legitimate interest in maintaining what Eliot Freidson (1961, 1970a, 1970b) has usefully labeled "professional dominance."

The patient usually relies on the physician for his knowledge about dosage, main effects, and side effects of the drug prescribed. But the physician may not give the patient all the knowledge that is available to him, because he does not want the patient to use that knowledge as a basis for disobeying medical orders (Lennard et al. 1972). Henry Lennard has given me a telling example. Certain of the tranquilizing drugs sometimes produce an unusual effect on male sexual functioning; while the man experiences orgasm, no ejaculation occurs. This naturally causes those who have the experience some anxiety. Since the drugs are given to relieve anxiety, Lennard asked psychiatrists why they did not tell patients that this might occur. "If I did that," ran the typical answer, "the patient might not take the drug and, *in my judgment*, he should run the risk of that anxiety in order to protect himself from his basic anxieties." Physicians also withhold information about side effects because suggestible patients often experience effects they have been told about, even when there is no physiological basis for the experience. They believe that this risk outweighs the risk of morbidity associated with lack of information, but I know of no definitive data on the matter.

Sometimes the physician does not give the patient adequate information about the experience the drug will produce because he does not have the knowledge himself. Research on drugs for medical use is organized quite differently from user research, and its organization creates substantial barriers to a free flow of information. Drug research is a highly specialized discipline, with its own journals, professional societies, and scientific world to which the physician does not belong. He does not follow the latest developments in pharmacology, read its journals, or attend meetings of its scientific organizations. So he depends for his knowledge of drug effects on such general medical literature as he keeps up with, on his immediate colleagues, and on the knowledge provided by pharmaceutical companies through their literature and salesmen (Coleman et al. 1966). Most of his knowledge, especially of new drugs, probably comes from the last source. Some physicians, especially those in specialized practices who see many cases of the same disease, may engage in casual experimentation similar to that done by illicit drug users, trying different dosages and treatments on different patients. They may then pool their observations with like-minded specialists and generate knowledge similar to that contained in drug-user cultures, with the same advantages and drawbacks.

Another serious barrier to the practicing physician's acquisition of knowledge about the drugs he prescribes arises from the organization of pharmaceutical research and manufacture. While pharmaceutical companies, the scientists who work for them, and the physicians who participate in their drug testing programs want to produce medically valuable drugs that will help physicians combat disease, they are also interested, as congressional investigations have shown, in profits (Harris 1964). They design their research to produce profitably marketable products which can be sold, via physicians' prescriptions, to the public, and which will also pass government tests of purity, efficacy, and lack of dangerous side effects. They look primarily for drugs which will produce (or seem to produce) effects on diseased patients, of the kind physicians want, or can be persuaded to want, to produce. They appear to investigate possible side effects only so far as required by prudence and the law. (We have no studies of the organization of pharmaceutical research laboratories, their characteristic patterns of investigation, their reward structures, and the relations between the two, so I have relied on more public sources [e.g., House Government Operations Committee 1971].)

Pharmaceutical research thus produces knowledge about the main effect a doctor might need to treat a patient. That is what the companies' advertising communicates to the physician. If he looks carefully, he can find material on side effects and contraindications, but it is not pressed on him. In general, companies do not seek or force on the practicing physician information which would lessen the profitability of a drug they believe has good commercial possibilities.

The physician, then, may not know that the drug has some effects it in fact has, or he may not choose to tell the patient when he does know. When, for either reason, the patient the drug is prescribed for does not know what it may do, he runs two risks. He may have experiences which are quite pronounced, extremely unpleasant, and even dangerous, but not realize that they result from his medication. As a consequence, he may continue to take the drug that produces the unwanted side effect. For instance, certain commonly prescribed antihistamines occasionally produce urethral stricture; allergic patients who take large quantities may experience this but never report it to the allergist because it does not seem to be in his department. If the condition becomes severe they consult a urologist. He may discover they are taking large doses of antihistamine and cure the difficulty by recommending one that does not have this side effect. But not all physicians know of the connection, and failure of the patient to report or the physician to make the connection can lead to serious difficulty.

The patient may also experience symptoms which have an insidious and gradual onset, and never recognize that there is any change in his condition which requires explanation. This was apparently the experience of many women who took birth control pills (Seaman 1969). They suffered serious and continuing depression, but it appeared gradually and seemed nothing out of the ordinary, so that they did not realize anything had occurred which might be attributable to the hormone. This reaction is especially true of drugs taken for medical purposes; the mood changes they produce will be so gradual as not to be noticed or will be attributed to psychological difficulties, changes in social relationships, or other causes unrelated to the medication. Thus, the physician may treat the patient who begins to experience mood changes as a neurotic, and the difficulty, when the user does become aware of it, will not only be undiagnosed but misdiagnosed. This must have happened frequently among early users of oral contraceptives, especially unmarried women, whom physicians often consider especially prone to neurotic symptoms (Seaman 1969).

In either case, the drug experience is amplified and the chance of serious pathology increases because the doctor has insufficient knowledge of the drug's effects to warn the patient, or because he chooses not to warn him. The patient, not knowing what is likely to happen, cannot recognize the event when it occurs and respond adequately himself or present his problem to an expert who can provide an adequate response.

As we have seen, knowledge accumulates in illicit drug-using groups when users are in touch with one another and communicate the results of their personal research to one another freely. Though the medical and scientific professions are organized in a way that ought to promote full communication of adverse drug reactions to practicing physicians, a recent study suggests obstacles which impede that communication (Koch-Weser et al. 1969). Hospital physicians were asked to report all adverse drug reactions, and, simultaneously, clinical pharmacologists made independent checks. From two-thirds to three-quarters of the adverse reactions to prescribed drugs verified by the pharmacologists were *not* reported by the physicians. Physicians tended to report those adverse reactions in which morbidity and danger were high, and in which the connection between the drug and the reaction was already well known. This means that the system works poorly to accumulate new information, although it is relatively efficient in reconfirming what is already known. Add to this the probability that patients are probably less likely than illicit drug users to compare experiences on a large scale. There is then a substantial risk that adverse information will never be accumulated so that it can be passed on to the drug's ultimate user for him to use in interpreting such events as occur subsequent to drug use.

Many of the user's difficulties in interpreting his experience will result from the stage of development of knowledge about the drug. I have argued elsewhere that adverse reactions to illicitly used drugs decline as their use increases and a fund of knowledge grows among communicating users, allowing them to use that accumulated wisdom to regulate dosage and deal with adverse effects (Becker 1967b).

A similar natural history may occur with the use of drugs in medical practice. Doctors seek drugs which will make a decisive and noticeable improvement in a patient's condition. Pharmaceutical companies and researchers attempt to produce such drugs. In the effort to produce a *noticeable* improvement, company recommendations, insufficient research, and physician inclinations combine to produce a tendency to prescribe dosages larger than required for the desired medical effect, large enough to produce serious side effects. Because the research done prior to use on patients has not looked thoroughly into possible side effects, no one connects these occurrences with the new medication. Where the drug is potentially profitable, as in the case of antibiotics, adrenocortical steroids, or oral contraceptives, its use will be heavily promoted and widely publicized, so that physicians will feel pressure both from patients and the example of their more innovative peers to begin prescribing the new drug. Massive use, combined with a tendency to overdose, will produce enough adverse reactions that someone will eventually investigate and establish the connection. More such reactions will occur before the information filters through the barriers already discussed, but eventually conventional dosages will be lowered and the incidence of adverse reactions will decline. When they occur, furthermore, they will be recognized and treated more effectively. Eventually, presumably, the number of adverse reactions will reach a minimum based on the number of physicians who are either ignorant of their character or who do not communicate their knowledge to patients so that the reactions can be recognized, reported, and treated.

The introduction of oral contraceptives appears to embody this natural history. When they were first introduced, both the manufacturers and prescribing physicians were determined to use sufficiently large doses so that they would not have to face the wrath of a pregnant woman who had been assured that *that* could not happen. The large doses produced serious side effects in a variety of organ systems, as well as severe psychological depressions. As knowledge of these effects became more widespread, many physicians (and others) did not wish to publicize them, since women who knew of them might refuse to take the pills. Eventually, doctors discovered that one-tenth the conventional dose was sufficient to produce effective contraception, with many fewer adverse reactions. With both physicians and users alerted by massive publicity, adverse reactions were more quickly reported and dealt with.

To what degree does the process I described occur because the investigation and production of medically prescribed drugs is carried on by profit-making corporations in a capitalist economy? Obviously, those elements of the process which reflect marketing strategies designed to maximize profits—focusing research on products likely to produce high sales at low costs and a relative neglect of potential side effects—would not occur in a noncapitalist economy. On the other hand, most of the other elements, reflecting as they do the interests of an organized medical profession as distinct from the interests of patients, would presumably occur in any developed society which contains such a group. The desire of physicians to achieve discernible results and to maintain control over patients would probably continue to influence the dissemination of knowledge from researchers to physicians to patients and, consequently, the kinds of experiences medical patients have as a result of using prescribed drugs.

Carlos Castaneda's account (1968) of his instruction in the use of psychedelic substances by Don Juan is the only one I know of the delegation of control to a religious, rather than a medical, agent. The relationship between the two, and its effect on Castaneda's drug experiences, appears similar to the medical model. Don Juan often gave Castaneda insufficient information with which to interpret his experiences and avoid unpleasant experiences, because he felt Castaneda's inexperience (for which read "lack of professional training") would make it impossible for him to understand, because he wished to retain control over his student's progress, and because he wanted his pedagogy to turn out the result he sought, even though the experience might be unpleasant or frightening for Castaneda in the short run and the result might ultimately be failure. The disparity between teacher and student goals parallels the disparity between physician and patient interests and goals, and some of the resulting experiences of the user who has delegated control appear similar.

Control by External Agents

People sometimes find themselves required to ingest drugs involuntarily, the whole process under the control of an independent agent who administers the drugs for his own purposes. The external agent's purposes sometimes conflict directly with those of the user, as when people find themselves the victim of chemical warfare (Hersh 1968) in the form of a poison-gas attack or a contaminated water supply. In other cases, the agent administers the drug because he believes it is in the best interest of the community to do so, as when people with tuberculosis or leprosy are medicated to prevent them from infecting others (Roth 1963). In such cases (and in such similar instances as the forced medication of mental hospital inmates and the administration of amphetamines to allegedly hyperkinetic schoolchildren) those administering the drug frequently insist, and believe, that the medication serves the ultimate interest of the user as well, however much he may wish to avoid it. In both chemical warfare and forced medication, the characteristic features of a serious disagreement about the legitimacy of the drug's administration and the consequent necessity of coercion to effect that administration appear. The crucial feature of the social structure in which the drugs are used, then, consists of an imbalance in power between those administering the drug and those to whom it is administered such that drug ingestion is forced on unwilling users.

Those administering the drug usually have goals quite divorced from anything the user might desire. Although physicians in ordinary medical practice have goals somewhat divergent from those of their patients, they must nevertheless take realistic account of the possibility that patients will cease coming to them unless the treatment proves satisfactory. When the one administering the drug has sufficient control that the user cannot escape, he can safely ignore the other's interests altogether, so that his actions can be designed solely to serve his own interests, personal or (more likely) organizational.

The emphasis on the interests of the person administering the drug shows up in the calculation of dosage. In contrast to the careful self-regulation characteristic of user-controlled drugs, and the attempt to prescribe a dose that will produce a result satisfactory to the user for whom one is acting as agent characteristic of agent control, external agents usually look for a maximum dose, one that will not fail to produce the result they seek. In the case of chemical warfare, they seek to kill or incapacitate those to whom the drug is administered, so they look for dosages in the range of the LD50 (the dose at which fifty percent of those dosed will die). In the case of mass administrations of tranquilizers in mental hospitals, they look for a dose which will allow patients to continue to take care of themselves but render them incapable of violence and totally suppress psychotic symptoms which interfere with hospital routine. In general, dosages are higher than in medically prescribed or self-regulated use, because they are meant to kill, disable, or control the target population, rather than cure their diseases or give them pleasure.

Since goals are set unilaterally, those administering the drug must use coercive measures to insure that the desired dose gets into its target. As the divergence in goals between the two parties increases, the difficulty of administration increases proportionally. Physicians often worry that patients will suspect that their prescription is not good for them and thus not take their medicine. Where the divergence is relatively great and obvious, as in tuberculosis and mental hospitals, hospital personnel usually supervise patients' ingestion of medication very closely; even so, inmates often discover ingenious ways of evading forced medication.

In chemical warfare, where the interests of the parties are diametrically opposed, the problem of an "effective delivery system" becomes extremely important, thus highlighting the degree to which other forms of drug ingestion rely on the voluntary cooperation of the user. Chemical warfare agencies concern themselves with foolproof means of dosing entire populations, and so work on such devices as aerosols, which guarantee ingestion by saturating the air everyone must breathe, or methods of contaminating urban water supplies. In their zeal to dose all members of the target population, they create for themselves a problem which does not bother those who administer drugs in a more selective way that requires user cooperation. A homely example is the policeman who, attempting to squirt a political demonstrator with Mace, neglects to allow for the wind blowing toward him and gets a faceful of his own medicine.

Those who administer drugs to involuntary users are either indifferent about providing those who get the drug with any knowledge about it or actively attempt to prevent them from getting that knowledge. Hospital personnel seldom inform inmates receiving forced medication about main or side effects or how they can best be interpreted. They may suggest that "this pill will make you feel better" or that "the doctor thinks this will make you feel better" or that "the doctor thinks this will help your condition," but seldom give more detailed information. The difficulties occasioned by lack of knowledge already discussed can thus arise, though they may be counteracted by the development of a user's culture among people who are confined in total institutions and subject to the same drug regimen.

Where destruction or incapacitation of the target population is the aim, those who administer the drug may wish to prevent any knowledge that the drug is being administered, or of its effects, from reaching those who ingest it. In this way, they hope to prevent the taking of countermeasures and, by preventing the use of available knowledge to reach an understanding of what is happening, create, in addition to the drug's specific physiological effects, panic at the onslaught of the unknown. It was just this phenomenon that both Army chemical warriors and those of the psychedelic left hoped to exploit by putting LSD into urban water supplies. Not only, they hoped, would the drug interfere with people's normal functioning by causing them to misperceive and hallucinate; in addition, people would not even know that they had been given a drug which was causing these difficulties and so would be frightened as well. (As it turns out, Mayor Daley need not have worried about the Yippies putting LSD into the Chicago water supply during the 1968 Democratic Convention. As Army Chemical and Biological Warfare investigators had already discovered, LSD breaks down rapidly in the presence of chlorine, and the Chicago water supply usually contains enough chlorine that one can easily taste it. This defect in LSD as a chemical warfare agent has led the Army to an attempt to produce a water-soluble version of THC [tetrahydracannabinol, one of the active agents in marijuana], which otherwise is most easily ingested in smoke.)

Conclusion

If drug experiences somehow reflect or are related to social settings, we must specify the settings in which drugs are taken and the specific effect of those settings on the experiences of participants in them. This analysis suggests that it is useful to look at the role of power and knowledge in those settings, knowledge of how to take the drugs and what to expect when one does, and power over distribution of the drug, knowledge about it, and over the decision to take or not to take it. These vary greatly, depending on the character of the organization within which the drugs are used. In illicit drug use, the effects of the drug experience depend on the social links and cultural understandings that grow up among those who use the drug. In the use of medically prescribed drugs, the effects reflect the profit orientation of pharmaceutical manufacturers and the characteristic professional dominance exercised by physicians. Where drug use is forced on people, the results reflect the unilateral exercise of power in the interest of the stronger party.

Naturally, these are pure types, and many of the situations we observe in contemporary society are mixtures of them. Many people, for instance, originally begin taking a drug because a physician has prescribed it for them, but then continue to get supplies of it in illicit or semi-licit ways; their use probably contains features of both user control and control by the user's agent. Folk medicine probably consists of a similar mixture, since folk curers may not have professional interests that diverge from those of their patients to the same degree the modern physicians do; then again, they may. I don't suggest that empirical cases will fall neatly into one or another of these categories, but rather that the pure categories I have discussed show most clearly how knowledge and power can influence the experience of a drug user. Much more needs to be known about the pure types I have described (for it may turn out that my analyses are one-sided and incomplete), as well as about the numerous marginal types that exist.

In the course of writing this, I became conscious of the ambiguity of the very idea of a "drug." Much of what I have said about use enforced by a powerful external agent could be applied without much change to our daily ingestion of the pollutants in air, water, and food. Is smog a drug? Why not? Many people consider the fluoridation of city water supplies an instance of chemical warfare against them, sometimes going so far as to attribute the action to a foreign enemy. Are fluorides drugs? Clearly, we label as "drugs" a somewhat arbitrary selection of the materials we routinely ingest. It might be useful to look at the entire commonsense classification of ingested substances to see how we decide to call some things "foods," others "drugs," still others "pollutants," and whatever other categories people use. We could then ask what the consequences of such differential labeling are. We take different kinds of regulatory actions with respect to foods, drugs, and pollutants. What are the differences? How do they affect the distribution of knowledge and power with respect to ingestion of these materials and, therefore, the distribution of various kinds of experiences among those ingesting them? By extending the analysis I have begun here with respect to drugs, we might gain greater understanding of such diverse phenomena as smog poisoning, malnutrition, and indigestion.

The analysis might similarly be extended, in another direction, from consideration of chemically induced physical and psychological experiences to those produced by diseases of various kinds. We can investigate, for example, the way information about the effects of diseases is generated—what kind of research? done by whom? with what ends in mind?—and how it is communicated—in what social channels? with what barriers to overcome? We can then see how the resultant distribution of knowledge affects people's responses to their symptoms.

Beyond that, and I believe of more general import, we can investigate the sociology of normal physiological functioning. Consider that medical symptoms exhibit themselves as departure from normal function: breath that is "shorter" than normal, appetite that is "less" than normal, pain that is beyond normal expectation, bowel movements that are "unusual," and so on. What is the folk wisdom with respect to "normal functioning"? How is it taught and learned? How does it vary from group to group?

4

DISTRIBUTING MODERN ART

The way art works are publicized and distributed affects how those works are made in the first place and how they are later understood. People interested in contemporary art—collectors, dealers, curators, critics, not to mention artists themselves—have begun to take that proposition seriously as they worry about what the alleged mammoth increase in the amount of "hype" and merchandising associated with contemporary visual art is doing to that art and the artists who make it.

Writing in the *New Yorker*, Calvin Tomkins noted that a painting by Julian Schnabel had been sold at auction for $93,000 and remarked that

> for a number of people, the Schnabel sale neatly epitomized the 1982–83 art season, which has been dominated by the attention paid to non-expressionist painting and by complaints that this attention was the product of publicity, "hype," and rampant commercialism. (1983:80)

Roberta Smith, in the *Village Voice*, said, after suggesting that Schnabel deserved a lot of credit for his accomplishments:

> At the same time, Schnabel has brought a circus-like atmosphere to his art and his career which has clouded the view. In his public persona, his preposterous titles, and the scaled-up emptiness of his worst work, he has acted out the Romantic old-fashioned idea of what it means to be an artist in such larger than life, often hilarious terms that he has turned himself and his work—for the time being quite hopelessly merged—into a cliche, making a mockery of the very things he has dignified: himself, his art, and painting in general. (1982)

John Bernard Myers, from whom I will quote again, voiced the worry this way in the *New York Review of Books*:

> But how then to account for the enthusiastic reception now being given a wholly new batch of painters, around New York for only a

few years, all of them in their early thirties or late twenties? [New, that is, compared to such aging stars as DeKooning, Sam Francis, Lichtenstein, and Stella.] Variously called New Realists or Neo-Expressionists, they have "arrived," from Germany, Italy, and the provinces of America. The new painters, for all their brashness and ineptitude, have attracted a lively market which admires big, splashy, noisy, turbulent canvases, filled with soft-porn and hard-core banality. The new collectors are willing to pay handsomely in the tens of thousands, and do. (1982:32)

I want to analyze these complaints and observations, and the situation that appears to be provoking them, comparatively. All works of art, after all, get distributed somehow, and they all show the signs of how they are distributed. To put this in a broad perspective, let's use the concept of *art world*, as I have developed it elsewhere (Becker 1982). Writers often speak of "the art world" when they want to refer to the most fashionable people associated with those newsworthy objects and events that command astronomical prices. I use the term in a more technical sense.

1. All art works involve the cooperation of everyone whose activity has anything to do with the end result. That includes the people who make materials, instruments, and tools; the people who create the financial arrangements that make the work possible; the people who see to distributing the works that are made; the people who produced the tradition of forms, genres, and styles the artist works with and against; and the audience. For symphonic music, the list of cooperating people might include composers, players, conductors, instrument makers and repairers, copyists, managers and fund raisers, designers of symphony halls, music publishers, booking agents, and audiences of various kinds. For contemporary painting, an equivalent list would include painters, makers and purveyors of canvases, paints, and similar materials, collectors, art historians, critics, curators, dealers, managers and agents, such auxiliary personnel as, say, lithographic printers, and so on.

2. Why make such a list? Because each of these *cooperating links* is a point at which the people making the art have to consider how to take into account how the person at the other end of the link will cooperate—what they will and won't do, and on what terms— or suffer the consequences. They have, for instance, to think about what it will mean to paint a canvas of a size that will fit into a home comfortably as opposed to one that will fit into a corporation head-

quarters or a museum. Taking the anticipated reactions of others into account, they can decide to tailor what they do to what others will likely do. They can decide to paint a canvas that is four by six feet because they know it will be easier to find a home for it than one twenty by thirty. In the same way, a composer might decide to write a string quartet rather than something for two ocarinas and bassoon, in part because there are many more string quartets to play his piece than two-ocarina and bassoon combinations. If artists decide not to do what others want, they pay another kind of price. Instead of giving up some of their freedom to choose, they have to give up time to do themselves what others might have done for them if they were more cooperative, train others to do it for them, or do without. In each case, the work shows the effects of their choice.

3. All the people who thus cooperate in making a work of art do that by using mutually understood conventions. All sorts of aspects of art works are governed by conventional understandings as to how they can be done. Some common examples are: musical scales, which are a conventional choice of just a few from all the tones available; the three-act play; the sonnet; the history painting; and so on. Such questions as size and shape, length, and appropriate subject matters are all decidable by reference to conventional understandings as to how things should be done. Conventional knowledge is what makes it possible for musicians who have never seen each other to play as though they had known each other for years. It is what makes it possible for knowledgeable viewers to respond to a painting or musical work. Because you know what *ought* conventionally to happen, you can be surprised by an innovation which would otherwise be meaningless. It didn't mean anything special to hear Bob Dylan play electric guitar unless you knew that he had always played acoustic guitar. Using conventions makes it easier for people to cooperate and get the work of art done. Changing or ignoring them makes it harder and cuts down the possibility of getting others to cooperate.

4. An art world, to give a technical definition, consists of the network of cooperative activity involving all the people who contribute to the work of art coming off as it finally does, using the conventional understandings they share. Most work gets made in art worlds. Some does not, whether it is the innovative work of art-world mavericks (e.g., a Charles Ives or Conlon Nancarrow) or

the naive work of a Simon Rodia (the maker of the Watts Towers) who never heard of such a thing as the art world and wouldn't care much about it if he had.

5. Art worlds are always changing, as conditions change, including who gets recruited, amounts of resources available, and kinds of audiences. The world of published fiction changed radically when eighteenth-century England developed a new class of literate servants and business people who could read such work and wanted to. The modern novel was born.

6. One implication of this analysis is that, if we remember that one of the cooperating parties in the production of any work of art is the audience, we can think of a work as coming into existence anew every time someone looks at it, reads it, or hears it. This reminds us, and gives us a way to think about, the fact that the physical object is in a real sense not the whole art work, which is always being reinterpreted. The interpreter helps to create the work's character as a result.

7. Art works get their value from art worlds, so conceived. I don't mean that art works have no agreeable or instructive or edifying or enjoyable qualities, only that they don't have them *in themselves*, but rather as they are commonly interpreted to have them, in a world of like-thinking people. Great works are great to people who know enough to understand them for what they are. We owe that thought to Hume, among others. And we must remember that art worlds often reinterpret work, finding some valuable that they thought less so, and vice versa. The works haven't changed, but their value has.

8. Perhaps the most controversial thing to be said here is that the quality of a work is not affected by the kind of system it is made in. Good work (generally so recognized) has been produced under every sort of system, including the most vulgarly commercial, ones filled with "hype," ones that intruded shamelessly on the artist's prerogatives. Think of the Hollywood film. It is hard to imagine, given the conditions under which movies are made, that there are any good films at all, but we know that there are. Or consider the Victorian novel, whose authors had to take into account what publishers insisted on if they wanted their works to see print. J. A. Sutherland (1976: 114–16) has shown, for instance, how Thackeray's *Henry Esmond* got some of its finest qualities from the intrusion of George Smith, a literate and concerned publisher who

wouldn't pay the author until he took more care than was his custom.

9. Perhaps the most important thing to be said, for our later discussion, is that the participants invest the whole apparatus with an aura of "rightness," so that this way of producing art seems moral and other ways immoral. Using classical ballet steps is moral and proper, while using more ordinary motions like running, jumping, and falling down is somehow wrong, an insult, a disgrace—to people attached to the world of classical ballet. To adherents of the world of modern dance, of course, it is a different story.

Distribution Systems

One aspect of the system of cooperation that is an art world is the network of personnel and activities involved in the distribution of the work artists produce. Fully developed art worlds usually have elaborate distribution systems which integrate artists into their society's economy, taking the artist's work and getting it to the people who might be interested in it, usually (but not necessarily) trying in the process to make some money for the artist and others so that the work can continue to be produced.

Keep in mind that work does not need to be distributed. Certainly it need not be distributed in the artist's lifetime or while the artist is still active. Emily Dickinson and Charles Ives, to take notorious examples, had almost none of their work distributed while they were living. Cases like these let us see some of the influences of distribution systems. If your work is not distributed, you needn't worry about the people in charge of distribution and how they will react to it. Ives, having given up on the possibility of getting his music played through the conventional system of symphonic programming, didn't care whether his work could be played or not, and wrote music that was thought, for a long time, to be "unplayable."

There are interesting variations among the arts in the effect of non-distribution. A novel which is not distributed still exists as a physical object, even if in typescript rather than letterpress. A play or musical work, on the other hand, exists only as a set of instructions to performers, not as the actual performed work. Paintings are like written works, but differ in their size and bulk. If you are not going to be able to move your work through the existing distribution system, you are better off as a novelist or photographer than a painter or sculptor. (In fact, Edward Levine [1972] says painters sometimes give up when they realize they have no more room for their unsold canvases.) Even though paintings exist physically without being distributed, that is misleading. If we think of an art work as requiring the active participation of audience members to complete it, then a painting is, in a way, like a play script or a musical score, a set of directions to viewers to look here, look there, and have this kind of experience. If no one looks, if no one has the experiences the painting might provide, in some real sense it does not exist, however sturdy it is as a physical object.

So painters want their work distributed, so that it may be completed by being viewed. In addition, distribution has a crucial effect on reputation. What is not distributed is not known and thus cannot be well thought of or have historical importance. The process is circular: what does not have a good reputation will not be distributed. Thus judgments about what constitutes great or important art are affected by the operations of distribution systems, with all their built-in professional biases. This is one basis for the current concern about "hype."

Whose cooperation does a painter or sculptor need to distribute work? A number of systems presently operate simultaneously. Each of them has to do the jobs that Francis Haskell outlined in his analysis of one such form, patronage: provide financial support, give the artist an adequate place to display his work, and give the artist a knowledgeable audience whose members can understand what he is about. At one extreme, private patronage, while not common these days, is not totally unknown (Marcel Duchamp is a relatively recent example). Public patronage exists, both in the form of fellowships and commissions, but provides no one with a steady and dependable source of income. Public sale for the mass market only occurs for kitsch, sold in the rows of galleries along San Francisco's Fisherman's Wharf, parts of Chicago's Michigan Avenue, and in the lobbies of Hilton hotels.

The gallery-dealer-auction system, which assumed its present form in nineteenth-century France, is the standard, and the one currently undergoing changes. As it now operates, and has operated for the last century, the system has the effect Raymonde Moulin describes in great detail, in her classic study of the art market in France (she focuses on France, but the situation is not very different anywhere in the world now): it totally confounds artistic or aesthetic and financial worth. If a work is financially valuable, it has an automatic claim to be aesthetically interesting, and the basis on which works get financial worth is that they have lasting aesthetic value. As Moulin says:

> The speculator [in contemporary art] makes two bets, intimately connected in the short run, one on the aesthetic value, the other on the economic value of the works he buys, the two guaranteeing each other. To win this double bet is to confirm oneself simultaneously as an economic actor and a cultural actor. (1967:219)

One of the chief functions of the discipline of art history in such a system is to ensure that paintings are not only aesthetically justified but also financially solid, that is, really what they are alleged to be and thus worth what is asked for them. Connoisseurship consists in knowing exactly the value of works, both aesthetically and financially.

As Moulin explains, the market in old and contemporary masters is relatively stable. Works once thought very important seldom become completely unimportant. If nothing else, they continue to have value because they are historically important. Of course, their actual market value fluctuates, as do the values of all collectibles, in line with the ups and downs of the financial markets. In particular, during recessions and depressions people who need cash sell art and prices drop precipitously. This has little to do with aesthetics, but is purely a matter of economics and investment policies.

The market in contemporary art, the kind we want to discuss here, is, according to Moulin, more speculative. Is it good and what is it worth are both more difficult questions to answer. Some of what goes on must be understood not so much by referring to questions of art and aesthetics but by comparison, say, to the phenomenon of new issues in the stock market. In both cases, information, and especially inside information others don't yet have, is crucial. You make money and enhance your reputation for fine aesthetic perceptions by making judgments about artists and works others will later accept as authoritative. New artists and new stock issues have yet to prove their worth. They prove it by becoming attractive to people who are knowledgeable. The process by which this happens is not new, and has always involved the manipulation of information.

Artists, dealers, critics, curators, and collectors all collaborate, in ways that are well known, to make new works valuable. A critic decides that some artists are doing work that is more important than others yet realize. Liking the work and thinking the artist deserves some help, the critic buys some and recommends it to people who find his or her opinions trustworthy. Some of these will be collectors whose purchases in themselves make the work more "important" and valuable. The collectors' purchases embolden a dealer, and together these influence others to buy the artist's work. When enough of this has gone on, a museum may be persuaded that the artist deserves an exhibition, and the work becomes even more valuable just because it now has the cachet of having been exhibited in such a place.

John Bernard Myers finds it difficult to understand who is the prime mover in this process:

> The question, however, of who creates the "market" for high-priced contemporary painting is not so simple as it would at first seem. Perhaps the most widespread view is that the market is the result of favorable reviews. Critics give people certainty of taste and knowledge. If enough writers say an artist is superior, then no doubt he is taken to be. Thus, there are those who maintain that the prestige and fortune of the Abstract Expressionists, among them Pollock, Rothko, Gottlieb, and Still, were created by Clement Greenberg. . . . [But Greenberg] has liked a wide variety of painters and sculptors, many of whom did not become famous or make money. (1983:33)

Myers goes on to make the same point about the alleged influence of reviews in the *New York Times*: some artists Hilton Kramer praised, for instance, have become very successful, others not so.

The solution is simple. Who starts the process is not crucial. But it only works if whoever starts it can convince all the other participants in the value-creating process to cooperate. What leads to that cooperation is a sort of bandwagon effect, in which (to put it in the best light) people see what the prescient forerunners saw. We can put the matter in a worse light by saying that now that everyone seems to agree on the worth of this new work, no one wants to be left out in the cold, perhaps financially, but certainly in the matter of taste and ability to see what everyone else sees and values.

In any event, this kind of activity calls into question the equation of artistic and financial worth. People buy "hot" young artists in the hope that they will have bought something that will simultaneously appreciate substantially in financial value and come to have a permanent reputation as a sterling example of the way the history of art was going and thus as a major work. Reputations are so volatile that, as is characteristic of any speculative market, no one can tell whether they reflect "true worth" or "mere hype."

The minute the automatic connection between aesthetic and financial value comes into question at all, it opens up other questions. Especially questions of corruption. Are critics who invest in work they find wonderful only feathering their own nests? Are collectors who sit on the boards of museums doing the same by recommending exhibits that will enhance the value of their speculative purchases? I don't at all mean that I think this is what's happening. It's worse than that. No one can tell if that is what is happening or not, including the people involved. The mixture of values is so complete that to pursue one objective that is estimable—wanting to own and support fine art—is to pursue the other—trying to make a killing.

Artists, of course, cannot be unaware of all this and are not. So they begin to make their work with an eye to how it will fit into the distribution system. Dickens, after all, wrote his narratives so that they reached dramatic climaxes in rhythms that coincided with the length of the serial publications in which they appeared. Composers write pieces of a specified length and instrumentation because that is what the systems that distribute their music—whether it is the symphony orchestra and concert hall or the avant-garde and the universities and music schools—can handle. In fact, artists almost invariably make their work with an eye to how it will be distributed. A purist, imagining a lonely artist communing with a muse, finds this appalling, but it is no more than common sense.

The reason there is a problem here is that it just is not, for the reasons I have suggested, possible to know whether people are being corrupted or not. Here is the dynamic. What everyone is interested in is something that is going to happen in the future: the development of an artistic career and a body of work, the development of a corresponding reputation. Neither of these is predictable. The artist's development cannot be manipulated, although people can try to influence it through criticism, suggestion, coercion, or temptation. The techniques of reputation-influencing are somewhat better understood, although not as well as practitioners of public relations like to let on.

The key variable is information. It is much like the stock market or the race track. Some people, of course, may have better judgment than others. Others, whatever the quality of their judgment, however, may have better information. And it may be more important to know who is buying, or interested in buying, a certain artist's work than it is to know whether it is really any good or not. Nor is that a matter of corruption because, after all, we usually rely on the judgment of people more informed than we are. The suspicion of corruption arises when the information is not public. In the stock market this is called "insider knowledge," and insiders are forbidden to profit by it.

The language of the contemporary art world has this speculative ring to it. No one wants to, or feels they can afford to, wait for the judgment of history. That will mean missing out. You won't be able to win the beautiful painting you would love to live with if you don't buy it now, because others will see how good it is and its price will vanish into the stratosphere. You won't be able to make a killing waiting for the judgment of history either; it will be old news and worth nothing.

This, finally, is where "hype" comes in. The mechanisms of publicity can be used to create a surge of mass behavior, a collective feeling that the boat is pulling out and we're not on it. Note that I used the word "mass." That is a technical term in sociology, used to denote the process by which large numbers of people individually decide that some particular course of action seems a good one, and all those individual choices converge on the same line of activity: they all buy Toyotas that year or decide to wear blue jeans to work or cut their hair in a new way or grow beards. No group gets together and decides to do any of that. It "just happens." Decisions of that kind are especially open to influence by advertising, publicity, and other communications aimed at people as individuals (as opposed, say, to them as members and functionaries of communities).

This points to what may be a historically unique feature of the contemporary art world (though I doubt it). The art world has in our time been a *community of taste*. Its members knew each other, met at parties and clubs, knew each other's tastes and possessions. They competed with each other, to be sure, for priority: to know first what others would eventually know, to esteem and collect a new kind of work marginally ahead of others, and so on. But they competed in a game they all knew with people they knew. They knew what "everyone" thought, and could not be led to think something was valuable unless the other members of their community agreed. They never had to worry about opening up the newspaper and being surprised by news of something that had gone on in the world of art. In such a community, hype is not possible.

Hype is possible, however, when an arena of social activity is not a community but rather is populated by a mass, in the technical sense I used the term above (not, by the way, in the pejorative and snobbish way characteristic of a lot of contemporary and classical social criticism). Without a community of taste to dominate the activity of the art world, people can *then* use the techniques of publicity to reach isolated individuals (or small coteries, which comes to the same thing) and make them feel that something important is going on which they know nothing about. *Then* you can create reputations which may be based on no more than talk and rumor. So the current situation is one in which the art market and world have grown to the point where there is not enough community to make that impossible.

Listen to John Bernard Myers describe the current situation (and we can be sure that he speaks for many others):

... what a gaggle of go-getters these turned out to be—all over town. The most nauseating group was the young married women with time on their hands specializing in "art for offices"—sometimes whole suites of offices where masses of brightly colored prints, drawings, and gouaches decorated the walls of jerry-built high-rises. Some specialized in cheering up doctors' and dentists' waiting rooms or placing kinetic light-ups and movables opposite operating chairs. Other entrepreneurs concentrated on the big corporate patrons. They engaged themselves in filling the lobbies, courtyards, plazas, and terraces of the new glass and steel edifices rising along Madison, Park, and Third avenues. Invariably this was done with tangles of bent cable, slabs of Corten steel, high-buffed stainless, or massive hunks of granite, both round and square.

Another group specialized in tapestries to lighten the grimness of vestibules and stairwells. Somewhere, in Ecuador perhaps, natives were hooking away at big zigzags, arcs, circles, rectangles, or polka dots of eye-filling intensity to soften the impact of elevator banks. New business was pouring into foundries in Long Island, upper New York State, or New Jersey to "fabricate" jumbo-sized constructions by artists famous, near-famous, or quite unknown, who prepared mole-sized maquettes for elephantine productions. These celebrations could be found on the lawns of benign industrial plants, secure amid the expensive landscape engineering, visible proof of business supporting art and improving the community. (1983:34)

We have heard this tone and language often enough in social history, every time an old elite loses its privileged position in some world. It is the way Wasp citizens of New York and Philadelphia reacted to finding the streets of their cities filled with peasant immigrants bawling at each other in strange languages. It is the way the old French elite of Quebec felt and talked when their towns filled up with the English managers and technicians who ran the new factories, people who had never heard of their old family names and cared less. It is the way the elites of rural California feel when the managers of the large corporations which purchased their lettuce ranches show no interest in preserving the old systems of deference that characterized their towns. (And why should the heads of those corporations worry about such things? Their children will not go to school with the children of *braceros*.)

In short, this is the language of a displaced elite. The sociologist W. I. Thomas once remarked that social disorganization is a stage between two stages of organization. The upheaval people like Myers observe will be replaced by a new kind of organization of the art world, one in which a new sort of community will dominate taste, collecting, and all the associated activities. I don't know what that will be, but it will very likely be along the lines Myers so feelingly describes.

Two questions remain. The first is: is any of this true? Does this guy know what he is talking about? I don't know if it's true or not, neither the diagnosis nor, especially, the prediction. I am not in the inside information game, so I don't set great store by making predictions of that kind. I am more concerned with the nature and dynamics of what is going on. So I invite you to think of this as a collection of working hypotheses, perhaps to be checked out by further observation.

The second question is, assuming that this is what is going on: is it good or bad for art? Here I really don't know. As I said earlier, we all know that art that we could all agree is first rate, whatever our critical commitments, has been made under the most unlikely circumstances. Artists do good and interesting work whether they are working for the mass market (like Dickens) or for an imperious royal patron. They do good work under politically repressive circumstances. It would be nice if there were a simple linear correlation between quality and circumstances of production. But there is not. So I am not convinced that the current importance of publicity and media attention to the world of visual art means that the work produced is necessarily bad. Without accepting his entire argument, let me close by quoting Calvin Tomkins again:

The deep anxiety that some people feel over having to decide what is or is not art is almost certainly heightened by the prevalence of large-scale publicity. Confusion on this score makes older works of art that everybody *knows* are art seem more desirable than ever— that, at least, is one interpretation of the buying fever at Sotheby's and Christie's spring sales (which received, by the way, a huge amount of publicity). The fact is that works of art (and their makers) have figured prominently in the public eye whenever lots of money was being paid for them. Contemporary works are going for very high prices today, and increasing notice is being taken of them as a result. This is not necessarily an impure, or even an unhealthy, situation. Some artists are going to feel neglected and bitter because of it, and others may feel unnerved by the competition, but that should not have much effect on what they do. If it did, then we could be fairly sure, for once, that what they do is not art. (1983:83)

PART 2

SOCIAL RESEARCH

5

RADICAL POLITICS AND SOCIOLOGICAL RESEARCH: Observations on Methodology and Ideology (with Irving Louis Horowitz)

With the increasing polarization of political opinions and positions in the United States, sociologists have become increasingly concerned about the political import of their work. Until recent years, most sociologists probably believed that sociology was somehow above politics, even though sociologists had often engaged in political activity, and political and sociological discussion had often overlapped. Events have now made it impossible to leave that belief uninspected. The disclosure that social scientists have undertaken research designed to further the interests of the powerful at the expense of those of the powerless (e.g., riot control at home and "civic action" abroad) showed how even apparently innocent research might serve special political interests. Prison research has for the most part been oriented to problems of jailers rather than those of prisoners; industrial research, to the problems of managers rather than those of workers; military research, to the problems of generals rather than those of privates. Greater sensitivity to the undemocratic character of ordinary institutions and relationships (ironically fostered by social scientists themselves) has revealed how research frequently represents the interests of adults and teachers instead of those of children and students; of men instead of women; of the white middle class instead of the lower class, blacks, Chicanos, and other minorities; of the conventional straight world instead of freaks; of boozers instead of potheads. Wherever someone is oppressed, an "establishment" sociologist seems to lurk in the background, providing the facts which make oppression more efficient and the theory which makes it legitimate to a larger constituency.

The belief that members of the sociological discipline are guilty as charged helps to account for the way many sociologists have responded to the attacks. They have not dismissed the charges. On the contrary, professional associations, scientific societies, the periodical literature, and foundations from Ford to Russell Sage have reviewed the political tenor of sociological work. Younger men have debated whether it was moral to be affiliated with the sociological enterprise. Older sociologists have searched their work and their consciences to see if, far from being the political liberals they imagined themselves, they were in fact lackeys of capitalist repression.

In the midst of these reconsiderations, positions hardened. The language of scholarly journals became increasingly polemical. Meetings thought to be scientific were disrupted by political protest and discussion. Presidential addresses at national and regional meetings were interrupted. All this was accompanied by, and in some cases was intimately connected with, political uprisings on entire campuses, in more than one of which sociology students played a key role. Some teachers found themselves unable to bear the discourtesies of their radical students. Some professors saw attempts to change the hierarchical relations of a department as an attack on the very idea of scholarship. They assumed that a student who called their ideas "bullshit" was attacking rational thought, and not simply using in public a critical rhetoric usually reserved for private meetings. Sometimes they were right, for some students seemed intent on cutting off debate and substituting for the free play of intellect a vocabulary designed exclusively to conform to a political position. The distinction was not always easy to make, and those making affronts were often as unsure of what they were about as those receiving them.

In situations of collective upheaval, persons and groups move to maximize their private interests. In this case, some sociologists tried to further their professional careers by judiciously taking one side or the other. Groups moved to secure power within professional associations. Some radicals seriously discussed taking over professional associations or university departments, having convinced themselves that worthwhile political goals might be served by such acts—though the resemblance of such maneuvers to similar careerist actions by doctrinaire groups of quite different persuasions in the same associations and departments was obvious. Elder sociological statesmen of every political stripe appeared, trying to gather "unpredictable youth" into their own sphere of influence. The rhetoric of radicalism appeared in every area of sociology.

Participants in these events found themselves confused. Members of the older "straight" factions, however, failed to note the confusion. They saw the actions as concerted expressions of radical or left sentiment. They could not see the conflicts of interests among radicals, blacks, Chicanos, women, and other "liberation" groups. The persistent emergence of differences among these groups made it obvious that the mere assertion of radical sympathies guaranteed neither concerted political action nor a uniform style of sociological analysis. The differences and confusions demonstrate the need for a clearer analysis of the political meaning and relevance of sociology.

Good sociology is often radical. A sociology which is not good, however, cannot be radical in any larger sense. But moral sentiments do not determine scientific quality. The reverse is more often true: the quality of sociological work determines the degree to which it has a radical thrust.

We insist on the isomorphism between radical sociology and good sociology in order to dissuade those who think political sloganeering can substitute for knowledge based on adequate evidence and careful analysis; to persuade others that their work has suffered from a conventional social and political attitude, expressed in the way they frame problems and in the methods of research they choose; and to demonstrate that there is a tradition of good sociology worth preserving, that the expression "good sociology" has meaning, and that the possibility of doing good sociology is not tied irrevocably to contemporary academic institutions.

Good Sociology

Good sociology is sociological work that produces meaningful descriptions of organizations and events, valid explanations of how they come about and persist, and realistic proposals for their improvement or removal. Sociology based on the best available evidence should provide analyses that are likely to be true in the linguistic sense of not being falsifiable by other evidence, and also in the ontological sense of being "true to the world."

In the first sense, generations of methodologists have developed procedures and techniques by which approximate truth can be reached. The sociologist achieves partial truths, always open to correction. While methodologists have dealt only with a small part of the problem of arriving at propositions and inferences likely to be true, the techniques they recommend as warranted are all we have; we will have to use them until we invent something better. With all their faults, interviews, participant observation, questionnaires, surveys, censuses, statistical analysis, and controlled experiments can be used to arrive at approximate truth. While the results to date are modest, some things are known because sociologists have employed these techniques.

Sociologists have done less well by truth in the second sense. While they know some things well, they can predict few things with accuracy. Humanists and scientists alike complain that sociology tells them only a tiny part of what they really want to know. Men want to know how the world is; sociologists give them correlation coefficients. Coefficients do help us know how the world is, and one need not accept the humanistic contention that unless sociology can reproduce the world in full living color it is worthless. Nonetheless, the charge stings. Sociologists' knowledge about real problems in society does not take them far.

If essentials are left out, the work cannot pass the tests that science poses for itself. The work cannot, to use the language of statistical analysis, account for much of the variance in the phenomena under study. In addition, sociological work loses its potential practical importance if it does not encompass the major processes and actors involved in those parts of the world to be changed. Therefore, work that is not true to the world has neither scientific nor practical value.

Why does so much sociological work fail to be true both to its own scientific standards and to the larger world? Some radical sociologists have insisted that political ideologies blind us to the truth because our political masters have paid us to produce research that will be useful in a different direction, or (more subtly) because our standard methods and concepts, reflecting political biases and pressures, prevent us from seeing what would be politically inconvenient. Many failures in sociological research result from simple ignorance, having little to do with either ideological bias or utopian fantasy. But we should examine those instances in which sociological research has been severely blemished not so much by ignorance as by bias.

Consider the charge that the concept of "accommodation," applied to racial relations, had a conservative effect (Myrdal 1944).

It implied that blacks accepted their lower position in American society and that therefore, because blacks did not complain, the situation was not unjust. But to say that racial relations in a given place at a given time were accommodative means only that the racial groups involved had achieved a modus vivendi and does not imply that the actors were happy or the system just. Whether any or all actors considered the system pleasant or righteous is a matter for empirical investigation. If the description of the situation as accommodative were true to the world, no evidence of conflict and resistance could be discovered because none would exist. To assume consensus would be bad sociology insofar as it assumed that, since there is evidence of accommodation, we can rule out the possibility of conflict. The concept of accommodation can be objectionable only if we insist that its use will necessarily cause sociologists to overlook or ignore conflict, exploitation, or resistance to change where they occur. But a full exploration of possibilities, as in Robert Park's description of the race-relations cycle (Park and Burgess 1921), applied evenhandedly, should spare sociologists such errors.

Much contemporary sociology is not true even in the narrow scientific sense. It is falsifiable by evidence contained in its own data or by evidence that could have been obtained had the investigator bothered to look for it. Sociologists tend to ignore the degree to which they fail to abide by their own methodological standards and consequently fail to achieve the scientific rationality to which they pretend. Where sociology allows political biases and generalized expressions of wishful thinking to affect its conclusions, it lacks truth in either of the two meanings discussed.

Radical Sociology

An immense variety of political positions have been announced as radical. Since the actual consequences of the label are so important to all the people involved, one cannot expect any definition to go undisputed. But most arguments over definitions turn on questions of the means by which agreed-on goals can be achieved or of the correct diagnosis of the ills that afflict society, rather than on the goals that radicals ought to strive for. Thus, most radicals will agree that a key feature of any radical political program is the reduction and eventual removal of inequalities in society, whether the inequality is of power, economic resources, life chances, or knowledge.

Likewise, most radicals will agree that a radically reconstructed society should maximize human freedom, especially when that is conceived as dialectically related to social order.

Radicals may not so universally agree on the necessity of permanent change and revolution as an ideal. We ourselves believe that every society and every set of social arrangements must be inspected for their potential inequalities and interferences with freedom, even those which seem to conform to one or another blueprint for a socialist utopia. The radical, so defined normatively, is never satisfied, never prepared to abandon the struggle for an even more egalitarian and free society. At the least, the better is the critic of the good.

Where circumstances compel a choice between individual interests, self-expression, and personal welfare, on the one hand, and social order, stability, and the collective good, on the other, such a radical politics acts for the person as against the collectivity. It acts to maximize the number and the variety of options people have open to them, at the expense of neatness, order, peace, and system. It regards conflict as a normal concomitant of social life and a necessary element in political action. Clearly, some definitions of radicalism are based precisely on collectivism. While we look for the convergence of personal and public goals, when we are compelled to make a choice, it is on behalf of persons.

The radical sees change as permanent and inevitable, but he need not accept all changes as good. Rather, he sides with the powerless against the powerful, and renounces coercion, terror, and control as methods of establishing truths about the world.

The posture of a radical sociology overlaps considerably with that of a radical politics. Radical sociology also rests on a desire to change society in a way that will increase equality and maximize freedom, and it makes a distinctive contribution to the struggle for change. On the one hand, it provides the knowledge of how society operates, on the basis of which a radical critique of inequality and lack of freedom can be made. On the other hand, it provides the basis for implementing radical goals, constructing blueprints for freer, more egalitarian social arrangements, the working plans for radical utopias. These constructive aspects are rooted in the positivist tradition, just as the critical aspects are rooted in the Marxist tradition. Both involve an explanation of radical goals, and both involve a repudiation of all forms of mystical, theological, and supernaturalist interpretations of events.

A radical sociology thus looks for explanations of social life and theories of society which assume that radical change is at least possible, and resists those theories which root inequality in "inescapable facts" of biology or social structure (Horowitz 1968). Since such assumptions are seldom subjected to empirical test, a radical sociology can just as reasonably assume possibilities that more conservative or pessimistic sociologies do not.

In the controversy between Kingsley Davis and Wilbert E. Moore (1945: 242–49) and Melvin W. Tumin (1953: 387–93), the real difference of opinion was not over the fact of social stratification in American life, or even over the existence of inequality. There were indeed differences of opinion at the factual level, but the core controversy concerned the tendencies of American society: whether the direction of the democratic society carried with it as a central agenda item the reduction and finally the elimination of inequality. If inequality is rooted in the nature of man, with only the forms of inequality changing and the types of oppressors shifting, then the goal of equality is itself suspect. Any radical sociology must explore the nature of inequality fully, and beyond that must assume the possibility of abolishing inequality and describing the machinery necessary to implement a more egalitarian social order (Dumont 1969).

It might be objected that this equation of radicalism and the search for equity itself represents a liberal "bourgeois" model rather than a radical paradigm, that true radicalism must uphold the banner of a particular social system, such as socialism. While this formulation is abstractly appealing and in fact is often employed by radical theorists, it omits the most important fact of our times: the need for a social scientific judgment of *all* available political systems. Any equation of radical perspectives with the demand for equity implies the universal claim to priority of equality in socialist systems such as the Soviet Union, no less than in capitalist systems such as the United States. To demand allegiance to any social system as the mark of a radical perspective is to ignore the one-hundred-year history of inequality within what has passed for socialism, as well as the far longer history of inequality under capitalism.

But the search for equity is only one side of the radical thrust. At least equal in importance is the investigation of the ability of society, as presently organized, to deliver equity. It is the assessment of that ability that divides radical and liberal analysts. The ability of established society to absorb new social demands of disenfranchised groups becomes a major concern of the radical. The historic concern of radicalism with problems of revolution expresses a pessimistic view of the present social and economic order's ability to absorb change.

No matter which of these several tasks a radical sociology undertakes, it finds itself providing the facts, theories, and understandings that a radical politics requires for its implementation. For a radical political posture without reliable facts and analyses is no more than insurrectionary art incapable of predicting its own successes or failures. Radical sociology provides relevant and trustworthy data, intellectual resources for measuring costs as well as benefits in realizing the insurrectionary act.

Conflict between Radical Sociology and Radical Politics

Radical sociology may create a tension with radical politics, pure and simple, by indicating the high cost of some desired act. For example, it may analyze the special features of the Cuban-Castro revolution and produce an explanation of why guerrilla insurgency was successful in Cuba in 1959 but tragically unsuccessful in Bolivia in 1969. It is by no means a simple matter to counsel the gathering of evidence instead of performing a revolutionary act. But the gathering of evidence distinguishes a radical sociology from a radical politics, without necessarily destroying the basis for their mutual interaction.

A radical sociology will base itself either explicitly or implicitly on the premises of a radical politics. In either case, it will produce knowledge that serves the purposes of radical politics, in any of a variety of ways.

Every group in power is bent on the protection of privilege. Therefore, every radical sociology must expose the nature of such privilege, unmasking forms of domination. This unmasking process creates dilemmas. It implies a ruthless stripping away of all mystery and cant, not just that of the Department of Defense but also that of the nation of Islam. One task of a radical sociology is thus to persuade the oppressed and radicals of the need for as total a dedication to what is true as to what they may deem good. It is here too that the issue between most contemporary forms of radical sociology and radical political action becomes enmeshed in controversy, since many forms of radical politics are themselves bound to canons of secrecy, perhaps more benign than conservative politics but ultimately no less destructive of the search for truth in society.

Every status quo—societal, organizational, or factional—thrives on myth and mystification. Every group in power—in a nation, a government, an economy, a political party, or a revolutionary cadre—tells its story as it would like to have it believed, in the way it thinks will promote its interests and serve its constituencies. Every group in power profits from ambiguity and mystification, which hide the facts of power from those over whom power is exerted and thus make it easier to maintain hegemony and legitimacy. A sociology that is true to the world inevitably clarifies what has been confused, reveals the character of organizational secrets, upsets the interests of powerful people and groups. And while uncovering error does not necessarily aid the interests of those exploited by an organization or society, it does at least permit equal access to the evidence upon which action must be based. Only if sociological work is good in the sense of explaining actual relationships of power and authority can it provide a force for change. Thus, work which is true to the world and explains the actual relations of power and privilege that envelop and determine what goes on in society will be politically useful to radicals, even though (importantly) those who do such work may not themselves be committed to radical political goals.

Sociologists already know the difficulties that come from doing work which exposes the operations of powerful groups in society (see the various accounts in Vidich, Bensman, and Stein 1964). In operating explicitly in behalf of radical goals and in cooperation with people engaged in radical political action, the sociologist will experience other characteristic difficulties. For instance, a good sociological analysis, explored fully for its political implications, may undermine one's own position of superiority and privilege. Thus, a radical sociological analysis of universities entails exposing the myths by which the professor who makes the analysis supports his own privileged position of tenure and income. Similarly, white sociologists find themselves producing work which undermines their unequal privileges vis-à-vis blacks; men undermine the bases of their social superiority to women; and so on. This is why the poor and downtrodden are never "radical"—what they do is "natural," in keeping with their "interests." The radical violates the canon of self-interest or group interest. The good sociologist carries radicalism a step further: he makes it a principle to transcend parochialism and patriotism in investigating the social context.

The radical sociologist will also find that his scientific "conservatism"—in the sense of being unwilling to draw conclusions on the basis of insufficient evidence—creates tension with radical activists. This results from the differing time scales of the two activities. The social scientist takes time to collect evidence, but the political activist must often make decisions prior to the compilation of adequate evidence. Under such circumstances, the political man will act; the sociologist can give him the best available evidence. Radical activism is not the same as the know-nothingism underlining the irrationalist "will to act," but rather a recognition that action may be induced by needs that cannot possibly await the supply of the social scientist's information. The lag between action and information explains, in part, the peculiar tension between the political man and the social scientist, a tension that often leads the activist to disregard the sociologist's advice and, correspondingly, often leads the sociologist to an overconservative estimate of the potential success of a dramatic political action.

Since radical politics and radical sociology are not the same, the two may conflict. What is the relation between political radicalism and sociological radicalism? Rosa Luxemburg acted as a revolutionist and as a leader of the Spartacists of the German Left Socialist movement, but at the same time she functioned as a radical, as a critic of Lenin and of the dogma of proletarian dictatorship. She did this at a moment of revolutionary euphoria when serious thinking was at a premium. It is her criticism which is now best remembered. The same can be said of Eugene V. Debs, whose importance in the Socialist movement lay precisely in his being above the fratricidal struggles for control of the Socialist party apparatus. Debs, the radical man, had little organizational power in American socialism. Far less concerned with organization than Daniel DeLeon, Debs alone emerged as the ecumenical figure for the Socialists (see Ginger 1949).

Radicalism, then, entails a critique of organizational constraints. Yet revolution can only be made on the basis of a theory of organization. This is why the roles of radical sociologist and revolutionary activist, while they may coexist, cause considerable tension within the person and between the organization and the individual. If the activist joins forces with other advocates for rapid change, the sociologist points out how limited the practical effects of these changes may be. The activist, achieving his goals, seeks to enjoy the fruits of his victory; the radical sociologist looks for new sources of inequality and privilege to understand, expose, and uproot.

The difference between political radicalism and sociological radicalism deserves further elaboration. While the two can be linked, they can also occur independently and may be quite distinct. Radical action and rhetoric are one thing, and a radically informed sociology is another. Confusing the two opens leftism to any professional opportunism of the moment. Political sloganeers can easily tailor their doctrine to the changing fortunes of political sects. Serious sociologists find it much harder to change their sociological practice to match their changing political beliefs. To teach the same courses in theory and method one taught twenty years ago, while shifting from support for the government to opposition, does little to change the political thrust of contemporary social science. One can use radical rhetoric and engage in radical political action while one's sociology, because of its failure to be good, leaves established myths and institutions untouched. This is only the radical manifestation of the dualist distinction between "fact" and "value" adhered to by most conservatives. The "values" shift and become anti-establishment rather than pro-establishment. But the world of "fact," or, as is more nearly true, the fantasy that passes for sociological fact, remains unaltered.

Radicalism and Causal Analysis

The intersection of sociological and political analysis, the common ground which allows a characterization of various kinds of sociology as having one or another political cast, lies in their mutual concern with causes of events. It seems clear that any necessary condition for the occurrence of an event may be considered a cause of that event, at least in the limited sense that if the condition were not present, the event would not occur. From this point of view, there is an infinite or at least a very large number of causes of any event. To use a *reductio ad absurdum,* the presence of oxygen in the atmosphere is a cause of class exploitation, since without oxygen there would be no people, and without people there could be no exploitation. All such physical conditions of human action are, in this extended and vacuous sense, causes. In a more restricted and less trivial way, the actions of every person and group that contribute, however remotely, to a social event occurring in the way it did can be seen as a contributing cause of the event, since in their absence things would have occurred differently. To take a not-so-absurd example, the actions of slaves constitute one of the causes of slavery, since they could (and sometimes did) refuse to act as slaves (even though the price might be death).

Even though there are a multitude of causes of any event, both scientific and political analysis concentrate on only a few of them—different analyses emphasizing different causes. How do sociologists choose from among the many possible causes those they will emphasize in their political analysis or investigate in their research? Sometimes they look for those potential causes which vary, or might vary, in the specific cases observed. Thus, social scientists ignore the presence of oxygen as a cause of social events, since it is a constant in human affairs (except, of course, for those rare situations in which its presence becomes problematic, as in a recent study of social relationships among the men who climbed Mount Everest [Emerson 1966]). Sometimes they choose causes for investigation with an eye to the "usefulness" of results. Insofar as analysis is meant to be useful as a guide to someone's action, sociologists look to causal analysis for the clues as to how things might be changed, how they might be kept the same, and what the cost of either course is.

These guidelines help somewhat but do not go far enough in cutting down the number of causes the analyst pays attention to. On further inspection, we can see that the assignment of causes to events has a political aspect. The way sociologists assign causes, both in setting up hypotheses to be studied and in announcing conclusions, exhibits the influence of a political point of view, however implicit or hazy.

When sociologists link a cause to an event or a state of affairs, they at the same time assign blame for it. An event occurred because certain actors did something that helped to make it occur; had they acted differently, the event would not have occurred as it did. If the event is judged to be morally or politically reprehensible, the sociological analysis, by isolating those actors as the cause of the event, blames them for its occurrence.

An analysis may also implicitly or explicitly place the blame for events on impersonal forces beyond personal control—human nature, the human condition, or the social system—and thus excuse the people whose actions appeared to be morally suspect by suggesting that they could not help doing what they did. Deterministic sociologies of every description perform this service for the villains they identify.

If sociology allows for choice on the part of human actors, then it can blame, by the way it assigns causes, any of the people involved, since they could have chosen not to do what they did. This has consequences for the political character of a sociological analysis. Volitional sociologies perform this service for the heroes they identify.

The sociological analysis of causes has practical importance. When some object or action is labeled as the cause of the event or situation, the analysis suggests what would have to be influenced or altered in order to make a significant change in that event or situation. Some things will be easier to change than others. The analysis may suggest that, under the circumstances, it is virtually impossible to change what must be changed in order to affect the situation. Alternatively, the analysis may focus on things easily changed in themselves but which have little chance of changing the situation. Every combination of the feasibility of intervention and of the magnitude of the expected effect can occur in a particular analysis.

When sociologists, in their investigation of causes, implicitly or explicitly assign blame for events and when they suggest what must be done to cause meaningful social change, they speak of matters that are also the subject of political analyses. Their analyses can be judged to be radical, liberal, or conservative by the same criteria used to judge political analyses.

In general, radicals will judge a sociological analysis as radical when its assignment of causes, and thus of blame, coincides with the preferred demonology of the political group making the judgment. Radicals will denounce analyses as conservative (and conservatives will denounce analyses as radical) when the assignment of causes blames people who "don't deserve it." Similarly, radicals may criticize analyses that suggest causes which, when we take action, are too easily influenced and will not produce sufficiently profound results (right-wing reformism or opportunism), or are too difficult to influence, thus leading to disillusionment and low morale (left adventurism).

Since radical political positions are more "unusual" and thus more visible in contemporary social science, it is radical sociologists who are most aware of these political connotations of sociological work. Most discussions of the problem have therefore been conducted by sociologists who conceive of themselves, or would like to conceive of themselves, as radical and who therefore focus on ferreting out the political implications of work that is not politically self-conscious. Both because of our own political position and for the sake of congruence with current discussions, we will take the same tack. It should be understood, however, that in a society where some version of radical politics was more common and dominated research in an unself-conscious way, a similar critique might be mounted from the center or right. In our own society, political judgments of the results of sociological work could as easily be made from those positions, though they could scarcely be designed to uncover hidden radical assumptions, since radical sociologists tend to make these quite explicit.

Examples of the political import of causal analysis are easily available. It is common knowledge that most black Americans live less well than most white Americans. Something ought to be done about it; people mostly agree on that as well. What causes this situation? Some explanations explicitly blame the victims themselves, by finding, for instance, that their own inherited defects lead to all their trouble (see the critique in Ryan 1971: 3–30). Many people found fault with Daniel Moynihan's explanation that some of the trouble lay in the disorganization of the black family (Rainwater and Yancey 1967). That explanation seemed implicitly to blame blacks for their own troubles by suggesting that they need not have been so disorganized. It did not emphasize the causes of that disorganization, which, when revealed, placed the blame on their oppression by the white community. The same analysis further suggested that it would be difficult to change things because it is quite difficult to change family patterns. The Moynihan analysis might thus be interpreted as having a conservative political thrust.

Consider the rash of ideological interpretations of student protest movements. Investigators may locate the causes of those protests in some characteristic of students themselves (e.g., Shils 1969; Feuer 1969), and thus implicitly suggest that it is the actions of students which, without the help of any of the other involved parties, produce all the trouble. Students are to blame while, by implication, others whose behavior we do not regard as a cause are not to blame. Alternatively, we can interpret campus disorders as political phenomena which arise in the same way as other political phenomena, and serve as a mechanism by which subordinate groups make hierarchical superiors pay attention to their demands for change (e.g., Becker 1970b; Horowitz and Friedland 1970). In such a case, the difficulty can be located in the disparity between what one group wants and what the other group is willing to give, and it becomes equally possible to blame those who refuse to give students what they want, since that refusal is one of the necessary conditions for the occurrence of the disorderly events.

Political and sociological analyses both operate under a potent constraint, which is that actions based on them should have the anticipated consequences. That remains a major test of any *scientific* proposition. If an analysis is factually incorrect, then political predictions will not come to pass and strategies will be discredited. Science will not validate propositions just because they appear ethically worthwhile; the propositions must be correct in the real world. In this sense, radicalism is a necessary, but not a sufficient, condition of good sociology.

The production of factually correct analyses involves a paradox. What sociologists need to know about any institution or organization in order to achieve radical goals is usually similar to what they must know to achieve conservative ends as well. Consider research on consumer behavior. Advertising and marketing experts, presumably lackeys of the capitalist system, have done research to discover how to make advertising more effective, that is, how to manipulate people so that they will buy what they might not have bought otherwise. Simultaneously, radicals have complained, though they have not done research on the topic, that advertising makes people desire commodities they do not need. Radicals agree that advertising works the way marketing people say it does. Radical sociologists presumably want to know how to lessen the impact of advertising and make people's choices free; they might be interested in how the process of choice would work in a situation devoid of the artificial influence of advertising.

Apart from the difference in the moral animus of the language used by opposing groups, both conservative businessmen and radical activists need, to further their opposing ends, the same knowledge about the process by which consumers choose products. If we had a decent theory of consumer behavior, empirically validated, then the radical, knowing how advertising works, would know where to intervene so that it would not work, and the marketing expert would know why his techniques fail and how to improve them. An adequate analysis of how things stay the same is thus at the same time an analysis of how to change them. Conventional, presumably conservative, analyses often fail to take into account matters radicals think important. If those matters are indeed important, then the conservative analysis which ignores them will be faulty and its predictions will not prove true.

Political commitment is revealed by the kind of causes sociologists include in their analyses, by the way blame is assigned and the possibilities of political action evaluated. It is revealed most clearly by ignoring causes conceived of as incapable of change when in fact they could be changed under certain conditions, and by regarding a situation as easily subject to change when in fact there are substantial forces perpetuating it. Such false assumptions make it likely that plans of action resting on them will fail. In fact, although it is often charged that American social science is (presumably successfully) engaged in helping oppressors keep subject populations in their place, the actions which are supposed to be based on these analyses often fail, precisely because they have failed to take into account important causes suggested by more radical sociological analyses.

Obstacles to Radical Sociology

If the foregoing analysis of causality is correct, it ought to be no more difficult to create radical sociology than other varieties already available. Yet, for all the stated need for a more radical sociology, we find mostly programmatic statements and little substantive work that could reasonably be so labeled. It cannot be that there are no radical sociologists, for they have made their presence known. Indeed, as we have suggested, even those who call themselves radical have trouble knowing what their sociology ought to look like; in fact, we can see that it often differs in no observable way from nonradical sociology.

Some radicals in sociology claim that there is no truly radical sociology because most sociologists, being liberals or worse, are on the take from the establishment and naturally do not wish to make analyses that will subvert their own material interests. These radicals further suggest that the organizations which distribute research funds and control publication are so dominated by liberals and conservatives that radical work cannot be supported or published. If we accept such statements as radical sociological work, the ease with which they too achieve publication and professional recognition suggests that they are not true (see Nicolaus 1969).

Those who conceive of themselves as radical sociologists find it hard to do identifiably radical research, while politically neutral sociologists do research useful for radical goals (in the sense that they discover causal relationships which can be used as guides for radical political action). That demands explanation. There seem to be three chief reasons for this lack of connection between radical sociology and radical politics: (1) the conservative influence of conventional technical procedures, (2) commonsense standards of credibility of explanations, and (3) the influence of agency sponsorship. Each of these, in its own way, deters the sociologist's full exploration of the range of necessary conditions that ought to be considered as potential causes of the situation he studies.

Most commonly used research techniques require the investigator to have worked out his hypotheses fully before he begins gathering data. If we conceive research as testing deductions made from existing theories (wherever those theories come from), then the data one gathers must be suitable for making such tests. One restricts what he finds out to what will be relevant to those hypotheses. Experiments, surveys, and paper-and-pencil testing necessarily restrict the range of causes eventually considered, by the simple technical fact of confining inquiry to what the researcher has in mind when he plans his research. But in doing research, we often find that we have failed to take into account many variables and causes that, on the basis of early findings, we see we should take into account.

With respect to the possibility of a radical sociology, what we leave out may not be important for the allocation of blame. But if what has been neglected, or made impossible to locate, is necessary to effect change, such research becomes less useful for radical political purposes by virtue of that gap. Even committed political radicals find themselves constrained by the research techniques they are familiar with. These techniques often leave out some things they would think important if they knew about them. Some techniques, indeed, require sociologists to leave out things they *know* might be important. Thus, it is difficult, though not altogether impossible, to study certain kinds of power relationships and many kinds of historical changes by the use of survey research techniques. If that is what one knows how to do, then he is stuck with what he can discover by that technique.

Another barrier to a radical sociology lies in commonsense conceptions of credibility. Every theoretical stance, including those defined as radical, makes assumptions about the character of the world. In particular, the sociological view of the world usually assumes that some people are more believable than others, that their stories, insights, notions, and theories are more worthy of being taken seriously than those of others. One of the chief reasons conventional sociology fails to uncover some important causes of events and situations is that it accepts the commonsense notion that the people who run organizations and are highly placed in communities know more about those organizations and communities than others, and therefore ought to be taken more seriously. The immediate effect of assuming the veracity of highly placed people is to leave out of consideration questions and problems that appear foolish from an elitist viewpoint (Becker 1967a).

Conventional sociologists might, for instance, find it reasonable to ask why some schools are more effective in teaching their students than others. But it violates common sense to suggest, even though research might show it to be true, that schools actually prevent people from learning what they are supposed to learn. We have similar official versions and analyses of most social problems. When we study those problems, we find it hard to free ourselves from official analyses sufficiently to consider causes not credited in those versions. This is not to say that other causes are necessarily operative, but only that sociologists often fail to look at them because they seem unlikely or bizarre.

Radical politics has its own set of official explanations, its own set of preferred causes, and one can err as badly by taking these for granted as he can by taking conventional causes for granted. Of course, radically oriented research will seldom leave out of account what conventional sociologists include, if only because it wishes to demonstrate that those analyses are wrong. Therefore, research organized on radical lines will probably be more inclusive and therefore more useful.

Agency sponsorship tends to put conservative limits on the search for necessary conditions (Blumer 1967). Although research is most commonly funded and sponsored by the government or foundations politically suspect from some radical point of view, the trouble does not necessarily arise from the political character of the sponsors. Rather, it occurs because, whatever their political persuasion, when agencies purchase research they are concerned with answers to particular questions, questions which arise for them as operational difficulties. They do not wish to spend their money on meandering investigations of God-knows-what. Therefore, the agreement between researcher and agency typically specifies a limited area of research, the limits set by the agency's conception of what the problem is and where its causes lie. Ordinarily, the agency will not see its own operations as one of the causes of the problem, and thus those operations will not be included in the area the researcher agrees to study; by implication, he agrees not to study them (see Platt 1971).

This discussion of barriers to unconventional radical sociological analyses allows us to look critically at some common notions of what constitutes radical sociology. Most of the common definitions of a radical style in sociology bear some relation to making the kinds of analyses we have now identified as radical. In every case, however, the connection is contingent rather than necessary. We need to understand the circumstances under which the phenomenon in question actually leads to radical analysis and when it does not.

When one does research for a government agency, that agency will want the questions to be studied in a way that makes it difficult to come up with unconventional and radical conclusions. But refusing to accept government funds does not guarantee a radical analysis, nor is all research paid for by the government by definition conservative. If a federally funded researcher has arranged conditions so that he has maximum freedom, he may very well produce radical findings. Having done so, he may find it difficult to get further research funds from the same or similar sources. The remedy for that is to travel light, to avoid acquiring the obligations and inclinations that make large-scale funds necessary.

Studying radical groups from a sympathetic point of view, though one need not be particularly sympathetic with them to do so, may be of great use. Those groups might be exceptions to sociological wisdom, based on more conventional cases, and might make us aware of causal connections sociologists had not seen before. Thus, the study of communal living groups might allow sociologists to see certain possibilities of social organization that are ordinarily masked if we examine only longer-lasting and more stable institutions.

The influence of the sociologist's life-style on his work becomes especially important in an era of theatrical politics. Wearing a Viet Cong button does not make one a radical any more than living in a suburb makes one a conservative. Nevertheless, wearing buttons, beads, or otherwise looking "freaky" may cause the person to have experiences (with police, fellow sociologists, or others) which will force him or her to question assumptions that might otherwise have been left uninspected. In the same way, living in a middle-class suburb might insulate the sociologist from some experiences and so lead him to incorrect assumptions about some matters of fact.

Personal involvement in political radicalism or affiliation with an organization that champions radical programs and positions does not necessarily lead one to do radical sociology. Such a political commitment might dispose a sociologist to search for causes and possible modes of intervention other analyses had left out. On the other hand, a radical sociologist might do research for his political allies which was no different in its style from the research other sociologists do for General Electric or Standard Oil. Such research might produce no more profound analysis of causes and would thus be no more useful to the movement than market research and an investigation of how to keep the native labor force happy have been for industry.

A radical rhetoric or ideological posture does not inevitably result in politically useful sociological work. Ideologically "correct" analyses cannot substitute for cogent, empirically verified knowledge of the world as a basis for effective action. Ideological radicalism cannot provide a workable understanding of the relative roles of China and India in the developmental process of Asia. Ideological radicalism cannot tell us how long it takes to make the transition from rural to urban life. Ideological radicalism cannot prove the merits or demerits of one or another form of economic investment. When radicalism without sociology is employed as a surrogate for truth, it becomes fanaticism—a foolish effort to replace substance with style. But when these limits are understood and expressed, sociological radicalism can help us measure the distance between where people are and where they want to go—between the society and the utopia.

In a period of railing and ranting against the social sciences, it is perhaps time once again to raise the matter of priorities for our age. It is the purpose of a meaningful sociology to demonstrate how it is that society and its institutions are on trial, and how it is that society and its organizations are undergoing crisis. When we keep this in mind and remember that sociology is part of society, and that sociology in itself means very little apart from the larger social tasks, then perhaps the sense and style of radical sociology will be enhanced, adding flesh and blood to its current programmatics and calling us back once again *first* to the criticism of society and only *second* to the criticism of other sociologists.

6

SOCIAL SCIENCE AND THE WORK OF HANS HAACKE
(with John Walton)

Hans Haacke's works resemble those of social scientists sufficiently to make comparison both provocative and illuminating: provocative because Haacke's work manages to make so much more of a stir than the social science research it superficially resembles; illuminating because the differences beneath the similarity arise from and tell us something of the organizational differences between the worlds of art and social science.

Even if Haacke imitated in every detail the methods of social scientists, his work would still be different. Any work gets its meaning from the traditions and organized practice of the people among whom it is made and to whom it is presented. The same work makes a different statement, is a different act, when it appears in an art world rather than the world of social science. Haacke, speaking to artists, curators, collectors, gallery goers, critics, and museum trustees, gets a different effect from the social scientist who speaks largely to other social scientists.

Despite these crucial differences, when Haacke investigates art as a social system, social scientists can interpret the results in the light of the traditions and organized practices of their scientific world. When we do that, we find ways of assessing Haacke's work that are unavailable within the art world proper. We likewise find that Haacke's "naive" social science uses interesting possibilities social scientists have not used, but might want to try.

In what follows, then, we view Haacke both as artist (i.e., as a participant in the art world whose activities he investigates) and a social scientist (i.e., as someone whose work can be viewed as an attempt to answer questions posed by social science theories and

This article originally appeared in Haacke (1975), a book devoted to the works of conceptual artist Hans Haacke. The works we refer to are all reproduced there and this piece should be read in conjunction with that book.

interests). This will do some violence to the conceptions readers hold of both art and social science, which is probably a good thing.

Methods of Studying Power

Haacke is mainly interested in the networks of relationships through which power is exercised in the art world and in the social, economic, and political bases of that power. He has explored that interest in a variety of projects reproduced in this book: studies of elites and their interconnections, studies of the provenance of paintings, studies of the social characteristics and attitudes of patrons of museums and galleries, and even (one might say) experimental studies of the activities of museum directors. His earlier studies of physical and biological phenomena relied heavily on the idea of *system,* and he has brought that concern to his studies of social phenomena as well.

Social scientists have used many methods to bring empirical data to bear on their theories about the distribution and exercise of power. For more than twenty years books and papers have appeared which identified the topic as *The Power Elite* (Mills 1956), *The Power Structure* (Rose 1967), *Community Power Structure* (Hunter 1953), and so on. This vast literature has never given a definitive answer to the question of how to study power. But it has had the consequence of introducing the idea of and the term "power structure" into common parlance. Without question, the term refers to something that makes intuitive sense to people with either a theoretical or practical interest in politics.

Speaking confidently of "power structures," social scientists promised what they never delivered: an explicit set of principles and procedures for the analysis of power. The failure to produce generally acceptable principles and procedures shows up in two ways. First, researchers, all claiming to study "power," have actually studied a great variety of things, ranging from personal influence in small face-to-face groups to corporate concentration, trends toward oligopoly, and the military-industrial complex. Second, researchers cannot agree on either methodological questions—should the unit of analysis be the individual or the institution—or ideological ones—is power distributed pluralistically or centered in elites?

Questions of theory, method, and ideology are interrelated. Scientists trained in different disciplines use different methods, make different theoretical assumptions, and arrive at different conclusions and different ideological positions (Walton 1966). If we consider the major approaches researchers have used, we can lay out the issues and assumptions involved, and place Haacke's work in relation to the social science tradition. We will set aside for the moment our awareness that Haacke is, after all, an artist producing works of art, and see what we can learn if we consider him a social scientist producing research.

Where some of Haacke's procedures appear amateurish or inadequate in the light of some notion of an acceptable social science standard, we propose to be pragmatic in assessing his results. If the method used produces convincing results, then we will not require Haacke to use all the methods of verification, all the safeguards against bias or error, all the rigorous and systematic procedures social scientists have devised to guarantee to one another and the public the validity of their results. Social scientists in fact do this themselves, because of the lack of consensus on methods just alluded to. This means that Haacke's work cannot be held to account, as some might attempt to do, for failing to be conducted according to rigorous scientific standards. No such agreed-on standards exist, and, while there are certain well-known precautions for avoiding bias, the practical constraints of the research situation (e.g., inaccessible or unavailable evidence) frequently require that the investigator make do with what data is obtainable—a practice recognized as justified as long as the researcher frankly reports the limitations imposed. Where the findings overwhelmingly point to a conclusion, a failure to use available safeguards against error makes little difference; the results may be so conclusive that even these potential errors would not change our interpretations, as some of the discussion below will make clear.

Social scientists studying power structure have used several distinctive procedures. Some use the individual as the unit of analysis, asking *who* is powerful or influential, *who* participates in the decision-making process, what the social and occupational backgrounds of the influential are, what constituencies they represent. The *positional method,* for instance, begins with a set of offices or positions assumed to be important: members of Congress (Matthews 1954), elected officials, judges, heads of large banks and corporations (Baron 1968), or members of such decision-making bodies as the President's cabinet, the Council on Foreign Relations, and so on (Domhoff 1970). The researcher uses available sources to report on the social backgrounds and interconnections of the people who occupy these positions (he may also interview them to get information not already available). Domhoff, for instance, concludes that U.S. politics is dominated by the "higher circles" of the upper class since a large proportion of holders of high positions are also listed in the Social Register or have other "blue blood" attributes.

Sociometric or reputational methods (Hunter 1953; Miller 1958) are similar though more elaborate, aiming at the identification of who is "really" powerful, whether those persons hold formal positions or operate "behind the scene." This procedure begins with a small panel of experts who hold a variety of positions in a community such that they may be presumed to be knowledgeable about local matters. This panel then is asked to identify the most important persons in town "when it comes to getting things done" or "promoting a major project." Tabulation of the nominations of this panel leads to a list of the highest vote-getters who are then designated as "influentials." Typically a second stage of this method involves interviewing the influentials to determine backgrounds, occupations, acquaintance with one another, and actual participation in local activities.

Organizational network methods take a similar approach but focus on the organization rather than the individual. Using this method, you identify key institutions, such as the largest banks and the largest nonfinancial institutions, and then determine the number of "interlocking directorates" linking them (the number of people holding directorships in two or more major institutions, e.g., Dye et al. 1973). One can also use such economic data as how much of a given corporation is owned or controlled by a given bank or family grouping (Knowles 1973; Zeitlin 1974).

Haacke's Guggenheim piece (Haacke 1975: 59–67) uses a version of these methods, tracing family memberships and corporate directorships to show the dependence of the Guggenheim Museum on Guggenheim family financial interests and the implication of those interests in the exploitation of the mineral wealth of underdeveloped countries. In particular, Haacke uses this form of research to indicate the role of one of the Guggenheim companies, Kennecott Copper, in the economy of Allende's Chile. In doing this, Haacke uses none of the elaborate forms of analysis characteristic of power structure studies in social science. Since all the facts can obviously be checked in public records by anyone who wants to take the trouble, their authenticity need not be guaranteed by any rigorous method of data gathering. Since he draws no conclusion, letting "the facts speak for themselves," no one can complain that his methods of manipulating data do not warrant his conclusion.

Social scientists also make use of *decisional methods* or *event analysis* (Dahl 1961). These methods criticize those just discussed for their reliance on mere reputations for power instead of on observations of the actual exercise of power. Decisional methods focus on key decisions and reconstruct their histories, seeking to discover who participated in making them. Analysts study several important decisions, to see whether the same people exercise power in all cases or whether the decision-making elite consists of different people for each issue or area of politics. *Historical analyses* (Mills 1956) do the same thing at the institutional level, trying to assess the shifting influence of major organizations and social sectors on large-scale social policy. How, for example, do such major social changes as war, depression, expanding governmental bureaucracy or corporate concentration affect the distribution and exercise of social power? Mills argued, for instance, that power in America had increasingly centered on the military, the higher levels of the federal executive, and the large corporations and documented his contention by tracing social backgrounds, common affiliations (e.g., prep schools, colleges, and clubs), and individual careers that moved from the military to corporate vice-presidencies or from industry to related federal regulatory agencies.

Haacke has not used either of these methods in anything like their original form. One might argue, however, that his provenances of the Manet and Seurat paintings (Haacke 1975: 69–112) are a form of event analysis, which show the sequence of events that constitute the career of a particular art work and indicate the influential people who helped the work become historically important. The provenance, of course, relies almost entirely on publicly available data (from *Who's Who,* reports of art auctions, and the like) and does not actually provide information on who decided to do what in relation to the work or the influences on those decisions. In that sense it does not go as far as event analyses usually do to remedy the complaint that while powerholders have been identified we do not see how they exercise their power, under what conditions, and to what ends. We learn that art dealers Richard L. Feigen, Heinz Berggruen, and Artemis S. A. collaborated in an elaborate sequence of events leading to the most recent disposal of the Seurat painting, but not who decided that it should be done that way or for what reason (though we have plenty of material on which to base a guess).

In this case, Haacke has followed one sort of analytic tradition in relying solely on publicly verifiable data which do not require interpretation to be used. Another tradition would have required him to interview Feigen, Berggruen, and others on the board of Artemis S. A., perhaps to gain access to their private meetings, and so to have become privy to the most minute aspects of this sale, of the interactions between participants, and to their private and collective thinking about what they were doing, had done, and were about to do. Practically, such a method might not be possible, for it depends on the participants granting the investigator access to ordinarily private affairs, and such permission would presumably not have been granted in this and similar cases. Indirect methods of gathering data, which require much more interpretive inference, are often necessary, but are naturally less useful.

One might also argue that Haacke used a form of experimental event analysis in the occurrences that followed the cancellation of his show at the Guggenheim Museum. He may not have intended, by offering to exhibit works depicting the social system of certain real-estate holdings in Manhattan, to provoke the museum director into canceling his scheduled show. But that was the result. The cancellation led to the firing of the museum curator, to the boycott of the museum by many artists, and, it has been argued, to a living demonstration of "the character of the cultural establishment within which artists have been forced to function" (Fry 1972). This vivid demonstration may not reflect direct pressure from the museum's trustees; Haacke himself thinks not, believing that subordinates often pursue their principals' interests more zealously than the principals themselves would. Nevertheless, it does demonstrate the exercise of power in the contemporary art world and thus provides important data about the process as well as the location of power.

In addition, Haacke has considered two aspects of power ordinarily included in social science theorizing about power, but seldom included in the research agendas that flow from the theories. Theories of power frequently allude to the relationship between the powerful and the powerless, suggesting that we understand power only when we understand the basis on which its subjects allow it to be exercised (Weber 1957). Theorists draw distinctions between power which is accepted as legitimate—authority—and coercive power, whose subjects do not recognize its legitimacy. But research seldom investigates the attitudes of the subjects of power. It would stretch matters somewhat to regard the polls Haacke conducted (Haacke 1975: 9–58) as investigations of the attitudes of powerless subjects of the rulers of the art world. But the polls do indicate that gallery goers overwhelmingly favor left-liberal causes, positions, and candidates, that they do not provide the financial underpinnings of the art world by purchasing art works, that they mistrust the wealthier people who do provide that support, and that they are in large measure people with some sort of professional interest in art.

These conclusions give us useful material on the ideological arrangements of the art world, on the relations of beliefs and social position, and on the degree to which those without power live in a world made by people who believe very differently from them. The other end of the ideological structure is documented in the metal plaques on which Haacke displays quotations from Nixon, Rockefeller, and others on the relations between art and business.

In what sense can these polls and quotations from speeches and corporate documents provide sufficient data of a quality to allow us to draw valid conclusions about the contemporary art world? It is clear enough in the case of the polls that Haacke has not followed standard procedures of questionnaire construction, sampling, or analysis. The questions, not by their wording but by the kinds of materials they probe, suggest strongly to the respondent the political position from which they emanate, and this conceivably might prompt some to answer in ways they think pleasing to the questionnaire's author, or vice versa. The analysis never proceeds beyond simple cross-tabulations of the answers to two questions. The samples consist of visitors to a gallery, some portion of whom answered the questionnaire; it is not known whether the nonrespondents differ in any important way, such as might influence their answers, from those who did fill out the instruments.

These all constitute flaws in Haacke's procedures but, in our judgment, not of sufficient magnitude to cast serious doubt on the conclusions we have already mentioned as indicated by the data. He has, first of all, followed scientific practice scrupulously in indicating all the circumstances of the polling, such that a skeptical reader knows all the precautions that need to be taken in interpreting the data and could even replicate the research if that was thought necessary. Though social science textbooks contain a multitude of rules about how research should be done, these rules are often impractical and cannot be followed exactly in the real-world situations in which research is done. In that case, working scientists do essentially what Haacke has done: do the best they can and inform the reader so that the findings may be discounted accordingly.

Second, Haacke's findings are very clear-cut. Many of the more elaborate procedures of survey design, sampling, and analysis are designed to allow the researcher to "tease out" (a suggestive phrase) findings from data which show no clear-cut pattern. When the poll shows that museum goers disapprove Rockefeller's policies by a ratio of two to one, it seems unlikely (on the basis of everything we know about museums and museum goers, which is the basis on which working scientists make these judgments) that sampling errors or the wording of the questions account for these results. It is not plausible that the full population of museum goers, had they answered, or that the population that did answer, had they been confronted with a question that sounded more pro-Rockefeller, would have produced data that showed that they were evenly divided for and against or that the majority actually favored Rockefeller's position.

Haacke's quotations from business and political leaders are made to stand for the ideology with respect to art of that segment of the American power elite. Haacke has here made use of a powerful device often used by social scientists, though seldom formally described as a "method." The device consists of demonstrating incontrovertibly that some event or utterance occurred even once, and then arguing that the conditions under which this happened are such that it must be a common occurrence, built into the fabric of the organization or society in which it happened. The demonstration is especially effective if it can be shown or argued that when the event occurred no one thought it very remarkable or out of line, but rather that it was accepted as an everyday and ordinary event; this can be accomplished when the reader understands that, had the event been out of the ordinary, some outcry would have followed. In the case of the plaques, we can see that these are the kind of statements political and business leaders make all the time. We know, further, that we have heard no one complain about these remarks, which enhances our willingness to accept them as straightforward evidence of the ideology about art current in the business and political communities.

Beyond the parallels between Haacke's methods and those of social scientists it is important to stress that each has something to learn from the other. Haacke may have made a contribution to social science method by adapting the art-historical technique of the provenance to the study of power. We can describe the technique more generally as one of following the history of ownership of a socially valued object (its "career"), thus tracing the outlines of some portion of an elite network; this is analogous to the way following an individual's career traces the outlines of a professional organization (cf. Hughes 1971: 132–50). This becomes more interesting when the objects traced begin with little value and gradually accumulate more, thus penetrating successively higher elite circles. Perhaps this method has not occurred to social scientists because there are few social objects whose value continually increases as that of some art works does. On the other hand, a great many objects continually lose value (for instance most cars) and these might make possible the use of a reverse form of the method.

In summary, Haacke has made reasonable use of variants of social science methods. His results are credible and acceptable by social science standards. Like many good social scientists, he has viewed the phenomena he studies as connected in a *system*. This has led him to the use of the multiple methods we have just reviewed and assessed, by means of which he can gather data on a variety of participants and events in the art world and give them, viewed as a system, more meaning than any one set of findings would have alone. The findings of each individual inquiry both rest on and reinforce the findings of all the other works, so that the analysis of the system, considered as a whole, is more credible than any one set of findings might be. (The logic of this kind of holistic analysis is explicated in Diesing 1971.)

Haacke's Theory of the Art World

Haacke has scrupulously refrained from enunciating an explicit theory of the social, political, and economic organization of the contemporary art world. The data he has accumulated and presented nevertheless clearly embody such a theory. One practice of organized social science which may prove useful to his enterprise is the habit of summarizing and collating results in a general theoretical form. One puts the available material together and extrapolates from it, describing an entire system or even an entire class of theoretically defined phenomena as though it were what the partial data accumulated indicate it might be. The procedure allows you to see where your data are leading, where the gaps that require filling are, and makes it possible to identify data which show that the theory is wrong and thus allow it to be revised on an empirical basis.

Haacke has not made his theory explicit, so we will attempt a brief summary. The theory describes both the organization of the contemporary art world and the processes by which it is maintained. The bottom layer of the art world consists of a relatively large (compared to the numbers of participants at other levels) aggregate of gallery and museum goers, the "public" for contemporary art. These people are typically young, upper-middle class, politically interested and left-liberal in their politics, artists, art students or otherwise professionally involved in the arts. They believe that the major institutions of the art world (especially museums) are run by people of a different political stance—that museum trustees, for instance, were Nixon supporters while gallery goers supported McGovern—and that those institutions, accordingly, are not responsive to their desires and tastes—that gallery goers like or tolerate politically engaged art, but that museums will not exhibit it. The members of this stratum do not provide much financial support for contemporary art; despite their class position, they are young enough that they have not yet realized their income potential. But they believe that the preferences of the wealthier people who back the art world, people whose politics they understand to be well to the right of their own, influence the kind of work artists produce. The public for contemporary art, then, believes that the work it is most interested in is ultimately controlled by people who have a view of the art enterprise contradictory to their own.

The evidence of the plaques containing quotations from business and political leaders, especially the Rockefeller brothers, shows that the public's suspicions are not wrong. These leaders, who furnish the bulk of the money supporting contemporary art institutions, do indeed view art differently: Nelson Rockefeller thinks it has no intellectual (hence, no political) meaning; David Rockefeller describes art as a good investment for corporate business; Frank Stanton thinks art is essential to business. The Guggenheim study shows further that the members of this top stratum of the contemporary art world—the trustees of one of the most avant-garde museums—get the income they use to support art from exploitative and imperialist businesses of the kind members of that world's public abhor, in this case Kennecott Copper, whose involvement in the fate of Allende's Chile the Guggenheim panels document.

The cancellation of Haacke's Guggenheim show (which we will continue to interpret as one of his pieces of research) demonstrated, as did the events surrounding the cancellation of the exhibition of the Manet provenance in Cologne, the role of the functionaries of contemporary art institutions (Haacke 1975: 137–40). They act to protect what they take to be the interests of their employers; it is possible, and even likely, that they overreact to the provocations offered by works such as Haacke's and that their trustees would not mind these exhibitions so much. (That supposition is something Haacke might check out in further works.) These events lay bare the process by which the financial control of art institutions actually affects the work of artists by controlling what is exhibited. Artists are presumably less likely to make works that are not acceptable to the major outlets in which they might be exhibited. Since the Haacke pieces that provoked these cancellations had political connotations, we can see the process by which politically meaningful work is institutionally discouraged. These events thus provide evidence that the public's belief that the work it finds interesting is discouraged by those who control contemporary art is correct.

The two provenances give information on another aspect of the contemporary art system, its financial arrangements. They suggest a number of conclusions. The two paintings appreciated enormously since they were created, and mostly in the past several years (the Seurat, purchased in 1936 for $40,000, sold for over a million dollars at an auction in 1970). The big jump in value came when the paintings ceased to be circulated among family members or a small group of upper-class acquaintances and moved into the open market. In these two cases, at least, while huge profits were made, the artists (long since dead) got no share of them. In both cases, the data suggest more elaborate financial arrangements than are explicitly described, but leave no doubt that investment for speculative gain is a major element. That, of course, is no news with respect to the market in contemporary art.

The irony involved in the case of the Manet merits remarking on. Here a man who was active in the financial affairs of Nazi Germany ends up arranging for the donation to a German museum of a painting held for many years by a German Jewish painter and finally brought to the U.S. by a prominent anti-Nazi refugee. It is not clear what the general theoretical import of this is.

Taken together, all of Haacke's materials seem to imply a theory that describes the contemporary art world as one organized around an endemic conflict between the interests of those who produce the art and the broader public which supports them ideologically, on the one hand, and the interests of the much smaller group of wealthy people and politicians who provide the big money supporting the system. Working through such intermediate institutional functionaries as museum directors, those who control the system act in various ways to control the output of artists and particularly to diminish and mute the political content of their work.

We think this is a fair summary of the theory implicit in Haacke's work. Much of the theory is at best *suggested* by the works Haacke has so far produced rather than being demonstrated in any more compelling way. His works do, however, touch on such key aspects of the contemporary art system, and such key persons in it, that the theory has a presumptive claim to acceptance. A social scientist might proceed by waiting to see what counterassertions were made disputing the validity of his theoretical claims, then organizing future work so as to test the validity of those counterassertions. We are not aware that anyone has actually disputed Haacke's findings. It would presumably be difficult to challenge the facts, since most of them are publicly available and easily checked. People might dispute the implicit theory in Haacke's work. But, being implicit, it is hardly available for dispute. We are not sure to what degree Haacke is willing to assume responsibility for the theory we have read out of (or into) his work, or for some other theory that he finds more acceptable. Insofar as he disclaims responsibility for the interpretation (as he has in Siegel 1971: "I leave it up to you as far as how you evaluate the situation. You continue the work by drawing your own conclusions from the information presented."), he makes it difficult to find the questions of validity which might orient future work.

But, of course, Haacke is not a social scientist; we have only been pretending that he is. He is an artist, and we now turn to a consideration of the *differences* between Haacke's work and that of social scientists, of the differences that are due to and illuminate the difference between the organized world of art in which Haacke operates and the organized world of social science in which studies of power are undertaken and presented. In short, we consider the two kinds of work as gestures that derive their meaning from the social worlds in which they occur.

Gestures in a Social World

Haacke, operating in an art world with methods and results in many ways similar to those of social scientists, gets very different and much more substantial reactions to his work than social scientists get, in their world, to their work. His work provokes reactions from relevant parties such that the reactions themselves provide further information about the original subject of the work, the exercise of power in the art world. In addition, the results of his work, having a kind of unarguably "valid" character, in fact are accepted by all the relevant parties as correct, which adds further to their provocative character.

Haacke's work has the appearance of unquestioned validity because the customary response of the art world to works of art no longer includes the possibility of questioning the veridicality of the statement the work makes. While appreciators of visual art could once include among the criteria by which they judged a work its faithfulness to the person or scene it purported to portray, the question of faithfulness is no longer of interest to anyone. We understand that a portrait, for instance, need not look anything like the person it portrays to be successful; it is enough that the image be formally interesting or emotionally compelling. (Photography has now acquired some of the burden of faithfulness to reality that painting and sculpture once carried; see Ivins 1953 and Gombrich 1960.) To say of a work of art, in any but the most extended metaphorical sense, that it is *not true,* is to make a meaningless remark.

Since the truth of an art work is not an issue, it follows that whatever else artists and critics discuss and argue about, the question of truth is not examined. Most contemporary works make little or no claim to truth; those that do tend to make the claim as Haacke's works do, by displaying facts that are regarded as self-evident and not requiring proof. Because the truth is self-evident, the meaning likewise is self-evident, and the steps by which one proceeds from fact to meaning need not be demonstrated or questioned. This is a rather tedious justification of Haacke's practice of drawing no explicit conclusions from his work, leaving that interpretive work as an exercise for the viewer. Confronted with the Guggenheim panels or the provenances, for instance, the viewer must search out the connections, keeping in mind in dealing with the data on the

Elgerbar Corporation that Mrs. Obre was born a Guggenheim and that Wettach and Lawson-Johnston are her sons by other marriages, while Stewart is her brother-in-law, and drawing the conclusions that information seems to warrant. But the premises and logical procedures by which those conclusions are reached seem, to all concerned, to be obvious and beyond question.

The reason we have been so tedious and long-winded on this point is because customary practice in the world of social science is very different, and because the difference has important consequences for the impact of the work. Haacke's work has great impact in its world because his conclusions are unquestioned. But no social science conclusion, particularly when the subject is of contemporary political interest, goes unquestioned, and it is only extremely rarely that the questioning is ever resolved into some kind of consensus of the scientific community. Social scientists question sources of data, procedures of analysis, interpretations, premises, assumptions—whatever can conceivably be questioned. They regard all conclusions as provisional. As a result, anyone who finds a particular conclusion or interpretation annoying or threatening can easily find a social scientist of as good reputation as the author of the distasteful conclusion to dispute it, to produce a counterconclusion, to produce data which threaten the validity of the unwanted result. If C. Wright Mills (1956) and Floyd Hunter (1953) find that American society is dominated by a power elite, Arnold Rose (1967) and Robert Dahl (1961) can be adduced in support of the conclusion that no power elite exists because America is in fact a pluralist society.

In short, Haacke's work provokes strong reactions because it appears, in some large part because of the conventional practices of the art world, as incontrovertible and patently true; no one questions it. It provokes those reactions for a second reason, which also requires a lengthy explanation.

Haacke presents his results in a way that openly flaunts the power of those whose power he exposes. The works he produces expose what the people implicated in them would presumably prefer not be exposed (if *exposed* is too strong a word, substitute *remind*). If, preferring that these things not be publicized, those involved cannot or do not stop the publicity, then they perhaps do not have the power they and others imagine they have. If, however, they do prevent the publicity, they can do so only by causing an even larger commotion in which not only the original materials are exposed, but also the attempt to suppress those materials. At its best, Haacke's work succeeds in presenting the powers-that-be of the contemporary art world with this Hobson's choice. In either case, what they do produces still further useful information about power in the art world.

We can remark on two aspects of this strategy and the reactions it provokes. First, what Haacke does can be conceived not as an exercise in power but rather as an exercise in bad taste. The powerful frequently view challenges to their power as lapses of etiquette (cf. Becker 1970b: 8–11). Haacke provides an example (in Siegel 1971: 20–21):

> Emily Genauer gave us a little glimpse of the larger base of the [Museum of Modern Art poll of attitudes toward Rockefeller's political position] in her review of the show. She wrote: "One may wonder at the humor (propriety, obviously, is too archaic a concept even to consider) of such poll-taking in a museum founded by the governor's mother, headed now by his brother, and served by himself and other members of his family in important financial and administrative capacities since its founding 40 years ago." With this little paragraph she provided some of the background for the work that was not intelligible for the politically less-informed visitors of the museum. She also articulated feelings that are shared by the top people at numerous museums. It goes like this: We are the guardians of culture. We honor artists by inviting them to show in *our* museum, we want them to behave like guests, proper, polite and grateful. After all, we have put up the dough for this place.

This works both ways. Defining a challenge to power as a lapse in taste is a way of denying its political import. Conversely, such a definition makes it possible to make a political statement out of an act of bad taste.

Second, this political challenge or failure to obey etiquette is possible because Haacke works in the same social space as those his work describes. His work thus differs profoundly from social science studies of the powerful, which typically occur as events in a world of social science quite separate from the world of the powerful people and organizations it describes. Haacke's work is displayed in, discussed in, is an event in an art world which includes among its integral elements (cf. Levine 1972) the dealers, directors, trustees, and collectors who appear in that very work. The subjects of power structure studies can ignore the books written about them because those books never impinge on or occur as events in the worlds they move in. They might think it in bad taste to find their corporate directorships discussed in detail, but they need not listen to such discussions or have their noses rubbed in their inability to prevent the discussions from taking place. Academic research appears in esoteric professional journals, or in papers read at meetings attended by disciplinary colleagues. An occasional finding achieves a momentary publicity in the daily press, but not more than that. Academic social science is sufficiently segregated from the worlds it describes, by virtue of its conventional practice with respect to the publication and dissemination of results, that scientists do not have the means to offer such provocations as Haacke does. Since they can so seldom do that, they equally seldom provoke the responses which provide even further information.

It is a sign of how segregated academic social science is from the worlds it describes that it is even difficult to imagine how it could achieve the same results. One way would be for social scientists to do research on their own world, on the world of universities, and publicize the results in the internal communications of that world. Probably the nearest approach to that occurred when people discovered and made public such matters as the character of contract research being done for the government by universities, the kinds of investments universities made with their funds, and the secret involvement of both universities and individual researchers with such government agencies as the Department of Defense and the CIA (e.g., Horowitz 1969; Ransom 1970). But those discoveries have not been followed up in succeeding and more systematic accounts of the nature of the university world; in that respect Thorstein Veblen's *The Higher Learning in America,* written in 1918, is still not surpassed. This is not to deny the existence of a sizable literature in such areas as the sociology of science and university organization; nevertheless, we think it fair to say that hardly any of this literature confronts the members of these worlds with the facts of power in them as Haacke's work confronts the art community. The closest parallel we know of was a study of Columbia University, its trustees, real-estate interests, and federal research grants, all of which indicated intimate linkages with the people and institutions Mills called the power elite (NACLA 1968). But, again, we do not know of any virulent reaction to this research.

In any event, it is studies of community and national power to which this point is most relevant. We have imagined the following as a way of seeing what social scientists would have to do to achieve an effect equivalent to Haacke's. William Domhoff (1974) has written a book on the informal associations of the rich and powerful, centered about the members of an exclusive West Coast summer camp called Bohemian Grove. Supposing Domhoff were to present his tabulations on large posters, pasted on the walls of San Francisco's Pacific Union Club, another organization to which many of the same people belong. *That* would approximate what Haacke's works do to the art world, and presumably would produce consequences for Domhoff and his work equivalent to the cancellations and other phenomena which have accompanied Haacke's exhibitions.

We do not argue that academic social scientists should necessarily attempt to produce the same kinds of effects Haacke has. To discuss the advantages and disadvantages of such procedures for the development of science would take another essay as long as this one, and one more relevant to another kind of audience. Suffice it to say that the intimate involvement of the rich and powerful in the day-to-day workings of the contemporary art world have provided Haacke with a resource not available to the academic social scientist, whose work is so segregated from the centers of social power. He has used that resource to produce art works with a substantial social science content and interest.

7

TELLING ABOUT SOCIETY

I have for many years spent summers in San Francisco, on the lower slope of Russian Hill or the upper reaches of North Beach; how I describe it depends on who I am trying to impress. I live near Fisherman's Wharf, on the route many people take from that tourist attraction to their motels downtown or on Lombard Street's motel row. Looking out my front window, I often see small groups of tourists standing, alternately looking at their maps and at the large hills that stand between them and where they want to be. It's clear what has happened. The map's straight line looked like a nice walk through a residential neighborhood, one that might show them how the natives live. Now, in the words of one young Briton I offered to help, "I've got to get to my motel and I am *not* climbing that bloody hill."

Why don't the maps those people consult tell them there are hills there? Cartographers know how to indicate hills, if that is required, so it is not a restriction of the medium that inconveniences walkers. I suppose, without knowing for sure, that the maps are made for motorists, financed by gasoline companies and automobile associations, and distributed through service stations—and drivers worry less about hills than pedestrians.

Those maps, and the networks of people and organizations who make and use them, exemplify the problem this paper deals with. An ordinary street map of San Francisco is a conventionalized representation of that urban society: a visual description of its streets and landmarks, and of their arrangement in space. Social scientists and ordinary citizens routinely use not only maps but a great variety of other representations of social reality—a few random examples are documentary films, statistical tables, or the stories people tell one another to explain who they are and what they are doing. All of them, like the maps, give a partial picture, which is nevertheless

This paper reports on work done with the help of a grant from the System Development Foundation of Palo Alto, California.

adequate for some purpose. All of them arise in organizational settings, which constrain what can be done and define the purposes the work will have to satisfy. This view suggests several interesting problems: How do the needs and practices of organizations shape our descriptions and analyses (call them representations) of social reality? How do the people who use those representations come to define them as adequate? Such questions have a bearing on traditional questions about knowing and telling in science, but go beyond them, as we will see, to include problems more traditionally associated with the arts and with the analysis of everyday life.

This paper reports on some explorations several colleagues[1] and I have made of these problems.

Representations of Society as Social Facts

People in a variety of scholarly disciplines and artistic fields think they know something about society worth telling to others, and they use a variety of forms, media, and means to communicate their ideas and findings. Comparative study of these ways of representing knowledge about society shows the common problems all such representations involve and the different solutions people develop in different situations.

We have tried to be inclusive in our comparison, including (at least in principle) every medium and genre people use or have ever used. Although that is not possible, we have tried to avoid the most obvious conventional biases, and included not only reputable scientific formats and those invented and used by professionals but also those used by artists and lay people as well. A list will suggest the range of things we looked at: from the social sciences, such modes of representation as mathematical models, statistical tables and graphs, maps, ethnographic prose, and historical narrative; from the arts, novels, films, still photographs, and drama; from the large shadowy area in between, life histories and other biographical and autobiographical materials, reportage (including the mixed genres

[1]The members of the research group at Northwestern University were Andrew Gordon, Bernard Beck, Robert K. LeBailly, Marjorie Devault, Samuel Gilmore, Lawrence McGill, Lori Morris, and Robin Leidner. A number of people at other institutions have collaborated with us: James Bennett of the University of Illinois–Chicago, Michal McCall of Macalester College, Rachel Volberg of the New York State Office of Mental Health, and Elihu Gerson and Susan Leigh Star of the Tremont Research Institute.

of docudrama, documentary film, and fictionalized fact), and the storytelling, mapmaking, and other representational activities of lay people (or people acting in a lay capacity, as even professionals do most of the time).

Modes of representation make most sense seen in organizational context, as ways some people tell what they think they know to other people who want to know it, as organized activities shaped by the joint efforts of everyone involved. We realized early that it was a confusing error to focus on objects, as though the subjects of our investigation were tables or charts or ethnographies or movies. It makes more sense to see these artifacts as the frozen remains of collective action, brought to life whenever someone uses them, as people making and reading charts or prose, making and seeing films. To speak of *a film* is shorthand for "making a film" or "seeing a film."

That's a distinction with a difference. Concentrating on the object misdirects attention to what a medium is formally and technically capable of, how many bits of information a television monitor with a particular degree of resolution can convey, or whether a purely visual medium can convey such logical notions as causality. Concentrating on organized activity, on the other hand, shows that what a medium can do is always a function of the way organizational constraints affect its use. What photographs can convey is in part shaped by the budget, which says how many photographs can be used and how they can be displayed, how much will be spent making them (how much film and photographers' time will be paid for), and by the amount and kind of attention viewers will put into interpreting them.

Seeing representations of knowledge about society organizationally means incorporating all aspects of the organizations they are made in into the analysis: bureaucratic structures, budgets, professional codes, and audience characteristics and abilities all impinge on telling about society. Workers decide how to go about making representations by seeing what is possible, logical, feasible, and desirable, given the conditions under which they are making them and the people they are making them for.

It makes sense to speak, in rough analogy to the idea of an art world (Becker 1982), of worlds of makers and users of representations: the worlds of documentary film or statistical graphics, of mathematical modeling or anthropological monographs. These worlds differ in the relative knowledge and power of makers and users. In highly professionalized worlds, professionals mostly make artifacts for use by other professionals: scientific researchers make their reports and inscriptions (see Latour and Woolgar 1979 and Latour 1983, 1984, and 1985) for colleagues who know as much (or almost as much) about the work as they do. In the extreme case, makers and users are the same people, a situation almost realized in such esoteric worlds as mathematical modeling.

Members of more differentiated worlds share some basic knowledge, despite the differences in their actual work. That's why sociology students who will never do statistical work learn the latest versions of multivariate analysis. Other professionals do their work for lay people: cartographers make maps for motorists who know just enough about cartography to get to the next town, and filmmakers make movies for people who never heard of a jump cut. (Of course, these professionals usually worry about what their professional peers will think of their work as well.) Lay people, of course, tell stories, make maps, and write down figures for each other. What gets made, communicated, and understood varies among these typical settings.

This makes it useless to talk of media or forms in the abstract, although I have already done that and will continue to in this paper. Abstract terms like "film" or "statistical table" are only shorthand for such specifics as "tables-made-for-the-Census" or "big-budget-Hollywood-feature-films." The organizational constraints of the Census and Hollywood are best thought of as part of the artifact made in those places. So our focus differs from the conventional one, which treats the artifact as the main thing and the activities through which it is produced and consumed as secondary.

The form and content of representations vary because social organization shapes not only what is made, but also what people want the representation to do, what job they think they need done (like finding their way or knowing what the latest findings in their field are), and what standards they will use to judge it. Because the jobs users call on representations to do depend so heavily on organizational definitions, we have not been concerned with what many people think a (indeed *the*) major methodological problem: given a particular representational job to be done, what is the best way to do it? If that were the question, one would set up a task—to communicate an array of numbers, for example—and then see which way of organizing a table would communicate that information most honestly, adequately, and efficiently (as people compare computers by seeing how fast they can find prime numbers). We have deliberately avoided judgments about the adequacy of any mode of representation, not taking any of them as the yardstick against which all other methods should be judged. Nor have we adopted the slightly more relativistic position that while the jobs to be done may differ, there is a best way of doing each of them. That isn't relativistic asceticism on our part either. It seems more useful, more likely to lead to new understanding, to think of every way of representing social reality as *perfect*—for something. The question is *what* it is good for. The answer to that is organizational.

Despite the superficial differences between genres and media, the same fundamental problems occur in every medium. The influence of budgets, the role of professionalization, what knowledge audiences must have for a representation to be effective, what is ethically permissible in making a representation—all these are common to every form of representation making. How they are solved and dealt with varies depending on organizational resources and purposes.

Such problems are debated in every field in which representations are made. Novelists worry about the same ethical dilemmas sociologists and anthropologists do, and filmmakers share our concern about budgets. The literature of those debates, and informal observations and interviews in those fields, have given us most of our data. We have also found the relatively recent literature concerned with problems of representation and rhetoric in the sociology of science very helpful (see, for instance, Gusfield 1981, especially pp. 83–108; Latour and Bastide 1983; Bazerman 1981; Clifford 1983; Geertz 1983; Bennett unpublished).

Making Representations

Any representation of social reality—a documentary film, a demographic study, a realistic novel—is necessarily partial, less than what one would experience and have available for interpretation in the actual setting. That is why people make representations: to report only what you need in order to do whatever you want to do. An efficient representation tells you everything you need to know for your purposes, without wasting your time with what you don't need. Makers and users of representations, then, must perform several operations on reality to get from it to the final understanding of social reality they want to communicate. Social organization affects the making and use of representations by affecting how makers go through these operations.

Selection. Every medium, in any of its conventional uses, leaves out much, in fact *most*, of reality. Even media that seem more comprehensive than the obviously abstract words and numbers we usually use leave practically everything out: film (still or moving) and video leave out the third dimension, smells, etc. Written representations usually leave out all visual elements. Every medium leaves out whatever happens after we stop our representational activities. Some breeds of sociologists like to point out that numerical representations leave out the human element, or emotions, or symbolically negotiated meaning—they use the criterion of completeness to criticize work they don't like. But no one, neither users nor makers, in fact ever regards incompleteness in itself as a crime. Instead, they recognize it as the way one does that sort of thing. Road maps, tremendously abstract and incomplete renderings of the reality they represent, are perfectly adequate for even the sternest critic of incomplete representations. They contain just what drivers need to get from one place to another (even when they mislead pedestrians).

Since any representation always and necessarily leaves out elements of reality, the interesting and researchable questions are these: Which of the possible elements are included? Who finds that selection reasonable and acceptable? Who complains about it? What criteria do people apply in making those judgments? Some criteria, to suggest the possibilities, are genre-related ("if it doesn't include this [or does include that] it isn't really a novel [or photograph or ethnography or table or . . .] any more") or professional ("that's how *real* statisticians [or filmmakers or historians or . . .] always do it").

Translation. We can think of translation, in a loose analogy, as a function which maps one set of elements (the parts of reality makers want to represent) on to another set of elements (the conventional elements available in the medium as it is currently used). Anthropologists turn their field notes into standardized ethnographic descriptions; survey researchers create tables and charts from field interviews; historians combine their index cards into narratives, character sketches, and analyses; filmmakers edit and splice raw footage into shots, scenes, and movies. Users of representations never deal with reality itself, but rather with reality translated into the materials and conventional language of a particular craft.

Standard ways of making representations give makers a standard set of elements to use in constructing their artifacts, including materials and their capabilities, such as film with a particular light sensitivity, so many grains of light sensitive material and thus a particular degree of resolution making possible the representation of elements of a certain size but not smaller; conceptual elements, like the idea of plot or character in fiction; and conventional units of meaning, like scenes or the wipes, fades, and other devices for indicating the passage of time in a movie.

Makers expect standard elements to have standard effects, so that consumers of representations made with them will respond in standard ways. We might define representations made when that condition obtains as "perfect." Since the condition never obtains completely, the more interesting situation is when it is met sufficiently that most people (and especially those whose opinion counts, because they are powerful and important) respond near enough to what makers intended that the result is "acceptable" to everyone involved. The criteria defining acceptability vary considerably. Take the issue of the "transparency" of the prose, tables, and pictures people use to report scientific results. Both the makers and users of scientific representations would like the verbal, numerical, and visual languages they use in their articles and reports to be neutral standard elements, which add nothing to what is being reported. Like a clear glass window, results could just be seen through them without being affected by being seen through anything. Thomas Kuhn (1962) has provided a reasoned argument that no such "transparent" descriptive scientific language is possible, that all descriptions are "theory-laden." More to the point, it is clear that even the width of bars in a bar chart and the size and style of type in a table, let alone the adjectives in an ethnography or historical narrative, affect our interpretation of what is reported. Nevertheless, all these methods of portraying social reality have been acceptable to scientific audiences, who taught themselves to overlook or discount for those effects of the communicative elements they had accepted as standard.

Standard elements have the features already found in investigations of art worlds. They make efficient communication of ideas and facts possible by creating a shorthand known to everyone who needs the material. But they simultaneously constrain what a maker can do, because every set of translations makes saying some things easier but other things more difficult. To take a contemporary example, social scientists conventionally represent race and gender discrimination in job promotions in a multiple-regression equation, a widely used standard statistical element which tells what proportion of the variance in promotions is due to the independent effects of such separate variables as race, gender, education, and seniority. But, as Charles Ragin and his collaborators (Ragin et al. 1984) have shown, that way of representing discrimination does not answer the questions either sociologists or courts ask. It does not tell you, and cannot, how the chances for promotion of a young white male differ from those of an older black female; it can only tell you the weight of a variable like age or gender in an equation, not the same thing at all. They advocate making another statistical element standard: the Boolean algorithm (details can be found in the article just cited) which represents discrimination as the differences in chances of promotion for a person with a particular combination of those attributes as compared to mean rates for a whole population. This *is* what social scientists and courts want to know. (Related and complementary arguments are made in Leiberson 1985.)

Some constraints on what a representation can tell us arise from the way representational activity is organized. Organizationally constrained budgets—time and attention as well as money—limit the potential of media and formats. Books and movies are as long as people can afford to make them and as other people will pay attention to. If makers had more money and people would sit still for it, every ethnography might contain every field note and every step in the analytic process (which Clyde Kluckhohn [1945] thought the only proper way to publish life history materials).

Arrangement. The elements of the situation a representation describes, having been chosen and translated, must be arranged in some order so that users can take them in. The order given to elements is both *arbitrary*—you can always see how it might have been done another way—and *determined* by standard ways of doing things, just as the elements are. Arrangement makes narratives out of random elements. It communicates such notions as causality, so that viewers see the order of photographs on a gallery wall or in a book as meaningful, see earlier pictures as the "conditions" which produced the "consequences" depicted in the later ones. When I tell a story (personal, historical, or sociological), the earlier elements "explain" those that come later; a character's actions in one episode become evidence for a personality which reveals itself fully in later ones (see McCall 1985: 176–79). Students of statistical tables and graphics are particularly sensitive to the effects of arrangement on interpretations (Dolby and Clark unpublished).

No maker of representations of society can avoid this issue since, as many studies have shown, users of representations see order and logic even in random arrangements of elements. People find logic in the arrangement of photographs whether the photographer intended it or not, and respond to typefaces as "frivolous," "serious," or "scientific," independent of the text's content. Social scientists and methodologists have yet to treat this as a serious problem; what to do about it is one of the things that gets passed on as professional lore.

Interpretation. Representations exist fully only when someone is using them, reading or viewing or listening and thus completing the communication by interpreting the results and constructing for themselves the reality the maker intended to show them. The road map exists when I use it to get to the next town, Dickens's novels when I read them and imagine Victorian England, a table when I inspect it and evaluate the propositions it suggests.

What users know how to do interpretively thus becomes a major constraint on what a representation can accomplish. Users must know and be capable of using the conventional elements and formats of the medium and genre. That knowledge and ability can never be taken for granted. Historical studies (e.g., Cohen 1982) have shown that it was not until well into the nineteenth century that most Americans were "numerate," capable of understanding and using standard arithmetic operations. Anthropological studies show that what such literary critics as Roland Barthes and Susan Sontag insist is the universal appeal to our sense of reality embodied in still photographs and film is no such thing. More professionalized fields expect users to become knowledgeable consumers of representations through training in graduate or professional school, although what is expected to be known varies from time to time. We expect sociologists to acquire a certain amount of statistical sophistication (for which read, in part, "ability to read formulae and tables"), but few departments expect their students to know much about mathematical models.

Users interpret representations by finding the answers to two kinds of questions in them (on understanding photographs as potential answers to questions, see Becker 1974). On the one hand, they want to know "the facts": what happened at the battle of Bull Run, where the slum communities of Los Angeles are located, what the median income of white-collar suburbs is, what the correlation is between race, income, and education in the United States in 1980, what it is "really like" to be an astronaut—questions, at every level of specificity, whose answers help people orient their actions. On the other hand, users want answers to moral questions: not just what the correlation is between race, education, and income, but also why the correlation is what it is, whose fault it is, and what ought to be done about it. They want to know whether the Civil War, and thus the battle of Bull Run, was "necessary" or could have been prevented; whether astronaut John Glenn is the kind of man who deserves to be President; and so on. On the most superficial inspection, almost any factual question about society displays a strong moral dimension, which accounts for the ferocious battles that so often occur over what seem to be minor matters of technical interpretation. Arthur Jensen's statistical mistakes upset people who are not statisticians.

Users and Makers

One important organizational dimension is the difference between makers and users of representations. We all play both parts frequently, telling stories and listening to them, making causal analyses and reading them. As with any other service relationship, the interests of the two sets of parties usually differ considerably, particularly when, as is so often true, the makers are professionals who make such representations full time for pay, and the users are amateurs who use such representations occasionally, in a habitual and uninspected way (see the classic analysis of routine and emergency in Hughes 1971: 316–25). A major difference between what we might call representational worlds is which set of interests dominate.

In worlds dominated by makers, representations take the form of an *argument,* a presentation of just that material which makes the points the maker wants to get across and no more (the current literature on the *rhetoric* of scientific writing referred to earlier makes this point). When making representations is professionalized, makers are likely to control the circumstances of their making, for all the reasons Everett Hughes pointed out: what is out of the ordinary for most people is what they do all day long. Even if others have substantial power, professionals know so much more about how to manipulate the process that they retain great control. Powerful others who support representation making over a long term typically learn enough to overcome that disability, but casual users seldom do. So professionally made representations embody the choices and interests of makers, and indirectly of the people who can afford to hire them, and thus may well not show the hills a pedestrian would like to know about.

In user-dominated worlds, representations are used as *files,* archives to be ransacked for answers to whatever questions any competent user might have in mind. Think of the difference between the street map you buy at the store and the detailed, annotated map I draw to show *you* how to get to *my* house. Lay representations are typically more localized and more responsive to user wishes than those made by professionals. (Another example is the difference between amateur snapshots, which satisfy their makers' need for documents to show to a circle of intimates who know everyone in the pictures, and the photographs made by journalists, artists, and social scientists, oriented to the standards of professional communities, discussed in Bourdieu 1965.)

Some artifacts seem to be *essentially* files. A map, after all, seems to be a simple repository of geographic and other facts users can consult for their own purposes. In fact, maps can be made in a great variety of ways, none of them a simple translation of reality, which has allowed formerly voiceless peoples to claim that the maps that dominate world thinking are "Eurocentric," the technical choices they embody leading to results that arbitrarily make Europe and North America look like the center of the world. That is, those maps embody the argument that Europe and North America are "more important."

Conversely, scholars routinely ignore the arguments contained in the scholarly papers they cite, merely rifling the literature for results which can be put to *their* purposes. In short, they use the literature not as a body of arguments but as a file of results with which to answer questions the original authors never thought of.

So arguments and files are not kinds of documents, but kinds of uses, ways of doing something rather than objects or things.

Some Organizational Problems: Misrepresentation

Sociologists in my tradition habitually seek an understanding of social organization by looking for trouble, for situations in which people complain that things aren't happening the way they are supposed to. You find the rules and understandings governing social relations by hearing people complain when they are violated. Every field of representational activity is marked by periodic violent, heavily moralistic debate over the way representations are made and used. The cries of "it's not fair" and "he cheated" would sound like the games of five-year-olds were the stakes not so much higher and the matters dealt with so much more serious. Analysis of the problem of *misrepresentation* illustrates the perspective on problems of method and technique this way of looking at things opens up.

For examples, anthropology students at the University of Papua in New Guinea complained that Margaret Mead's *Growing Up in New Guinea* was unfair because it repeated the derogatory stories her informants had told about the students' ancestors, for whom they had a traditional contempt. The students did not complain that what Mead reported was untrue; they agreed that those people had said such things. Nor did they complain that Mead presented the stories as fact. Rather, they complained because their own ancestors, whom Mead had not studied, used to say equally terrible things about those other people, and Mead had not given them equal time.

These complaints exemplify the class of complaints which arise from self-interest: "You made me [or mine] look bad!" The first assistant physician of the mental hospital Erving Goffman studied complained wistfully (in the footnote Goffman donated to him) that for every "bad thing" *Asylums* noted he could have produced a balancing "good thing": for the victimizations of patients Goffman reported he would have told about the newly painted cafeteria (Goffman 1961:234). The citizens and politicians of Kansas City, Missouri, complained that the 1960 Census underreported the city's population by a few thousand, thus keeping it from sharing in the benefits state law gave to cities over half a million (a law designed to help St. Louis some years earlier). Almost everyone whose organization is filmed by Frederick Wiseman complains that they didn't realize they were going to end up looking like that.

The practice of more or less fictionalizing reportage, as practiced by Norman Mailer, Truman Capote, and Tom Wolfe, among others, has provoked another kind of complaint. The distinguished journalist John Hersey (1980) pointed out that these writers not only made things up, but insisted on the right to make them up in the name of a higher truth. Hersey argues that that is all right in writing labeled as fiction, which carries on its license the legend "THIS WAS MADE UP!", but not in journalism. There

> the writer must not invent. The legend on the license must read: NONE OF THIS WAS MADE UP. The ethics of journalism, if we can allow such a boon, must be based on the simple truth that every journalist knows the difference between the distortion that comes from subtracting observed data and the distortion that comes from adding invented data.

Hersey adds, interestingly, that distortion by omission is acceptable, because

> the reader assumes the subtraction [of observed data] as a given of journalism and instinctively hunts for the bias; the moment the reader suspects additions, the earth begins to skid underfoot, for the idea that there is no way of knowing what is real and what is not real is terrifying. Even more terrifying is the notion that lies are truths.

But many critics of print and broadcast journalism (e.g., Molotch and Lester 1974; Tuchman 1978; Gitlin 1980) complain exactly that it leaves out what people need to be able to assess issues properly. And it's easy to imagine readers who would be as much at ease "instinctively hunting out" additions as Hersey is going after subtractions, as long as they knew that it needed to be done; in fact, I imagine that many of Wolfe's readers, as well as newspaper readers and television viewers, do just that.

Hersey, whether or not we accept his judgments, points to the sociological core of conflicts over representations of social reality. No report in any medium or genre, following no-matter-what strict rules—not even our own most up-to-the-minute state-of-the-art inventions—will solve all problems, answer all questions, or avoid all potential troubles. People who create reports of any kind come to agree as to what is good enough, what procedures need to be followed to achieve that good-enough condition, and that any report made by following those procedures is authoritative enough for ordinary purposes. That protects professional interests and lets the work and that of the people who use it proceed, guaranteeing the results as acceptable, believable, and capable of bearing the weight put on them by routine use for other people's purposes. These standards define what is expected, so that users can discount for the shortcomings of representations made according to them and, at least, know what they are dealing with. Hersey's analysis accepts this state of affairs as normal, standard, and proper. It is what I had in mind when I said earlier that every way of making a representation is "perfect": that it is good enough that people will accept it as the best they can get under the circumstances and learn how to work with its limitations. People claim that misrepresentation has occurred when the standard procedures have not been followed, so that users are misled by thinking a contract is in force which is actually not being honored.

People also claim misrepresentation when their interests are harmed because the routine use of acceptable standard procedures has left something out which, if it were included, would change the interpretations of fact, but more importantly the moral judgments, people make on the basis of the representation. This usually happens when some historical shift makes new voices audible. The people Mead studied did not read anthropological monographs and so could not criticize them, but their descendants can and do.

In either case, the problem of misrepresentation is a problem of social organization, of a bargain once good enough for everyone being redefined as inadequate. A large number of problems which crosscut genres and media can be similarly analyzed in organizational terms: the ethics of representation, the problem of the authority of a representation, or the influence of context on content.

Conclusion

This all implies a relativistic view of knowledge, at least to this degree: The same reality can be described in an enormous number of ways, since the descriptions can be answers to any of a multitude of questions. We can agree in principle that our procedures ought to let us get the same answer to the same question, but in fact we only ask the same question when the circumstances of social interaction and organization have produced consensus on that point. That happens when the conditions of people's lives lead them to see certain problems as common, as requiring certain kinds of representations of social reality on a routine basis, and thus lead to the development of professions and crafts that make those representations for use. As a result, some questions get asked and answered while others, every bit as good, interesting, worthwhile, and even scientifically important are ignored, at least until society changes enough that the people who need those answers come to command the resources that will let them get an answer. Until then, pedestrians are going to be surprised by San Francisco's hills.

8

STUDYING PRACTITIONERS OF VICE AND CRIME

Ideally, we would gather data on deviants by observing them as they go about their characteristic activities or by interviewing them about their experiences.[1] But in studying deviants we face all the problems that observation and interview occasion in any social group, and additional ones as well; or perhaps it is only that those problems are exaggerated. We must find people who engage in the behavior we want to study. We must assess the degree to which the people we find resemble the ones we have not been able to find. We must persuade, manipulate, coerce, or trick the people we find into furnishing us with the data we need for our analyses.

But the feature that makes deviance of interest to us (or at least one of the features) is precisely what makes the job so difficult. Because the activity in question is ordinarily stigmatized and is very likely to be legally punishable as well, those who engage in it do not make that fact publicly known or easily available. We may have trouble locating practitioners of the vices we are interested in, or locating them in such a way as to allow us to get any information about their deviance, because they will not engage in it in our presence or because they will not admit to us that they engage in it. Still, studies of deviance have been made, so the task is not impossible.

Gathering Data Directly

ACCESS AND SAMPLING

Factories do not give lists of employees, complete with names, addresses, and phone numbers, to anyone who asks for them; nor

---

[1] I have refrained from any complicated definitional discussions of what deviance is. In what follows I will be talking about the problems of studying people who engage in conventionally (and, usually, legally) disapproved forms of behavior and the patterns of collective reaction—the worlds—they move in. I focus primarily on such traditional vices as sexual misbehavior and the use of forbidden drugs, but occasionally refer to various forms of more ordinary crime as well.

do unions readily give out lists of their members. Many colleges sell lists of students publicly (largely for the convenience of other students, to be sure), but no hospital makes a list of patients so easily available (though new mothers sometimes wonder how else all those salesmen found them so soon). In all these cases, however, the list exists, or could be compiled. A researcher with proper credentials and justifications might persuade the proprietors of the list to make it available to him for purposes of drawing a sample from which data might be gathered. Alternatively, since the locations where characteristic activities take place are known to some specific official, a researcher can similarly learn and use them as a sampling universe.

No such officially complete list of participants in any deviant act exists. I suppose that, in some sense, none could, since the acts are unofficial. In any event, the researcher must draw his sample from a universe whose limits, units, and locales are known to him fragmentarily. Conventional sampling theory has unfortunately ignored this problem; but a conventionally mathematical approach might not be of great help. Strategies of sampling based on the sociological characteristics of the population that interests the researcher are likely to be much more fruitful in the study of deviants.

1. If the researcher, in his own private life, has achieved access to circles in which the deviant activity occurs, he can use that access for research purposes. I made use of my contacts among dance musicians (I had been a musician before I was a sociologist) to get interviews about marijuana use, an activity then relatively more common and more open among musicians than among others (Becker 1963:45). Similarly, Ned Polsky (1967:44–46) used his established position as a billiards buff and amateur hustler to gather data on pool hustlers and their activities.

This strategy solves the access problem conveniently; you at least know someone to observe and interview, and can attempt to have them introduce you to others and vouch for you, thus setting up a kind of snowball sampling. Since you are known, and known of, in your prior capacity, few doubts as to your trustworthiness arise. It is probably wise to reveal your research purposes, because your questions probably require explanation. In addition, such openness will explain your otherwise unaccountable desire to meet more and more practitioners of the vice under study. If it can be said that, by consenting to be interviewed, deviants are helping you (as one of them) to earn an academic degree or a scientific living, they may be very willing to cooperate. Deviants who know your purposes may cooperate so that the "true story," which they feel they can trust you to tell, can get to the public through your research report. Your participation will, of course, be limited both by what is conventional among the group under study and by what you are willing to do yourself; more researchers, presumably, will be willing to participate in after-work crap games than to engage in prostitution, even though the arguments in favor of completeness of data are equally compelling in the two cases.[2]

The representativeness of your data will depend on the degree to which all those you might want to study belong to a connected network. If, at one extreme, the activity is a solitary one (embezzling, kleptomania, masturbation), there are no circles to belong to that would give access to subjects of study. If everyone involved knew everyone else, to know one would be to know all and participation at all would solve the problem. If (as was probably true of marijuana smoking when I did my original study) a number of worlds where the activity is carried on overlap only slightly, this strategy may afford you good coverage of one subgroup, but only beginning leads or none at all to other groups. This may be the case in studies of homosexuality, where there seems to be little overlap of the quiet and respectable homosexuals studied by Evelyn Hooker (1965, 1967), the teenage hustlers studied by Albert Reiss (1961), and the participants in encounters in public toilets studied by Laud Humphreys (1970).

2. When you believe that you know nothing and have no contacts, the only sure method of getting at least some beginning information is to interview deviants who have been legally processed as a result of apprehension for a deviant act. This usually means interviewing incarcerated deviants, a strategy that has much to recommend it. For one thing, there is probably no quicker way to accumulate a large sample. No other location has so many deviants whose deviance is publicly known and who thus might as well talk to you as not. In addition, some activities occur in so private and solitary a way that subjects could not otherwise be found. How else, for instance, could Donald Cressey (1953) have found embezzlers to

---

[2]I do not mean to argue that one way is better than the other, for that judgment depends on what one wants to study. Nevertheless, the choice of methods constrains what one *can* talk about. Compare, for example, James Henslin's (1967) detailed dissection of the smallest features of gambling behavior with the necessarily more macroscopic analysis in James H. Bryan (1965).

interview? Successful embezzlers disappear, as do successful "missing persons." You can find only the failures who are caught.

That, of course, is a chief criticism of studies based on imprisoned populations: they use samples that are unrepresentative in a peculiarly bad way, for there is reason to suppose that, with respect to many forms of deviance, those caught differ in skill, in mode of operation, or in some other important way that is tied to their failure. Professional criminals, it is said, arrange for the "fix," and so amateurs are vastly overrepresented in prison populations; and amateurs, it might be argued, are more likely to have psychological difficulties, with obvious consequences for the validity of etiological theories of deviance based on such samples.

A second major criticism suggests that imprisoned deviants do not talk or act as they might in their native habitats, any more than animals in a zoo behave as they would in the wild. No longer operating in their normal circumstances, they now respond to vastly different controls, and in particular may think that by telling their story in one way or another they can use the researcher to influence the authorities on whom their fate depends. They may tell only "sad stories," self-justifying tales of how they got where they are. Clearly, studies using imprisoned populations should recognize the limitations this stratagem introduces. It should not be used simply because it is convenient, but only when some more compelling reason of structurally restricted accessibility requires it.[3]

3. If deviance were common enough, rather than being a rare occurrence, one might study it by questioning random samples of the total population or some approximation thereof, relying on this screening procedure to produce a sufficient number of cases for intensive study. For relatively rare activities—heroin addiction or incest, for example—this is an incredibly wasteful method. But some studies have found quite justifiable the assumption that particular deviant activities are common. This is a particularly useful device when you have some other research reason for the larger interviewing program. Thus, Alfred Kinsey and his associates wanted to study sexual activity in human adults and interviewed normal populations (as well as others) on the assumption, proven correct, that they

[3]Polsky (1967:117–49) argues this position forcefully. D. W. Maurer (1968) takes strong exception in a review of Polsky's book.

would find large numbers who had engaged in various deviant sexual activities as well as the "normal" ones presumably more widespread. Self-report studies of delinquency (reviewed in Hardt and Bodine 1965) rely on essentially the same device, and Reiss (1961) discovered teenage "queer hustlers" by routinely asking boys interviewed in a larger delinquency study whether they had ever engaged in the activity.

This approach is probably most useful when you are interested in the distribution of a great variety of deviant activities in the general population. It becomes progressively less useful as you focus in detail on some specific deviant activity, subculture, or world. To study the perspectives and structures characteristic of such worlds, you need detailed information on other people with whom the interviewee interacts. But while an interviewee who volunteers for a Kinsey-style interview in effect agrees in advance to regard questions about himself as legitimate, he may draw the line when asked to "incriminate" others, never having agreed to that as a fit topic for discussion. And the requirements of the larger study may interfere with such specialized inquiries (although they need not, as the Reiss study demonstrates).

In any event, this strategy produces a population of subjects if, but only if, the activity occurs commonly. Then Kinsey-like procedures will generate much information, and care should be taken to allow for specialized inquiries into particular topics, making use of informants and contacts produced by the larger screening.

4. A variant of the preceding approach likewise assumes that deviant activities, though hidden, occur quite frequently. Instead of contacting large numbers of people and inquiring directly about their activities, however, one advertises for volunteers in places where the sought-after deviants would be likely to hear of one's research interest and then waits for them to turn up. Nancy Lee (1969) used this strategy in her study of women who had had illegal abortions.[4] She first inquired among her own acquaintances and then asked doctors, birth control clinics, and other likely sources to spread the word that she wanted to hear from women who had had the experience and were willing to be interviewed about it. She ultimately achieved contact with over one hundred women, who either granted

---

[4]Clark E. Vincent (1961) used similar procedures in his study of illegitimate births.

her personal interviews or completed a questionnaire for her. One can advertise in this informal way or even use more public media to make known one's research.

This device produces willing volunteers who speak freely of their experiences and activities. Interaction with them is no problem, but sampling becomes difficult. You end up only with volunteers, so you can expect, as the debate over Kinsey's research suggested, that they will not represent the full range of experiences and social types to be found in the universe. It probably works best when one is investigating activities that can be expected to be fairly common in the general population or, alternatively, when one has some knowledge as to the specialized population within which it might be profitable to advertise. It may be the only feasible approach with activities, like abortion, in which each participant engages only once or a few times, which generate no subculture or continuing organization unique to those who have had the experience, but which are of at least potential interest to some much larger group (as abortion is likely to be to women in general).

5. You can induce deviants to reveal themselves by offering some service they desire and perhaps cannot get elsewhere, then taking advantage of your knowledge of them to ask for research data. James Bryan (1965) began his study of call girls when he discovered that a patient to whom he was giving psychotherapy was in that profession, and interviewed her. Not surprisingly, other call girls she knew felt they needed the same therapeutic services, and Bryan got part of his sample that way. Deviants frequently look for unconventional sources of medical, legal, and psychiatric services, either because they cannot afford what is conventionally available or, as is often true with regard to medical services, because they do not like the embarrassment and harassment they experience from conventional practitioners. Anyone who provides these services free or in a more neutral fashion will have plenty of people to study.[5] The advantages and disadvantages of this approach resemble very closely those of the preceding one.

[5]Dr. David Smith and his colleagues at the Haight-Ashbury Free Medical Clinic have achieved such a relationship with the hippie population of that San Francisco community and have been able to gather a great deal of important information on drug use and other medical problems. For early reports on this material, see articles by Smith and others in the *Journal of Psychedelic Drugs*, published at the clinic.

6. Finally, the researcher can locate himself in those areas or places where the deviants he is interested in habitually or occasionally congregate and then either simply observe them or take the opportunity to interact with them and gather information in a more direct and purposive way. This strategy in some ways solves the problem of sampling very neatly. If you regard as your universe all those who engage in the collective activity under observation, then those who do not show up to be observed by definition do not belong to the group to be studied; problems arise only in considering whether there are other places that could have been observed, and assessing how the observed activity fits into some larger pattern of related activities. For example, you may study gay bars but wonder how the activities observed there fit into some larger pattern of homosexual activities in the community.

Other problems of this strategy include finding the proper locations for observation and choosing and playing an appropriate role once you are there. Locations can often be easily discovered with the help of a knowledgeable informant. An experienced cab driver can often tell you where homosexual bars may be found, or where pimps and prostitutes or thieves and gamblers hang out. Newspaper reporters may have similar kinds of information, as may bartenders, policemen, or a lone member of the deviant group with whom one already has made contact.

Supposing you have found your observation post, what role will you play once you are there? The chief choices are to disguise yourself as one of the deviants (we have earlier considered the case where one comes by this role honestly), to be one of the service personnel associated with the location (a waitress in a homosexual bar, for example), or to make yourself known as a researcher. The latter choice gives you great freedom to pursue your scientific interest, for you need not tailor your words or actions to what would be appropriate to an occupant of either of the other roles, but can instead ask and do a great variety of things, offering science as the justification. Furthermore, you can avoid incriminating or distasteful participation in deviant activities on the reasonable grounds that, while you are perhaps sympathetic, your personal inclinations run in another direction. Many researchers feel, however, that to be known as an outsider will severely limit the amount of information one can get. I know of no definitive evidence on the point, but informative studies have been accomplished by this method, suggesting that the limitation can be overcome.

If the social scientist wants to study settings in which there is no opportunity to introduce himself as a researcher, he probably has no choice and must pass as a deviant. If he is not seen by others as a deviant in these situations, he will be seen as a tourist, policeman, or something else unwanted, and the people he wants to study will simply refrain from the activity he has come to observe while he is there, or perhaps drive him out so that the activity may resume (Sherri Cavan [1966:216–26] has described the way habitués of a gay bar get rid of sightseers). To avoid these unpleasant results, the researcher must discover some role in the deviant world he can comfortably play that will allow him to get the information he needs (see Black and Mileski 1967).

Humphreys (1970) used this strategy with great success in his study of homosexual activity in public toilets. These activities, of considerable sociological interest, take place without conversation between men who have very likely never seen one another before, but they will not take place in the presence of anyone suspected of being a policeman or a "straight" person. How then can one observe them? Humphreys discovered that a role existed for voyeurs, who simply watched and also assisted in the action by looking out for intrusions by dangerous outsiders. By performing as lookout, he was able to observe a large number of homosexual acts and develop an ethnography of this behavior. He also observed the license numbers of the cars men drove up in and used these to discover names and addresses of men he had personally observed engage in homosexual acts. He then interviewed these men, using a standard interview from a contemporary health survey, and so acquired a great deal of information on aspects of their lives other than sexual, which he then compared with similar information from a control group included in the larger survey.

It should be clear that no one of these strategies solves all the problems; each has its advantages, each costs something. The nature of the topic under study constrains the choice of method; you cannot use methods that assume the existence of an organized deviant world, for instance, where none exists. The nature of your social connections and experience constrains the kinds of roles you can play and will be willing to play. The deviant world one wants to study may be divided into several somewhat separate segments, such that various methods will be necessary for each; any study of homosexuality must reckon with this. In general, the situation calls for methodological flexibility; a researcher may use several approaches to the same topic as time, his resources and capabilities, and the situation allow.[6]

I have spoken of participant observation and interviewing as though they were almost interchangeable, largely for convenience in discussing problems of sampling and access. Although most deviant activities can be studied by either method, the results differ, each limiting you in a different way. The choice depends on the relation between the character and frequency of the activity, the goal of your research, and the costs and difficulties of each method. Take abortion as an example. Given the way the activity is carried on, you probably cannot get much information on the experiences of the women involved if you choose, as Donald Ball (1967) did, to observe an abortion mill in operation. You can get that information by interviews after the fact, as Lee did, but you then sacrifice knowledge of the professional side of the activity. Where people engage more continuously in the activity, or where there is not such great social distance between the various categories of participants, observation may allow you to get both kinds of data.

WHAT TO ASK; WHAT TO OBSERVE

Ask "How?"—not "Why?" I think it a good idea in research on any topic to avoid asking people *why* they have done something when you really want to find out *how* it came about that they did it. When you ask why you are asking for, and will receive, given the conventions of our common speech, a justification, an explanation, a selection from the currently available vocabulary of motives. We very often want just that, but we should never mistake it for an account of how something came to pass (see Mills 1940).

This caution applies with exceptional force to studies of deviants. If their unusual activities have come to the attention of friends, relatives, colleagues, or enforcement officials, they will have been asked repeatedly why they did what they did. In thinking of the difficulties they have had, they may even ask themselves the same question. And so they are likely to have stock answers and sad stories prepared for the researcher's version of the same old question.

[6]There are limiting cases in which it appears impossible to locate any kind of sample. See the account of an attempt to study a mildly deviant activity, the use of health foods, in Peter Kong-ming New and Rhea Pendergrass Priest (1968:250–54). For examples of various approaches to another problem (drug use), see *Journal of Health and Social Behavior* 9 (June 1968), a special issue on recreational drug use.

It is much more effective, if one wants to learn the sequence of events leading to some pattern of deviant activity, to ask *how* the thing happened. "When did you first do *X*?" "How did you happen to do that?" "Then what happened?" "How did that work out?" Questions that probe for the concrete details of events and their sequence produce answers that are less ideological and mythological and more useful for the reconstruction of past events and experiences. Such an interrogation can and should include questions on the subjective aspects of events: "What did you think when that happened?" "How did you feel about that?" But the answers to such questions should be interpreted with respect to the historical context of events elicited by the other questions. If the interviewing is carried on as part of a program of field observation, the researcher can focus his questions on current events, asking simply for descriptions of what is going on and explanations in the form of descriptions of further phenomena likely to be of interest. Though general doctrinal discussions have some interest, you need specific, situation-bound data for detailed analysis of social structures and individual careers.

In general, to ask why something happened shifts to the interviewee the analytic job that the researcher himself should be doing. An interview should elicit the concrete descriptions from which such an analysis can be made, rather than the amateur analysis the interviewee might be able to provide.

Argot. Deviant activities tend to generate a special language, at the least to describe the esoteric events, people, and objects involved, and perhaps as a matter of symbolic differentiation from nondeviants as well. How should the researcher take account of this language?

He must, of course, eventually learn to understand it. But he need not be too quick to demonstrate that he does, for he can get very good information by insisting that his informants and interviewees explain the special language to him. In so doing, they will have to make the explanations and provide the examples he needs for his analysis. Many researchers find it hard to feign ignorance or admit it when it is real, wanting to appear knowledgeable, either to make themselves feel good or to assure the interviewee that he can talk safely and that what is said will be understood. The latter reason may apply, but the other alternative should be considered. (If the researcher is passing as a member of the deviant society, then he must, of course, exhibit the necessary degree of linguistic ability.)

However the researcher resolves this dilemma, he will, as he would in the study of any form of collective action, want to pay close attention to nuances of language. Unusual terms or unusual uses of conventional words signal areas of central concern to the people under study and provide an opening analytic wedge, as the term "square" did in studying musicians (Becker 1963:85−91) or "crock" did in studying medical students (Becker and Geer 1957). Differences in the use of deviant argot may serve as useful indicators of generational differences among members of the group, of differences in degree of involvement in its activities, or of differences in the segment of the deviant world one belongs to (Lerman 1967).

Organizational variation. Deviant activities, as the discussion of access will have made clear, may take place in a solitary fashion, each deviant constituting a private world unto himself, or they may, at the other extreme, occur in a complex and segmented world. In the latter case, the researcher should make the structure of that world a topic for study, using that knowledge, as it accumulates, for sampling purposes as well.

In more complex worlds, a typical axis of differentiation for which the researcher should look centers on the relation of the deviant activities to the conventional world. One group will believe secrecy the best policy and act accordingly. The "closet queens" of the homosexual world, the quiet pot smokers recognize that, at some price in spontaneity and fun, they can carry on deviant activities without ever revealing to outsiders that they do so. Another segment frequently opposes such prudence, insists on "flaunting" their deviance publicly, has a lot of trouble as a result, fights for "equal rights" for their brand of deviance, may support "defense" organizations (such as NORML and the Mattachine Society), and are in general much more visible to researchers as well as to the public than the first group.

In addition, the researcher may discover segments defined by the differing degree of involvement of their members in the characteristic activities of that deviant world. Some persons might reasonably be called professionals: purveyors of necessary items used by members, proprietors of locations and establishments where the activities take place, or sellers of specialized services. Drug wholesalers, proprietors of gambling casinos or gay bars, and homosexual prostitutes exemplify this segment. Another segment consists of ordinary members deeply involved, people who participate frequently in characteristically deviant activities: "drag queens," addicts, and the like.

Still others partake only occasionally, are much less committed to "the life," and have a correspondingly complex life in the conventional world, and one more important to them: the occasional drug user, the part-time whore. Finally, there are the sightseers, experimenters, and novices, who, even while they investigate the deviant world, still retain for themselves the option of having nothing to do with it after all.

The researcher should look for these typical forms of differentiation and organize his work so as to gain some kind of access to each of the parts. Alternatively, he should learn at least enough about the matter to know how what he has observed or been told about stands in relation to the rest of that world he has not been able to explore fully. For many sociological purposes, he need not have samples of all segments in representative numbers; that is, the members of the various segments in his sample need not constitute the same proportions of his total sample that they do of the universe. His first order of business should usually be to discover the full range of social types, roles, adaptations, and styles of life that surround the deviant activity he is studying, for the discovery of a new type is likely to have great theoretical import.[7]

Typical situations. Certain typical situations and events arise in relation to most deviant activities; look for them and make them the focus of study. It pays, first of all, to get a good understanding of the deviant activity itself, insofar as it occurs publicly enough to be observed or is talked about freely enough to allow such understanding. By learning about the activity, one comes to appreciate the contingencies for action it creates and the effects these have on other aspects of collective action in the deviant community. Since lay people have many unfounded beliefs about deviant activities, which the sociologist for lack of any better knowledge will probably share, one should observe them simply to get rid of those conceptions; to learn, for instance, that drug users do not typically engage in sexual orgies following ingestion of drugs. In addition, the activity itself may be of great theoretical interest. Humphreys's study of homosexual activities in public toilets, for example, represents an extreme case of coordinated activity occurring on the basis of tacit bargain-

---

[7]A general perspective on the development of theory from research data is presented by Barney G. Glaser and Anselm L. Strauss (1967).

ing, a topic Thomas Schelling (1963) has treated on a much more abstract level.

Other typical situations worthy of special attention include the process by which novices are introduced to the deviant activity and taught how to carry it out, and the concomitant process by which they are inducted into whatever community may exist around the activity. The "coming-out" parties given some homosexuals are an extreme and formalized instance of this, but more informal analogues are common, except of course where the activity is carried on in a solitary fashion; even then, the person may invent such occasions for himself, as transvestites do when they appear in public in the clothing of the opposite sex.

In more organized deviant communities, look for the more or less formal educational situations in which the novice learns the culture of the deviant community. Bryan (1966) describes the elaborate procedure by which a call girl is taught her trade and the ideology associated with it; but he also shows—an important caution for sociologists who take the notion of deviant subculture as given rather than as something to be discovered empirically in each case—that girls learn the ideology but neither believe it, act by it, or permit it to influence their other ideas.

Since deviant activity is sometimes illegal and always stigmatized, deviants discovered by the conventional community can expect to be publicly labeled as deviant, to suffer various sanctions, and to have the normal order of their lives grossly interrupted and changed. Make a point of observing or asking people about the situations in which deviants are apprehended, the consequences of apprehension, and its effects on other aspects of their lives. In addition, look for the effect of this constant element of danger on the organization of the deviant community, and for differential attitudes toward it and actions with respect to it on the part of community segments.

Indirect Approaches

In addition to the direct methods just discussed (or, in rare cases, instead of them) the researcher may employ various indirect ways of getting at his subject. He can ask about and observe the operations of related people, groups, and organizations, and he can also search several relevant kinds of literature and archival records for useful material.

OTHER PEOPLE

We can learn about the contingencies of deviant lives and organizations by studying the operations of the professionals who
come into contact with them. Who these people are will depend
on the kind of deviance we study, but likely candidates for our
attention include doctors (especially psychiatrists), who may be
called on to provide diagnostic or treatment services; lawyers, who
serve as prosecutors, defenders, or counselors; and police, public
and private, who may be officially charged with enforcing laws
prohibiting the deviant activity or may have decided themselves that
they ought to. What these people do needs to be taken into account
because of its immediate effects on the people we study, and we
sometimes find it easier to observe certain key activities by participating as one of them or in their company. For example, it is
probably easier, at least for a male researcher, to discover some things
about the operations of prostitutes by observing, as Jerome Skolnick
(1967) did, members of the vice squad as they go about their daily
work of regulating and arresting whores.

In addition, specialists accumulate a great deal of practical experience and lore. They know what kinds of things go on, who is
who in the deviant community and where he may be found, relevant
local history, and a host of other things a researcher can use. Ju-
dicious cultivation of informants in these ancillary groups is sound
practice.

We may also wish to study the activities of nonspecialist nondeviants, of ordinary lay people whose own actions on occasion
figure importantly in the lives and experience of deviants. The most
important lay people to observe are family members, work colleagues, and members of the general public. A number of studies
(e.g., Sampson et al. 1965) have investigated the reactions of family
members to the fact or suspicion of mental illness in a family member. Edwin Lemert's remarkable study (1962) of paranoia used data
gathered from family members and work colleagues to demonstrate
that paranoid delusions of persecution were not delusions, that these
others, on their own testimony, actually did the things the putative
paranoid complained of. Richard Schwartz and Jerome Skolnick
(1962) used an ingenious field experimental technique to show that
employers were less likely to offer jobs to applicants who had been
tried or convicted of a criminal offense.

Studies of the attitudes and actions of the general public can be
quite revealing, especially with respect to questions of when deviant

labels are applied and what the consequences of the application are. John I. Kitsuse (1962) queried lay people about their contacts with homosexuals, discovering that there was both little consensus about what kind of behavior identified someone as homosexual and great variation in responses to such an identification, from violent assault to complete disregard.

OFFICIAL STATISTICS

Sociologists' past reliance on officially gathered statistics about deviance has provoked a number of severe and telling criticisms. I think it is now clear, though some may disagree, that police statistics, for example, tell us more about police than about criminals or delinquents, reflecting the degree to which officials decide to act against potential deviants in the community. But when we study deviance we may want to know about police behavior, so that the same statistics, so interpreted, become a valuable resource, telling us about levels of enforcement activity and suggesting possible variations in such activity with respect to subgroups in the deviant community. (See Kitsuse and Cicourel 1963; Cicourel 1967; and Biderman and Reiss 1967.)

While it is doubtful that police statistics can be used uncritically to learn about the etiology or causes of deviance, they can be used in conjunction with other information to learn many things of value, especially when there is no other practical way of gathering information. Mary Owen Cameron's study of shoplifting (1964) compared police and court records with the much more complete records kept by the store detectives who originally apprehended the thieves, and the comments of the detectives themselves on their own detection procedures, to arrive at estimates of the social class, age, and ethnic distributions of shoplifters.

As the above example suggests, police are not the only ones who keep potentially useful records. Many forms of deviance never come to police attention, being dealt with either by private policing agencies, as in industrial theft and embezzling, or by laymen in a more informal way. Agencies offering services to deviants sometimes keep useful records and may even collect data for research of their own that can be adapted for sociological use. The researcher should scout around for potential depositories of such records. Once he has located them, he will have to inquire carefully into how they were compiled—who gathered the information, under what circumstances, from whom, using what questions or data-gathering forms—

before deciding to what use they can be put. No agency's records should be accepted as accurate on faith; likewise, no agency's records should be dismissed as worthless without careful inspection and inquiry into how they are made up.

PUBLISHED SOURCES

A variety of published sources may contain useful information, depending on the form of deviance. Professional and scientific journals often contain articles on forms of deviance and related topics. If one is interested in drug use or sexual misbehavior, for instance, medical, pharmacological, psychiatric, legal, and police journals are likely to be useful. Most forms of deviance provoke diagnoses of mental illness from somebody, so that psychiatric journals are especially fruitful sources. One should routinely consult the *Quarterly Index Medicus* and *Psychological Abstracts* for leads to this literature, and their appropriate counterpart in law for law-review notes, discussions of public policy, and the like. In using this literature, keep in mind that the facts it reports were not gathered by sociologists for sociological purposes. Quite the contrary. You will have to distinguish carefully between the facts reported (keeping in mind that important facts may not have been reported) and the theories and opinions advanced. The former may be used to test your own theories. The latter may provide profitable material for an analysis of ideologies about the "problem" aspects of the deviant activity. Alfred Lindesmith's work on opiate addiction (1968) provides a classic model of both uses of available literature. He uses cases reported by physicians to test his own theory, reinterprets older findings, and uses the theories of physicians and enforcement officials as data for an interpretation of the social problem of addiction.

Another important source of data consists of legislative hearings. State, city, and federal hearings often deal with problems of deviance, since legislative action is frequently thought necessary to deal with the problems caused by the deviant activity. Legislators and their committee staffs interrogate witnesses of many kinds: police, proponents of changes in the laws, alleged lawbreakers, and so on. They do not always ask the questions we should like asked, but often enough they do; and sometimes they ask questions we might not have thought of. When the witnesses have been subpoenaed, investigators may get answers to questions, under oath, that sociologists might like to ask if they had the nerve. Some of the material in the hearings of Estes Kefauver's Senate committee on organized crime provides invaluable material for an analysis of that elusive topic.

Many forms of popular literature—newspapers, magazines, books—contain material that can be used for analyses of popular stereotypes of deviants and for analyses of propaganda designed to shape those stereotypes. Thomas Scheff (1966:55–101) analyzed comic strips, jokes, and other forms of popular culture to show how their treatment of residual deviance teaches members of our society the categories of "sane" and "insane." I used the incidence of popular articles about marijuana as a measure of the propaganda activity related to passage of the federal law banning its use (Becker 1963: 141), and Jerry Mandel (1966) traced the history of the stereotype of the assassin related to the use of hashish. Very little work of this kind has been done, and many possibilities remain to be explored.

Finally, organized deviant groups often produce a self-justifying literature that may also serve some of the functions of a trade magazine: autobiographical documents, reports on legal, medical, and scientific aspects of the deviance, editorials denouncing discrimination and repression, news of important events, and advertisements for other magazines and books of interest to practitioners of that particular activity (such as the easily available magazines published by nudist and homosexual groups). This material serves, as I have suggested with respect to other published sources, both as a storehouse of fact for testing your own theories and as raw material for an analysis of ideology. In addition, such magazines can be used to advertise for possible subjects of study; Taylor Buckner (1964), for example, reached some transvestites in this fashion.

Ethical Problems

Every conceivable topic of sociological study is probably a matter of moral concern to someone and thus poses moral and ethical problems for the researcher. Deviance certainly does, and, like the technical problems already considered, the moral problems center on the deviant status of the activities and people studied. What attitude should we take toward that deviant status? How should we respond to those activities?

GUILTY KNOWLEDGE

Unless we study apprehended deviants, we will inevitably know things that, under some strict construction of the law, should be reported to the police. If we do report what we know, we will probably not be able to continue our research. More to the point, we will probably have explicitly or implicitly violated a bargain we have made with the people under study, an agreement not to use the information we get to injure the people who give it to us. If the people studied know we are doing research, they will necessarily have assumed such a bargain on our part (see Hughes 1971:524– 29). If we have been studying them secretly, then we have gathered information in a way another citizen might, and I see no directive that applies to the sociologist *qua* sociologist. I think it repugnant and dishonorable to use information so gained to destroy people's characters and lives, though I do not know any scientific basis for that judgment. But none is needed; one's personal ethic should be enough. I do not mean to imply that the use of secretly gathered data in ways that do not harm the respondent is immoral. On the contrary, such data may be used for profoundly moral ends, as when Humphreys (1970) uses his analysis of homosexual encounters in public toilets to show how police victimize participants in those encounters.

What if law-enforcement officials demand access to our data? To my knowledge, this has not happened yet, but it probably will soon, as deviance and political marginality become more intertwined, both in fact and in the minds of enforcement officials. Lewis Yablonsky (1968) has suggested that we arrange in advance with relevant officials for immunity and that we seek legislative relief from these contingencies. But advance arrangements may require us to make bargains we would rather not make (though that is not necessarily so); legislatively granted immunity seems to me unlikely to come about soon. At present, I think we must be willing, if the occasion arises, to shield our informants as some journalists have done, even at the expense of legal sanctions.

TO PARTICIPATE OR NOT?

Researchers often feel that if they want fully to understand the deviants they study they should partake themselves of the forbidden activity. They want to share the experience itself, and the feeling of illegality as well, in order better to frame hypotheses and interpret data. But the activity may seem to them distasteful, frightening, immoral, disgusting, or any combination of these. What should they do?

I think it indisputable that one need not engage in an activity to understand it. If not indisputable, the proposition is at least a necessary assumption if we are to have a communicable social science. Otherwise, no white sociologist could write about blacks or blacks about whites; men could not write about women or women about men. In spite of the romantic yearnings of researchers and the earnest ideological assurances of some deviants, scientific requirements do not force us to join in deviant activities.

But our scientific purposes often require us to hear about and on occasion to observe activities we may personally disapprove of. I think it equally indisputable that one cannot study deviants without foregoing a simple-minded moralism that requires us to denounce openly any such activity on every occasion. Indeed, the researcher should cultivate a deliberately tolerant attitude, attempting to understand the point of view from which his subjects undertake the activities he finds distasteful. A moralism that forecloses empirical investigation by deciding questions of fact *a priori* is scientifically immoral.

WHO PROFITS?

A final ethical question arises because investigation of any area of deviance ordinarily discredits some portion of the general body of conventional belief. Major institutions, having either promulgated the discredited views or tacitly condoned them, find themselves under attack because the investigation shows them to have been wrong. To be sure, an investigation may be equally likely to discredit antiestablishment views of the matter; but then, no one of any established importance has supported those views or stands to lose when they are discredited. Thus research might show that, contrary to the claims found in some homophile literature, homosexuals are no more sensitive than normal males. This will not occasion the outcry that might arise if research showed that they were less neurotic than normal males, for that would discredit the views of important spokesmen of medicine, psychiatry, and the law.

This is not the place to rehearse this argument in detail (see Becker 1967a and 1970c:105–22). The researcher, briefly, must take into account the consequences of making his research public. Will his findings support popular views that he nevertheless feels morally unjustified, as might occur if a libertarian sociologist discovered that drug use actually caused brain damage? Or will they support unconventional views he feels morally unjustified, as when a more conformist sociologist might discover that drug use could be good for people? I think personally that the scientist must report his findings. I can also understand why one might suppress an obviously misinterpretable finding in situations where it will be misused for immoral ends, though I would not be happy to do so.

Conclusion

Technical problems of research reflect the peculiarities of the social groups we study.[8] In solving them, we simultaneously learn something about the social structure under observation and something about the methods we use. When we adapt our "ordinary" methods to a specific research setting, we do so because something about the setting is organized so differently from what we expect that we cannot ignore its effect on our techniques. The adaptation also shows us what we have been taking for granted in applying the method in "ordinary" situations and makes us aware that even there our routine technical assumptions may be incorrect.

Since we stigmatize and punish deviant activities, the people who engage in them usually take care not to be discovered. Their secretiveness takes a variety of organizational forms, and each variation complicates the technical problems of sampling, for instance, in a special way that requires us to find special solutions. We learn how the activity is organized by finding out what we must do to locate its practitioners: an activity carried on in a solitary way may require us to advertise, while one carried on collectively allows us to gather cases by observing likely settings. We learn which category any particular case falls into by seeing what we have to do to accumulate a sample.

The problem of sampling deviants also shows us that conventional sampling techniques assume, as a condition of their effective use, that we have enough information about the location of the elements of the universe to construct a sampling frame properly.

[8]See, for example, E. E. Evans-Pritchard (1940:15): "Azande would not allow me to live as one of themselves; Nuer would not allow me to live otherwise. Among Azande I was compelled to live outside the community; among Nuer I was compelled to be a member of it. Azande treated me as a superior, Nuer as an equal." See also the discussion of possible legal problems associated with studies of campus disturbances in *Science* 165 (July 11, 1969): 157–61.

Alternatively, they assume that what we want to study occurs so frequently that sampling on conventional criteria will turn up sufficient instances of what we want to study. By studying deviance, we learn how badly we need new theories and techniques adequate to the general problem of sampling hidden universes of rare items.

Similarly, to take another instance, because we think deviant activities wrong, they become matters of interest to persons deputized to catch wrongdoers or to treat, cure, and rehabilitate them once they are caught. For this reason, we can find useful information in the hearings of legislatures, the records of police agencies, and the archives of the helping professions. But deviance is controversial, and the arguments over the validity of such material alert us to the general problems of using material gathered by others for their own purposes. It is no wonder that the most penetrating critiques of official records come from the field of criminology, critiques relevant to every research enterprise relying on such materials (see Morganstern 1963).

The study of deviance is risky business, studded with traps and pitfalls. It is perhaps comforting to know that our very troubles, seen properly, can help us learn.

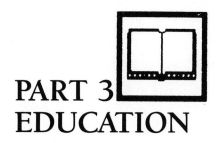

PART 3
EDUCATION

9

STUDYING URBAN SCHOOLS

People have been studying schools and education ethnographi-
cally for a long time. Anthropologists, following the lead of Margaret Mead and others, have made the socialization of children into
a culture a major concern, and what happened to children in contemporary Western schools could be seen as an example of that
process. Sociologists likewise long have been interested in schools.
In fact, Willard Waller's classic, *The Sociology of Teaching* (1932), is
probably the first ethnography of a contemporary American school.
    Waller was not very careful about his methods. He had not really
done ethnography so much as he had been the classic participant-
as-observer, making the best of his job as schoolteacher by noting
the interesting phenomena occurring around him. But his work had
one hallmark of good ethnography. He saw and reported a fact,
central to the institution he was observing, the existence of which
no one there would admit: He said that children did not want to
go to school and that adults forced them to, so that the natural
state of social relations in the school was conflict. That seems obviously true, today as then, and yet the people who take that statement and its implications seriously (e.g., the writings of Holt [1967]
or Herndon [1968]) still create controversy. Waller did work of the
kind Erving Goffman (1983) specified as the proper mode of sociological inquiry:

> unsponsored analyses of the social arrangements enjoyed by those
> with institutional authority—priests, psychiatrists, school teachers,
> police, generals, government leaders, parents, males, whites, nation-
> als, media operators, and all the other well-placed persons who are
> in a position to give official imprint to versions of reality. (1983:17)

    In many ways, that aspect of Waller's work, and its reception and
use, relates to a problem I want to focus on here. Ethnographic
studies of schools, and perhaps especially of urban schools, have a
paradoxical quality. On the one hand, the ethnographic study of
schools has a long and honorable pedigree. Waller published his

book in 1932, and work in the tradition has never stopped. Community studies usually pay attention to schools and education, and many researchers have spent years in close unfettered observation in schools. On the other hand, ethnographic studies of schools always have been suspect in the field of education, if not in the fields of anthropology and sociology in which the tradition originated. Ethnographic studies have been suspect even though they frequently produce results the face validity of which is apparent, and even though they do not have the obvious flaws of other styles of research common in schools.

Suspicion toward ethnography shows up in many ways. The most obvious—at least the way it most often comes to my attention—is the defensive posture of people in education who do such work. They are not neurotically and unrealistically defensive, either; they are defensive because they are always being attacked. Ethnographers of education do not receive the professional courtesy that allows unavoidable and irremediable flaws in one's methods to go unchallenged. Every version of research on schools has such problems, yet most of it gets done. But examining committees approve experimental research designs with well-known but conventionally accepted flaws, while balking at students' proposals to do ethnographic research. So I get a lot of phone calls from students and young faculty in education who are looking for legitimation for what they want to do; I'm sure that most people in the field get similar calls all the time. Our flaws have to be accounted for and justified every time—unless we meet among ourselves, and even then much of our attention is devoted to the attacks we will face when we get home.

Why should ethnographic research in education produce good results and still have such a bad reputation? This paradox has two major causes. One is the way scientific research in education came to be used to justify the failures and discriminatory results of the operation of educational institutions. The other is the inability of ethnographic research to be useful, in that or any other way, to educational practitioners.

Anthropology Isn't Psychology

Education, as a field of professional scholarly activity and as a public institution, was captured early by the field of psychology. The premise was that education consisted of putting information and skills into the heads of children and other ignorant people. It thus needed a science of learning and, secondarily, of teaching (as opposed, for instance, to a science of school organizations or educational situations). The science that could provide the knowledge on which to base methods of teaching was psychology, the science of the inside of people's heads. This coincided with psychology's decisive turn toward scientism, experimental modes of thought and procedure, and quantification. I'm not familiar enough with the history of psychology to know why this happened, or how and when it did, but it certainly happened. And education people, looking for theories and methods to justify a "professional" approach to their own work, found everything they needed there.

We all know what followed. First came the enormous growth and success of the testing industry, which quickly assumed authority in areas of major educational concern. Psychological scientists devised tests, some allegedly measuring native ability, others allegedly measuring achievement. As a further consequence, scientific students of the process and institutions of education began their never-ending discoveries of "how best to" do whatever someone who ran schools and similar institutions thought ought to be done. They discovered, for instance, how best to teach children to read. The only thing wrong with these discoveries was the rapidity with which they were replaced by new, contradictory discoveries. In this, education resembled the entire field of child development on which it has always been parasitical. As we all know from our own experiences as children, if not as parents, child development is the field that for decades alternately has advised everyone, on the basis of good scientific evidence, to feed their babies on demand or on a schedule.

Why did the institutions and leaders of education accept the authority of such a patently fallible group of authorities? I want to develop a hypothesis here, although I have not done the work required to verify it. Briefly, the idea is that increasingly over the decades institutions of education found themselves in a situation in which they had to prove that they were being fair, in the face of substantial and obvious evidence that they were not. In that situation, quantitative scientific psychology provided the required proof. I'll begin the argument by noting that education's swoon into the arms of quantitative scientific psychology coincided with the broad democratization of public education. State and federal governments began to believe that every child was entitled to an education provided free of charge by the state and that every child was capable of profiting from such an education.

I accept the first of those propositions philosophically, and I believe that the second one is empirically true, but contingent. Every child *can* learn what an education is supposed to give, but not all children can learn it taught in the same way, nor can they all learn it on the same schedule. The routinization of education that came with its growth as an industry—its development of standardized methods to be applied *en masse* to batches of students (to hark back to another theme of Erving Goffman's)—meant that everyone who came to school had to be equipped physically, mentally, culturally, and in every other way not just to learn but to learn something presented in just *one* of the many ways it might have been presented. People who could have learned something taught in "way X" are out of luck if it is only taught in "way Y" in their school. Similarly, someone who could have learned a body of material in fifteen weeks may fail if it comes in a ten-week package. (The latter point sticks in my mind because of my daughter's experience some years ago, when she switched from San Francisco State College [as it was then known] to the University of California at Berkeley. She reported that, while the courses in calculus in both places covered the same material from the same book, the Berkeley class covered it in ten weeks while State took fifteen. I will leave it as an elementary exercise for the reader to work out the arguments by which Berkeley faculty might then have "proved" that this difference made Berkeley a better school. Anyone who wants extra credit also can assess the logical basis and adequacy of those arguments.)

If an institution purports to do a job uniformly over an entire population, basing its claim for financial and other support on the successful doing of that job, and then fails to do it, the people responsible for the institution (and thus for its failures) have some explaining to do. Suppose public health officials had guaranteed to wipe out an epidemic disease like polio by following a procedure of universal inoculation. Suppose, further, that they succeeded in wiping it out in that portion of the population with the highest income, but that rates, while coming down some, were still high in poorer classes. Insofar as they had guaranteed universal results, they would have a big public relations problem.

The proponents of public health might have explained their failure by some characteristic of the people they had not been able to protect—a genetic flaw, perhaps, which made a vaccine not work.

That is just what educators did. Rather than ask why their methods did not work universally, as they had claimed, they "found" that certain measurable characteristics of students accounted for their ability to learn. As for the others—well, either you have it or you don't, and they just don't have it. Too bad! I am, of course, caricaturing a complex matter here and making unnecessarily cruel fun of serious and well-intentioned people. Or . . . is that really the gist of that argument?

Whatever the fairness of my caricature, educators did have a problem. They had promised the moon but could not deliver it. It might have been better not to promise the moon, but they were stuck with that. So, as the saying goes, they blamed the victim. But many people will not accept that diagnosis, most of all the representatives of the people who have been characterized as wanting. How can you persuade skeptics to accept your diagnosis? That is where the scientific psychology of the 1920s and beyond becomes useful. Almost everyone accepts, as a practical matter, what seem patently obvious facts of everyday life, no more than common sense: some people are smarter than others and that is why some people fail in school and others don't.

But how can we tell who is smarter and who is dumber, so that we can see if that is true? More to the point, how—if we are running a school system—can we make those distinctions in such a way that no one can complain that we are being unfair? This brings us to the heart of my speculation. If we are in perpetual danger of being accused of favoritism, discrimination, or racism, we need to be able to show skeptics, legislators, friends, and enemies that we reached our conclusions by a method that is fair and defensible. We cannot explain that we are promoting Dick and Jane because they come from good families and are keeping Tom and Harriet back because they don't; not in the America we live in, even if that is the reason, and even if there are plenty of countries in which that explanation might be acceptable.

Which methods are fair and impartial? Bitter experience has shown that almost any method that leaves discretion in the hands of the people using it can be misused in a discriminatory way. Any method that lets a judge's "subjective" judgments come into play may produce a quite improper result, improper in the sense of being offensive to the standards we want to uphold—a discriminatory result instead of a fair one. (I am not talking here about the results of fair methods that produce the results discrimination might have, e.g., the racial segregation produced by a "color-blind" sorting on economic variables.)

So everyone agrees that "objective" methods are better. Objective methods seem most clearly objective when they are quantitative, when the judge seems to be doing no more than laying down a ruler alongside something and noting where it falls on the ruler's scale; no room for subjective discrimination in that, or not much. If there is unfairness, it is built into the procedure. It is part of the ruler, and that is where it has to be looked for, the way Allison Davis (1950) and Kenneth Eells (Eells et al. 1951) looked for it and found it in the construction of intelligence tests. But those discoveries don't have what is called "face validity," and are much less convincing than the obvious parallels between test results and common observation. Kids who test dumb usually look and act dumb in school. That their dumbness may be the result of deep cultural differences between what they know and feel comfortable doing and what the schools require doesn't alter that.

Let me remind you of two well-known cases. Murray and Rosalie Wax and Robert Dumont (1964) reported that the native American children who tested dumb, and who also looked and acted stupid in reservation schools, were responding to a setting that systematically devalued what they did know (including the Sioux language) so that they could not display their abilities. They resented it and acted accordingly. Similarly, Jane Mercer (1973) reported (and here I simplify some complex relationships) that mental retardation was a disease children got by going to school. Before they started school, others might (or might not) think them a little slow to catch on to things, but they could perform adequately. When they got to school, however, and were tested, school personnel "discovered" their retardation. Since these children almost always were from groups whose culture differed significantly from that of the school (Hispanic or black), they had the usual problems and looked dumb enough to make the diagnosis seem reasonable.

Because so many children's troubles with schools are based on cultural differences of this kind, the schools are in a particularly difficult position. The children they fail with are often members of political minorities of whom the schools are specially wary. Courts and legislatures alike may want to catch them discriminating. They don't want to be caught doing that. On the other hand, other constituencies want to prevent what they define as "reverse discrimination."

The schools cannot win. What they *can* do is use methods that they can claim are scientific so that the troubles that arise will be visited on someone else. In other words, objective, quantitative, scientific research provides educators with defensible explanations for their failure to deliver on their own various and contradictory promises. That prejudices the entire education establishment in favor of such research and against anything else, especially against qualitative research that relies on the sensitivities and seemingly unrestrained judgments of individual researchers.

Ethnographic research therefore runs afoul of a deeply held belief, one embedded in the operations of major institutions. I don't mean to accuse educators of venality. I don't think they say, "Hey, if we let people do this kind of research it will spoil our explanation of why we can't do the job." But I do think that reasons like that are part of what lies behind the religious zeal with which people in the education industry espouse quantitative research. That zeal, in turn, helps account for their difficulties with, and complaints about, ethnography.

Anthropology Studies (and Judges) Everybody

Thus, educators, responsible for the successes and failures of educational institutions, understandably mistrust ethnographic studies that provide no rationale for the institution's failure to produce acceptable results with lower-class students. Worse yet, ethnographic research, with its emphasis on understanding social organizations as wholes, makes it impossible to confine research to uncovering the shortcomings of students. If you study schools by giving students tests, you may find out that the students have not learned what they are supposed to, but you will be studying the teachers and administrators only indirectly. Ethnographers, however, routinely study *everyone* connected with the school. Most ethnographers of schools have had to deal with the surprise (and sometimes shock) of teachers and administrators who discover that the ethnographers aren't just going to look at the students or subordinate members of the organization, but regard everyone in it, from top to bottom, as fair game for investigation. "You mean you are going to study us?" That immediately, and always, opens up for them the possibility that we are somehow going to find out that "it" (whatever "it" is) is their fault. They may not know what "it" is, but they can usually see that someone who hangs around long enough, nosing into everything, is bound to find *something* that is their fault. If we insist on sitting in their offices and observing them at work, and not just observing students, we may find out some things they'd rather we didn't.

In fact, we will *always and necessarily* find out those things. Institutions, in the voices of those who lead them and thus are responsible for them to the rest of the world, always lie about how well they do their jobs. "Lie" is a strong word; the people involved probably prefer to think of what I am talking about as statements of goals that somehow turned out not to be as easy to achieve as they had hoped. But people who don't quite live up to their goals year after year perhaps ought to be more cautious, so I'll stick with "lie."

Ethnographers—who hang around forever—are going to see the reality behind the statements of intention. Worse yet, they are going to see that the reality is no accident but is built into the fabric of the organization. Administrators and others involved in an institution do not mind the discovery of "a few bad apples in the barrel." (That is the usual phrasing in complaints about studies of police departments.) But they do mind the conclusion that the barrel makes good apples into rotten ones, and that is what ethnographers always are discovering and saying.

In fact, all research on schools has overtones of evaluation. We can't help that. Even if we don't intend our work to be evaluative, the people we study will take it that way, for the good reason that everyone else does and will hold them responsible for whatever we find out that anyone thinks untoward. The quotation from Goffman cited earlier attests to that. It is hard for any of us to avoid making those grossly evaluative judgments ourselves. When we thus "expose" the inadequacies of one level of an organization, the people at the higher levels don't mind, as long as the results don't suggest that it was *their* fault. Even ethnographies draw boundaries around organizations, leaving some things out of the field of what is to be studied. So long as we leave the higher-ups out, they won't mind a little ethnography. But eventually we almost always get them into the picture and, if we don't, someone else will look at what we have found, take the logical step, and do research at the next higher level. The investigations of the My Lai massacre are a case in point.

Studying higher-ups leads to some funny confrontations that make clear the difference between scientific organization and the bureaucratic hierarchy and self-protectiveness of schools. Years ago, two researchers produced a book that described sociologically the operations of a well-regarded educational program. They had done their research in the town where their university was located. When the book was published and the school principal saw it, he called the chairman of their department and asked, angrily, "Do you let your people publish stuff like this?"

Anthropology Is No Help

Beginning in the 1960s educators lost some of their autonomy, some of their control over their institutions. The giant sums that came to them as a part of the national effort to raise the educational levels of poor people, and especially poor blacks, carried some conditions. The most important for my argument is that the schools got no blank checks. They had to produce results, and it would not do to blame the children for failure. That was exactly why they were getting the new money: to discover or create new ways of teaching that would be successful with children for whom the old ways had failed. The shift from an emphasis on learning—what made learning hard for children—changed to an emphasis on programs and what about programs made them fail to produce the promised results.

Conventional evaluations might say you had failed to do the job, but could not tell you, except in the most indirect and tortured way, what caused the failure. People at various levels of the educational establishment worried about this in different ways. Those who handed out money for experiments that were supposed to produce startling new results worried about being cheated and wondered whether the experiments were being carried out as promised. If there were results, did they come from the new methods that were being touted as producing them, or were they an artifact of the selection of those exposed to the new methods? Were the experimenters "creaming" the population, attributing to new methods results that were really due to the superior ability of those who took part in the experiment? If so, such chicanery proved hard to document. School administrators and educational researchers are skilled manipulators of records. So it seemed like a good idea to observe these programs closely, and to have the observations made by people who were not part of the educational enterprise. Such people might be more "objective," even though they didn't use objective methods.

From another direction, many school people sincerely wanted to do a better job for students with whom they hitherto had failed. They understood and accepted all the liberal arguments. What they needed were new methods that worked. Many of them distrusted "objective" scientific research that evaluated them and found them wanting or that produced yet another in the long list of "innovations" that soon proved no better than those of their predecessors. Conventional psychologically oriented testing research could not help them, they were convinced, and they saw hope in the "depth" of ethnography, in its unarguable closeness to the facts of everyday school life, in what had to be its relevance to their problems.

Both groups were disappointed, although in different ways. The basis of the disappointment, most generally, was that anthropologists and sociologists remained social scientists, oriented toward their native disciplines rather than toward the discipline and institutions of education. If the people monitoring the new experiments expected anthropologists to police the experiments they were supporting, they were wrong. Anthropologists have good reason to avoid working for the established powers, having been stung on that score before. We all know that we cannot continue to do research if we go around telling bosses that the workers are goofing or stealing. If we tell research administrators that their experiments are phony, we will not do any more research.

I'm not sure how anthropological researchers solved this problem in all the places they encountered it. It was one of the great difficulties. Even when anthropologists were quite firm in their refusal to squeal that way, guilty teachers and local administrators (who often really did have something to hide) worried that they might. If a local administrator received money for an innovation but used it to cover routine expenses and never did the experiment—who should the anthropologists tell about that? This often erupted as an argument over who would be allowed to see the anthropologists' field notes, in which the incriminating evidence likely was to be found. Administrators, concerned with running a tight ship, could not understand why they were denied relevant evidence. Social scientists remained loyal to disciplinary standards, for in the long run they would make their professional lives in social science, not in school organizations. Concerned with the long-range consequences, for themselves and the field, of letting their data be used for nonscientific purposes, they would not cooperate.

Similarly, anthropologists and sociologists were unlikely to produce "solutions" to the problems of educators who wanted to do
better. The understanding produced by our research and theory
may be fine-grained and detailed enough to produce solutions, but
not ones that will meet the criteria that operate in the educational
setting. What I mean is this: We often can see what is causing the
trouble, why some technique of teaching or administration is having
an effect exactly opposite to what people want and hope for. But
what we see as the cause is not something the people who look to
us for help can do anything about. Or, at least, they can only do
something about it at some cost so great that they are not willing
to pay it.

Here is an example. When Blanche Geer, Everett Hughes, Anselm
Strauss, and I produced a draft of our study of a medical school
(eventually published as *Boys in White* [Becker et al. 1961]), the
doctors in that school who read it—the more thoughtful and dedicated teachers—wanted us to make recommendations. For instance,
we described (apparently convincingly) how students studied for
exams. Student study methods were the usual ones: cram as much
factual material as you can into your head just before the test and
forget it all afterward. That appalled teachers. They wanted students
to take a more professional attitude toward their work. We explained
to them that they provoked this sort of studying by the kind of
exams they gave, which called for exactly that sort of fragmented
factual knowledge. "If you want students to study differently," we
said, "you can do it by giving them a different kind of exam. What
do you want them to know?" They wanted students to be able to
make a physical examination, take a medical history, establish a
diagnosis, and plan a course of treatment. Our ethnographic knowledge immediately suggested how this could be done: give each
student one or two patients to examine and treat, and then let the
teachers evaluate how well they had done it.

The faculty looked glum when we said that. What was wrong?
That, one said, would take a lot of time, and they all had their
research to attend to and their own patients to take care of. Our
solution would work, of course, but it wasn't *practical*. That is the
difficulty. What a social scientist identifies as a cause is usually something the people can't do anything about. So we fail the serious
educational reformers on the firing line as well.

Why do we produce such useless advice? Because we are loyal
to the traditions of our disciplines, which tell us that these are the

kinds of answers worth having, the only kind that will work in the long run. (I believe that, but I can see that it means that practitioners are never going to be happy with the results of my research in educational institutions.)

The implication of all this is that ethnographers of education are never going to work their way out of their bad reputation. Not, at least, as long as they keep on doing good work and the schools keep failing at their job. Not as long as we come up with impractical solutions to chronic problems. Some fun!

A SCHOOL IS A LOUSY PLACE TO LEARN ANYTHING IN

Institutions create myths to explain to their participants and the public generally what they do, how they do it, why society needs it done, and how successful they are. Every institution fails in some measure to do the job it promises, and its functionaries find it necessary to explain both that they are trying to do better and that the disparity between promise and performance does not exist, is not serious, or occurs only rarely. Institutional apologias divert our attention from the way the very organization of an institution produces its failures. Further, they divert us from comparisons which might show how others, under a different name and rhetoric, actually perform the institution's characteristic function more effectively.

Schools tell us that people learn in them something they would not otherwise know. Teachers, who know that something, teach it to their pupils. Schools are said to pass the cultural heritage of our society to succeeding generations, both generally in elementary and high school and more differentiatedly in colleges and graduate and professional schools. Finally, while educators readily admit the shortcomings of schools, they do not conceive that anything in the essence of a school might produce those shortcomings or that any other institutional form might do the job better.

Though the evidence is both too vast to master and too scanty to allow firm conclusions when the great number and variety of schools is taken into account, it suggests that schools do not achieve the results they set out to achieve. Students do not learn what the school proposes to teach them. Colleges do not make students more liberal and humane (Jacob 1957: 5), nor do they have any great effect on students' intellectual development and learning (Astin 1968). Medical-school training has little effect on the quality of

Reprinted from *American Behavioral Scientist* 16 (September–October 1972): 85–105. Copyright © 1972 by Sage Publications.

medicine a doctor practices (Petersen et al. 1956; Clute 1963). Actors considered expert by their peers have seldom gone to drama school (Hoffman n.d.). The spectacle of elementary and secondary education gives credence to James Herndon's wry hypothesis (1968: 79) that nobody learns anything in school, but middle-class children learn enough elsewhere to make it appear that schooling is effective; since lower-class children don't learn the material elsewhere, the schools' failure to teach them is apparent.

This brief and selective review of the evidence suggests that educational mythology presents an unrealistic picture of the efficacy of schooling. If schools are ineffective, we can consider how their organization might contribute to that ineffectiveness. Our studies of trade schools and apprenticeships allow us to compare the two and see how the organization of each interferes with doing the job it sets out to do.

The following characterization of how schools work grows out of the continuing comparisons generated by our study of trade schools and on-the-job training situations (reported in Geer 1972). The various studies have highlighted one or another dimension of educational organization which I have then applied to conventional schools as well. The comparison suggests structural reasons for the schools' educational failures. By constructing an ideal type, a model of a school at its most school-like, we can understand the dynamics of more mixed cases.

Schools

COMPLEX SUBJECT MATTER

We set up a school to teach arithmetic or reading, barbering or beauty culture, when we think the subject matter too complex and difficult to be learned in haphazard ordinary life. The student, we say, must master certain "basic" conceptions before he can understand the more complicated structures erected on that base; otherwise he will flounder unnecessarily and never really understand the little he learns. Further, he will suffer a confusion that may be emotionally upsetting, even traumatic, and thus compound the difficulties of learning.

The complexity may lie in the subject matter itself. We think it foolish for a person who cannot read to start by attempting written material of the variety and difficulty one might run into in the ordinary world. We give him simplified materials—short words, simple sentences, a small vocabulary. We teach mathematics by starting with simple concepts of number and relation; we think it easier for children to learn "addition facts" than more abstract conceptions.

The complexity may lie in the social situation the student will later use his knowledge in rather than in the material itself. Techniques of barbering may not be complicated, but we believe a student may have difficulty learning them if he must simultaneously take into account the possible reactions of customers whose hair he has butchered in a beginner-like way. So we set up our school in a way that minimizes the student's anxiety. Barber colleges recruit customers by providing cheap haircuts. Anyone who pays seventy-five cents for a haircut forfeits his right to complain; if he wants a three dollar haircut, he knows where he can get it, and so does the student barber, who masters his anxiety over complaints by writing his customers off as skid-row winos or cheapskates. Similarly, teachers in the barber school Clyde Woods (1972) studied made it their business to tidy up particularly bad jobs done by students. (Medical schools use similar mechanisms.)

CURRICULUM

In principle, a curriculum could be tailor-made for each student; the complexities of the subject could be simplified to achieve the uniquely best way for him to learn. In practice, schools develop standardized curricula. They arrange the material in some order of increasing complexity, an order usually thought of as the "natural" or "normal" way to approach the subject. They decide what minimum amount of knowledge will be acceptable. They decide on a schedule, time periods in which the student is to learn particular batches of material. They produce, in short, a curriculum, which rests on a conception, usually uninspected, of a normal student who can do that much work and grasp that much material in the time allotted. The eleven-week quarter and the fifteen-week semester are common examples. Anyone who could learn the material more efficiently if it were presented in a different order will have difficulty, as will anyone who needs more or less time than allotted.

Schools could teach students individually, and occasionally make provision to do so. More typically, they process students in batches, treating them as if each were the prototypical normal student for whom they constructed the curriculum. Being part of such a batch naturally constrains the student to behave, as best he can, as though he were prototypical; it is the easiest way to fit into the collective activity he is part of.

TEACHERS

The curriculum necessarily differs substantially from what competent practitioners of the skill or art in question know how to do, for they do not divide what they know into more and less basic components and seldom see any particular order in which what they know should be presented to a learner. Furthermore, competent practitioners in a subject matter area know only by accident, if at all, the skills of teaching. The inability of competent practitioners to teach planned curricula arises equally with such general topics as arithmetic or reading and with specialized skills like cutting and setting hair or driving an automobile. I may be a proficient user of mathematics and a skilled driver and unable to teach a child either one. Ordinary practitioners in a particular subject, finally, have other things to do than teach beginners, and are ordinarily not available for instructional tasks.

So schools require teachers whose principal work is to teach the planned curriculum to batches of normal students. While teachers want to do their work in the easiest, least troublesome way, they also wish to demonstrate to themselves and others that their work produces results. Do a teacher's pupils know something, when he finishes the standard curriculum, that they did not know before, something worth knowing, something attributable to his efforts? Is it a true grasp of the material such that the student can use it in everyday life? Can he read well enough to get about in a literacy-demanding society? Does he know the craft skills (of welding, nursing, haircutting, teaching, writing, or whatever) well enough to work adequately with professional peers? Has he mastered the liberal arts well enough to use the knowledge and sensibility they provide to enrich his private life and inform his public activities?

Teachers assume that the student is as inferior in knowledge as he usually is in age (Geer 1968). They assume that what they know, the student needs to know. They may want to take his opinions into account, but they do not propose to let him decide which portions of the curriculum he will learn. They insist on having the upper hand in the relationship, searching for ways to augment and solidify control when it is disputed.

Because the teacher devotes his full-time effort to teaching, his own knowledge of what actual situations require may be faulty. This is especially obvious in trade schools, where the trade may change substantially after the teacher leaves it, but it occurs in varying degrees in more academic schools as well. Uncertainty about the teacher's knowledge aggravates problems of control and deepens everyone's sense that school training may not be adequate and may require some checking.

PUPILS

Teachers necessarily have pupils. The relationship might be interesting if pupils had more power over its dimensions and content, but the major say on those matters, by common consent of both parties, belongs to the teacher. Students typically (though not always) concede that the teacher knows more about the subject they want to learn than they do; if he did not, there would be little point in studying with him. (Students may refuse to concede the teacher's superiority when they attend school, as they often do, for some purpose other than learning: to avoid being charged as a truant, to secure a draft exemption, or to meet a legal requirement for some other desired activity.) They want to learn and expect that the teacher will help them, even though his activities seem to have no immediate or discernible relation to that goal. When they lose faith in his authority, they refuse to accept the standard curriculum, and the teacher's job becomes more difficult; he must persuade or coerce students into doing what he thinks best.

Students want to know whether they have learned something as they proceed through the curriculum. Their desire may reflect an uncertainty about the curriculum itself, but more likely reflects a concern with their own abilities. They think a normal student should be able to learn what the curriculum proposes in the time allotted. Are they normal? Have they learned what they should? Do they just think they learned it, while in truth they missed the point or are doing it the wrong way?

They ask themselves these questions because the school often fails to tell them whether their understanding is correct, their skill adequate. They need the answers to see whether their allocation of time and effort needs change and to confront deeper questions about the suitability of what they have attempted. Is this the right course for me? The right school? Do I want to spend any more of my life in pursuits like this? These questions arise for graduate students, students in professional schools, and students in trade schools equally, though trade school students have made a lesser commitment and can more easily take remedial action if they decide they have made a mistake.

TESTS AND EVALUATIONS

The setting in which teachers teach and students learn will be quite different, of necessity and by design, from the world in which students use what they have learned. The materials taught differ from the fully complex materials the world contains. When the student completes the work the school lays out for him, neither he nor his teacher can be sure there are not crucial differences between what he has been taught and what will later be required of him. So teachers—who want to know how their students will fare when they leave school—students—who wonder whether they are truly prepared for the tasks they will now have to do—and the rest of the world—which wonders what it can expect of the graduates—combine their desires for a working knowledge of what is being accomplished in a demand for tests and other evaluative procedures. A formal program of evaluation tells teachers they are doing their job competently, students that they have learned what they came for, and employers, parents, legislators, and others that the school is doing what is expected of it.

The chief problem in testing students and evaluating their performance is to concoct tests isomorphic to the real-world situations in which the student will exercise his skills. How do we test whether a student can successfully cut the hair of a fussy, middle-class executive who worries about his looks, when the only material available for him to demonstrate his skill on is a sixty-year-old drunk who falls asleep in the chair and whom both student and instructor know cannot and will not complain? Beauty colleges (Notkin 1972) solve this problem (as does the state barber board in conducting licensing examinations) by requiring the examinee to provide his own subject (usually a relative or friend); medical schools do not let students perform important or dangerous procedures without supervision by more experienced, licensed physicians. Neither solution is fully effective, since each avoids some of the most serious difficulties in social relationships. But both represent a high in isomorphism between school and practice compared to the written examinations and problem-solving exercises graduate schools, to take a notorious example, habitually use. These more typical examinations differ in gross ways from the tasks examinees will later be called on to do. It is commonplace, but true, to suggest that such tests mainly measure the ability to take tests.

We seldom argue that conventional tests measure the actual skills students are supposed to have learned. Rather, we believe that the test, while not a direct measure, is nevertheless highly correlated with the ability to exercise those skills, though the mechanism by which the alleged correlation occurs is seldom investigated or demonstrated. Common observation suggests the belief is unfounded; we seldom find hard evidence of such correlations. Instead, we rely on test results for want of anything better. In any event, the skills required to perform well on school examinations may not be the same skills required to perform adequately in the situations the school trains people for.

Another difficulty, in addition to the divergence between test and real life, is that tests are usually taken at the convenience of the tester, at a time set by the periodicity of the normal curriculum, at the end of the quarter, semester, or year, when the designated material has been covered. The test thus does not measure a student's ultimate knowledge, but his knowledge as of the time of the examination. This feature, among others, increases the student's anxiety, so that the conventional test in some part measures not knowledge, but the student's ability to withstand or cope with anxiety (Mechanic 1962).

SCHOOL REWARDS AND STUDENT CULTURE

Schools seldom use evaluations of students' performances in an advisory way, to help the student discover areas of weakness which can be strengthened by a changed allocation of effort. Instead, they incorporate the results of such evaluations—grades will do as the generic term—into permanent records, on whose basis people and institutions make decisions bearing on students' futures. Schools vary in the degree to which they allow examination results to become fateful beyond their immediate academic relevance. If grades have fateful consequences, students find it necessary to orient their efforts toward getting good ones; if tests are not isomorphic to the situations in which the abilities being tested will be used, students will have to divert time and effort from what the school wants to teach to what is needed for a good grade. This untoward consequence occurs only when tests do not measure and require the knowledge the school wishes to teach. When the two are the same, the school's reward system evokes exactly the learning teachers desire.

We found an extreme example of the constraint grading and evaluation exercised on students' allocations of their efforts in our study of a college (Becker et al. 1968). Students' grade-point averages, being the chief measure available and presumably reasonably accurate, fair, and comparable, affected most other rewards a student might want (or not want to be denied) during and after college. For example, college rules specified a minimum grade-point average for initiation into a fraternity or sorority, for holding major office in campus organizations, and for staying in school and graduating. Grades also affected a student's chances of getting into professional or graduate school, as well as the kind of job he might get on graduation. Grades even affected his social life: he might find it harder to meet eligible girls if he did not belong to a fraternity or could not participate in extracurricular activities because of low grades; girls were often reluctant to get involved with anyone who might flunk out. Since whatever a student wanted had to be paid for in high grades, few students felt they could safely avoid learning what was needed for tests. It is hard to say what the desired outcomes of a college's educational efforts are. But if they are a change in values and the acquisition of certain intellectual skills, students might be diverted from such goals by the necessity of studying for exams not requiring those abilities.

When what tests require differs from what the school wants to teach, and when the school rewards good test performance heavily, the structure of the school will systematically divert student effort. In this sense, and to the degree that these conditions are met, schools are structurally self-defeating. Where students have the opportunity to interact and develop collective conceptions of their situation and how it ought to be handled, they may develop a student culture which amplifies and extends this effect. When students agree they must do certain things to give a good performance for evaluation, and when that information is passed on to new students, each student need not experience the disparity and the constraint himself. He knows beforehand, in the way any functioning culture allows us to know, what is coming and how to deal with it. A student culture which advises grade-getting as an optimal strategy decreases the likelihood that students will attempt other strategies, though it does not make that impossible.

Since some students do learn some things that schools want to teach, the above analysis deals with the extreme case. Where some of the conditions outlined above do not obtain, schools will be more successful than the analysis suggests.

On-the-job Training

The chief alternative to learning things in school is to learn them on the job, especially if we define on-the-job training broadly. So defined, it includes not only the conventional apprenticeship in a trade, but all the casual learning that goes on in the course of everyday living, the kind of learning Paul Goodman (1968) and John Holt (1967) have called to our attention as the way children learn to talk and most other things. Think of living your daily life as a job to give the notion its full meaning. Though I speak mainly of occupational training, keep the larger relevances in mind.

The apprentice learns on the job, in the place where people do in a routine way whatever members of his trade do. He finds himself surrounded from the outset by the characteristic sights, sounds, situations, activities, and problems he will face as long as he remains in the trade (if we reasonably assume the trade does not change in the short run). The butcher's apprentice (Marshall 1972) works in a meat market, where journeymen break down carcasses, cut them into conventionally defined pieces of meat, trim them, price them, and package them. The apprentice ironworker (Haas 1972) works on a building under construction, where journeymen place beams and girders, rivet and weld them together, place rods for reinforced concrete, do finishing work, and take dangerous walks on narrow beams in high places. (Similarly, the small child, learning to talk, lives in a world in which most of the kinds of talk that go on, simple and complex, go on around him in person, on the radio, or on television [Goodman 1968]). Thus, the learner sees the kind of work he is to learn in all its tangled complexity from the first day, instead of being introduced to those complexities a step at a time in a carefully constructed curriculum. He suffers whatever traumas may arise from realizing all there is to learn. Some apprentices give up their ambitions quickly when they realize what they have gotten into, but those who remain have a pretty good idea of what they are in for from the start. They see the technical difficulties, the dangers, the social complications that may arise with employers and customers, and even the informal requirements of making it with one's work peers.

One consequence follows the immediate accessibility of the full round of activities characteristic of an apprentice's trade. He can participate in these activities right away or on any idiosyncratic schedule he can work out with his fellow workers. No one can learn everything at once, but no principle or rule prevents the apprentice from learning a little of this today, a little of that tomorrow, things in some order no one ever thought of before, or learning to the point where he wants to stop and then switching to something else. He need not, when he wants to learn a certain procedure, wait until its time in a prearranged schedule; nor need he learn something he is not ready for, thinks uninteresting, frightening, or unnecessary. The learner makes his own curriculum.

TEACHERS

This curriculum is created with the aid of people who know more than he does, who must be persuaded to assist him or at least not to interfere with his own efforts. Because the learning situation is the real work-world—an actual meat market or construction site—no one functions as an official teacher. Everyone has his own job to do, his own set of occupational constraints and rewards. The apprentice does not have a teacher's time and attention guaranteed to him as does a pupil in a conventional school.

This leaves the actual training to the apprentice's own initiative. Competent practitioners will teach him if he can persuade them to, and actual training is thus in some part a function of such formally extraneous traits as the degree of his aggressiveness. A pushy punk learns more than a quiet young man. An ideology common among journeymen suggests that if an apprentice is any good, he will make you teach him; if he does not push, he probably does not have what it takes. This differs diametrically from a conventional school in which learning occurs at the teacher's initiative: you move on when the teacher thinks you are ready.

In such a system, no one rests his self-esteem, reputation, or claim to having done a decent day's work on the amount his students learn. While everyone cares in general that the apprentices eventually learn their trade, no particular person can be blamed or has it on his conscience if any particular apprentice or group of apprentices fails to learn. Teaching is no one's job in particular, so it is no one's fault if no learning occurs.

Two consequences follow from the failure to assign teaching responsibility. On the one hand, when teaching does occur, it is not overlaid with the teacher's own worries about how he is doing; teacher and apprentice can concentrate on the learner's difficulties. Where the teacher has no responsibility, he cannot misuse or fail to meet it. On the other hand, an apprentice may not be taught anything, since he may not be aggressive enough to force anyone to teach him.

EXTERNAL CONSTRAINTS

The characteristic virtues of each kind of learning situation breed characteristic difficulties and vices. Schools divorce themselves from the problems of the everyday world in an effort to make learning easier. They thus create a need for evaluative mechanisms and thus divert student effort from learning to efforts to be evaluated more highly. On-the-job training, in and of the everyday world, provides a realistic and individualized learning setting. But it does that at the cost of making teaching and learning vulnerable to potent external constraints.

The chief constraint arises from setting the educational encounter in a real-life enterprise which has its own problems and imperatives. Meat markets have, as their main purpose, to sell meat profitably to customers. Ironworkers work for a company whose main business is to construct a building or a bridge. Interns (who also undergo a kind of on-the-job training) work in hospitals whose main business is to treat illness (Miller 1970). Each enterprise requires potential learners and teachers alike to contribute what they can to the success of the enterprise as the price of continued participation.

But the required contribution may prevent teaching or learning. Potential teachers may not have time for it, because of the press of more important business. When journeymen butchers prepare for a steak sale, they do not have time to teach apprentices. When senior physicians handle medical emergencies, they have no time to teach interns. Opportunities for on-the-job learning vary inversely with the amount of work the enterprise must turn out.

Similarly, the apprentice's labor and time may have to do necessary work for the total enterprise that no one else wants to do. An apprentice ironworker's first jobs are fire watch (looking for possible fires set by sparks from welding and riveting operations) and getting coffee for the journeymen. These jobs are not entirely uneducational—going for coffee prepares the novice to "run the iron"—but apprentices do them not for that reason but because people want them done and the apprentice, lowest man on the totem pole, gets the honor. Apprentice meatcutters start out running the wrapping machine, which packages, seals, and labels the meat. The wrapping machine requires no skill, and working on it falls to the one who cannot do anything else; the work may familiarize the novice with the various cuts of meat, but is not a big step in becoming a butcher. An apprentice may run the wrapping machine for three years in a large meat department solely because the other workmen, knowing more, can be profitably used elsewhere. Hannah Marshall (1972) saw one apprentice work on the wrapping machine for three months until a new apprentice was hired; then apprentice 1 was taught new skills while apprentice 2 ran the wrapping machine. No further new apprentice was hired, and apprentice 2 continued to run the wrapping machine. Someone had to. The first apprentice received superior training by the accident of being hired three months earlier and thus being advantageously placed with respect to the needs of the total enterprise.

Another external constraint limiting the opportunity to learn lies in the potential cost—to fellow workers, employers, customers, or the public—of allowing an unskilled apprentice to undertake some task. Because teaching hospitals may be held liable for the damage done a patient, they limit what medical students can do to patients in furthering their own learning. Ironworkers do not allow apprentices to do things that might jeopardize the safety of fellow workers. Meatcutters give apprentices more practice cutting up meat in markets that serve poor populations. The cost of mistakes made on cheap cuts of pork can more easily be absorbed than mistakes made on the expensive steaks sold in markets in more well-to-do neighborhoods.

Some of the things a novice ought to learn (or would like to learn) may occur infrequently during his period of training. A school would make some provision to cover this material, so that the student's competence would not depend on the accidents of history. Medical schools compromise, necessarily, on this point; they systematically *teach* about various diseases, but whether a student has clinical experience with those diseases is left to the chance of whether a patient with a certain disease appears during the student's tenure.

Gross effects of the external environment on the learning situation result from changes in the economy. A depression (or the memory of one, in some trades) may cause journeymen to fear the competition of too many qualified workmen. In consequence, they systematically withhold training and keep apprentices at the classic apprenticeship tasks of sweeping the shop and running out for coffee. Boom times make it harder to get prospective trainees; with more work to be done, apprentices must quickly be pushed into more responsible positions; if they feel ill-used, they may quit, and the enterprise needs their labor to meet its commitments. Under these circumstances, a trainee may be taught thoroughly and rapidly.

In short, what one can learn on the job and who will teach it depend on contingencies unrelated to education or training. The learning situation exists to do some quite different job and is subject to the constraints emanating from the external world, any of which may interfere directly in the novice's training. Many of these interferences have nothing whatever to do with any attribute of the novice, neither his skill or aptitude, nor his aggressiveness and initiative. The defect is structural.

EVALUATION

Even if people who learn on the job never take formal examinations, they do not escape evaluation, which occurs continuously as they go about their daily business. Everything they do is what people in that line of work do, and everyone in a position to observe their performance can immediately see whether they have done it satisfactorily. No person with special training need be present to make the evaluation; most people on the scene can do it. The evaluators not only know the work the novice attempts, but are the very people the novice must please to be successful. On-the-job training thus avoids completely any disparity between what the school tests and what the real world requires. Because the evaluators are part of that real world and what they require is the test, the two are the same.

Placing the process of evaluation in the midst of the work setting has interesting consequences:

1. The learner can take his tests any time he feels ready. Every novice will want to test himself or allow himself to be tested to convince both others and himself that he has mastered some important skill. In schools, tests can be taken only at stated intervals, when the tester gives them; often the student must take them at the time they are given or suffer a serious penalty. Since the on-the-job trainee's test will consist of doing something that could be

done every day (or almost every day, allowing for weekly or seasonal variations in workloads), he can take it at his discretion, simply by announcing that he thinks he can do a particular task. Someone will give him the chance, and both novice and observer can see the result. The test is self-scoring and self-interpreting, since the product either does or does not pass muster in the same way the world usually evaluates it.

2. Because the test consists of performing some routine task, an apprentice can take it repeatedly, without having to wait for any special time, until he finally performs successfully. Unlike the typical school, in which scores are averaged over some time period, only the last test counts. Since the test can be repeated, and since the learner takes the test when he feels ready, he feels less anxiety than over a conventional school test. The results are less fateful.

3. Because his progress is immediately observable, the learner can make a good or bad reputation among the people he will be working with once he has become a full-fledged member of the group. The possibility can cause considerable anxiety. School typically shelters the student from having his bad mistakes known to the people he will eventually join, but mistakes made on the job are fully seen by those people. Further, while school does not let really serious mistakes occur (because it simplifies the curriculum in ways making that impossible), learning on the job allows costly, even fatal, mistakes to occur, because the actual work cannot be successfully sealed off. An apprentice meatcutter can ruin an expensive side of beef; an apprentice ironworker can unintentionally cripple or kill another worker. In each case, that reputation may dog the perpetrator for years, especially if he harms a valued colleague (Forsyth and Kolenda 1966: 132).

4. Testing on the job is not restricted to technical material. It includes all the relevant human relations skills as well. Jack Haas (1972) provides a detailed example in his analysis of "binging." Ironworkers must demonstrate their ability to participate adequately in this earthy teasing before those already established accept them as trustworthy. Schools do not test these skills; on-the-job situations invariably do.

5. Because the testing occurs so much at the insistence of the novice, and because he may not wish to be tested in all or even in very many areas, a person who learns on the job may never be tested on a great variety of matters. Insofar as testing has value for either the learner or those who have to work with him or use his services,

that value may well be lost. (This is another way of saying that the apprentice may not be taught more than a few of the trade's characteristic skills.)

RELATIONS TO THE WORLD OF WORK

Educators, as I have already suggested, construct a standard curriculum which includes what they regard as the essential elements anyone must learn to be certified as knowing particular subjects, or as fit to occupy a particular social or occupational position. As we have seen, learning on the job in no way assures that any student will learn such a common core of knowledge. In this, learning on the job realistically reflects the character of most jobs and occupations.

Everett Hughes (1971: 311–15) has suggested that any job or occupation, any named kind of work, actually consists of a bundle of tasks. Some of those tasks may be taken to be symbolic of the whole, as when we think of courtroom pleading as the definitive legal task. Ordinarily, no single member of the occupation does the full range of tasks associated with it. Differentiation and specialization characterize most kinds of work, so that a member of the occupation may actually do only one or two tasks from the bundle. A school requires students to learn the entire bundle, in case they are called on to perform any of them, but on-the-job training allows a student to learn, at a minimum, only one, while still becoming a full-fledged member of the trade. On-the-job training thus reflects realistically the demands of the labor market, operating on the assumption that, if a person can get a job doing one of the tasks in the bundle, he knows enough to be an acceptable member of the trade.

Ironworkers present an interesting example of this phenomenon. The characteristic and symbolic act that marks the "real ironworker" is "running the iron," working high above the ground while standing on a four- to eight-inch steel beam. Running the iron takes more nerve than some recruits have, but their failure either to take that test or, if they try, to pass it, does not mean that they cannot be ironworkers. They can do one of the other jobs, requiring more brawn than nerve, such as placing rods for reinforced concrete construction. They will not get the considerable glory that goes with doing the tasks that require bravery, but they can still be ironworkers.

The work world, in short, accommodates to what people can do. Apprenticeship and job training prepare people for such a world. They avoid a recruit's difficulties with some portion of the standard curriculum, at the cost of producing a member of the trade who knows less than the complete body of knowledge that might be expected of him.

Conclusions

I have been discussing ideal types. Real-life educational situations usually contain some mixture of school and on-the-job styles of teaching and learning. Thus, medical schools, beauty schools, and barber colleges are schools, but with strong on-the-job emphases. On the other hand, meatcutters and ironworkers may take classes in some subjects. Ordinarily, when we are anxious to teach people something, we remove teaching from the job and organize a school. The above analysis has as its chief implication that schools are lousy places to learn, precisely because we establish them without considering the circumstances under which other ways of proceeding, perhaps less organized, might be more efficient, more humane, or both. Another equally important implication is that on-the-job training is often no better, for the same reason. The analysis has in general been pessimistic, making it appear impossible for anyone to learn anything. Since people do learn, the analysis is clearly insufficient, and I would like to end by considering how this learning occurs.

I do not suggest that students learn *nothing* in school, only that they typically learn what the school does not intend to teach and do much less well with what the school focuses on. We found an excellent example of this in our study of college students. Students learned effective methods of operating politically on campus. But in academic subjects they devoted themselves to getting good grades, a time-consuming activity that presumably accounts for the lack of attitude change Philip Jacobs (1957) reports and the lack of effect on academic achievement Alexander Astin (1968) uncovered. The explanation is that they learned their politics on the job, by acting in the political arena of the campus. Imagine what would happen if someone gave a course in "Operating on Campus," complete with texts, tests, and grades. Students, busy learning how to pass the tests, would never become the effective politicians campus political life produces.

People learn, in spite of the obstacles our analysis suggests, because the schools and job situations in which they learn seldom approach the extreme conditions of these ideal analytic types. Schools are effective, when and where they are, because tests sometimes require what teachers want students to learn, because teachers do not always connect a multitude of other rewards to academic performance, because students are sometimes incapable of developing a culture which maintains and spreads counter-faculty perspectives. On-the-job training is often effective because someone does have time to do a little teaching, because the enterprise allows enough leeway for the apprentice to make some mistakes without costing others too much, because the things that can interfere with his learning are fortuitous occurrences rather than structural necessities.

On-the-job training, then, for all the difficulties I have mentioned, is more likely to produce educational successes. Nevertheless, I do not propose that we immediately convert all education to an apprenticeship model. Substantial difficulties are associated with that model. Students may be denied the teaching they want, due to the exigencies and constraints of the real-life situation in which the training occurs. Students may learn very little of what we would like to see them know, even though they will probably learn a little something.

Nor is it easy to set up apprentice-like training situations. It requires the specification of educational goals in a more exact way than is common in schools. When schools state "educational objectives," they generally content themselves with pious generalities. If you want to create an on-the-job training situation, you must go much farther and find a place in the everyday world where people ordinarily act just as you wish your trainees to act, where the very skills, attitudes, and sensibilities you wish to inculcate are embodied in the daily activities of people trainees will be allowed to associate with. It is often difficult to find a place which wishes to be used as a site for an educational enterprise.

In addition, we sometimes cannot specify our objectives clearly. We may believe that we are training people for an unknown future. We do not know what we want them to know, because we cannot specify the problems and situations they will have to cope with. This may be because the situations that lie ahead of them are too complicated for us to deal with in detail or because we believe the world is going to change so much that we cannot forecast how things will be and thus what a person will need to know to act effectively. Given such a diagnosis, we generally settle for inculcating proper orientations from which students will be able to deduce correct lines of action in specific circumstances, general skills which can be used in a variety of situations, and an ability to learn new material as it becomes available.

We will always have schools, because we will often find ourselves in the dilemma of preparing people for unknown futures. A minimum use of the present analysis might then be to broaden educators' perspectives so that they will be aware of the possibilities of apprentice-like training that may be available to them (Beck and Becker 1969) and not engage unnecessarily in activities that actively defeat the very ends they seek. Such irrationality can only perpetuate the troubles our schools are already in and deepen the mistrust so many people have of them.

11

MODEST PROPOSALS FOR GRADUATE PROGRAMS IN SOCIOLOGY
(with Bernard Beck)

Sociologists continually review the programs of graduate training they provide, both in their own institutions and in the discipline generally. They conduct their reviews under the prodding of their own consciences, of factions that feel some particular portion of the field is being slighted, of government agencies that grant funds for certain kinds of expansion, and, most recently, of disgruntled graduate students who wish more voice in what is happening to them.

Surveying our own experiences and the experiences of others as they have been reported to us in casual conversation,[1] we have concluded that the typical approaches to revision of the graduate program consist of minor tinkering with a badly running machine that requires major overhaul or replacement. We have therefore concocted a number of plans, perhaps only slightly more radical than these, which show how conventional approaches cripple themselves with uninspected assumptions about what can properly be called into question and what must be left unquestioned.

By common agreement, the primary business of graduate education is to help students become people who, when they have left school, will do good sociological work as teachers and researchers. We have made this the chief criterion against which we assess both conventional practice and our own proposals. We recognize, however, that others may have other goals, either as additions or alternatives to the one stated. The chief alternative goal suggested in connection with graduate training consists of a desire to prevent

[1]We owe a great deal to our colleagues at Northwestern for jointly creating a department in which it is possible to make proposals of the kind contained in this paper and have them discussed seriously. We have profited greatly from those discussions.

people who will do bad work from being certified as sociologists. Compared to the goal of helping people do good work, this is a conservative decision rule (Scheff 1966:105–27). We have invariably resolved any conflict that arises between these two goals, and such conflicts arise, in favor of helping students become good sociologists, for reasons we make clear in connection with the particular issues involved. One lesson we have learned from our analysis is that one cannot assume that the two goals never conflict.

In speaking of conventional approaches to revision of the graduate program, we refer to such matters as departmental revision of the number and kind of required courses, revision of the form and number of Ph.D. preliminary examinations, and similar matters.[2] These are the matters with which faculty, frequently with great reluctance, will experiment; they may increase the theory requirement or decrease the statistics requirement or even, in a mad moment, do away with required courses. They will not, as a rule, seriously consider doing away with evaluation procedures entirely.

The currently fashionable introduction of students into the process of deciding on degree requirements and other departmental affairs cannot be counted on to change this picture. Conventional wisdom suggests that students will wish to reduce requirements, but we suspect that students probably exhibit the same mixture of opinions as the faculty in about the same proportions, and thus act as a conservative force. When they demand a voice, they may desire no more than to lighten some of the required burden or, in some perverse instances, to make it heavier. Their demands may reflect passing contemporary judgments of what is important, so that they insist on courses in a particular technique much talked of at the moment, or in some presently topical substantive area. They will probably not question such basic features as the existence of a graduate program or the awarding of degrees.

Idiosyncratic variations and special circumstances do not prevent the problems of graduate departments from being remarkably similar, as are the categories to which those problems are conventionally assigned. A very short list will still include most of the issues ordinarily raised: admissions (including financial aid); required courses and programs; comprehensive examinations; thesis management; and degree granting. Not only are the elements of the list conven-

---

[2]For a sampling of current approaches, which exhibit a great deal of variety, see Borgatta (1969), Blalock (1969), Horowitz (1968:129–58), and Sibley (1963).

tionally invariant; so is the order in which they are supposed to arise in the student's career. In constructing our own proposals we have found it useful to violate those conventional conceptions of order.

We have generated our proposals by means of some simple techniques that may have general interest. When we discussed matters of graduate instruction, both with our departmental colleagues and with sociologists elsewhere, we made it a practice to take absolutely seriously all statements made to us about the purposes of some way of doing things, but we did not accept the implied argument that those purposes could be achieved only by doing things just as they are now done. Instead, we searched for other ways—any ways—of achieving the same ends. The notion of a Sociology Symposium as a way of achieving the educational effects imputed to general examinations arose in this way.

When one proposes unconventional alternatives, he frequently elicits outraged reactions. These are very helpful, especially if their outrage leads discussants to attempt a counterargument by the technique of *reductio ad absurdum*. When one proposes some minimally radical alteration in current programs, discussants may demonstrate its impracticality or frivolity by carrying it to its logical but, in the context of conventional practice, preposterous conclusion. But the conclusion seems preposterous only because the discussant relies on some major premise left unstated; at this point, one can extract the implied major premise and inspect it carefully to see whether it must be treated as axiomatic or whether it can perhaps be replaced by some alternative premise.[3] With a new premise, the otherwise preposterous conclusion can be taken seriously and may be very near to a workable solution to some important problem. The Matriculation Degree Award Plan outlined below arose from a discussion in which one of our colleagues suggested facetiously that perhaps we would like to award the Ph.D. on entrance into the program. When we make problematic the implicit premise—that graduate departments must certify the competence of graduates—the notion no longer seems preposterous.

A final principle we have followed is to separate from one another the various purposes said to be achieved by conventional arrangements, searching for solutions to each separately. It is much easier

---

[3]The basic technique of extracting implied major premises is described in Hughes (1971:212–19).

to solve simple subproblems than to replace such an omnibus package as preliminary examinations, which are alleged to be both evaluative and pedagogical. We may have trouble finding another device that will do both jobs, but less trouble finding individual solutions to the problems once they are separated.

Some readers will consider our proposals outrageous; others may think them not outrageous enough. Most people, whatever their moral judgment, will think them impractical and utopian, and wonder whether we can possibly be serious. The question of seriousness takes two forms: Are we in earnest when we offer these proposals? And are the proposals offered as practical courses of action? With regard to the first question, we disclaim any implication of frivolity. We offer our proposals as plans we would like to see put into effect for the purpose of improving graduate education. We do not, of course, suggest that they all be adopted, since some are clearly alternate ways of achieving the same ends, distinguished according to the kinds of subsidiary problems they create. But we have not devised these plans for comic effect, nor have we offered them ironically, simply to expose absurdities of the present system.

We are of two minds on the issue of practicality. On the one hand, most of the things we suggest will be unpalatable enough to make their passage by any faculty group unlikely, under current conditions. On the other hand, conditions change. What is impractical and not to be countenanced today may well seem conservative and reasonable tomorrow. Practicality depends on relative costs, and if, for whatever reason, the balance of costs that makes today's style of graduate program a bargain were to shift, then the costs associated with our plans might no longer seem excessive. Think of these proposals, then, as possible practicalities for some other time, which might soon be upon us.[4] (Etzioni [1968] describes a department whose time had come.)

Required Courses

Most graduate programs require a core program, a minimum set of courses all degree candidates must pass satisfactorily. Where the

[4]We have, not surprisingly, found it a good deal easier to discover the difficulties in conventional practice, difficulties we all experience at present, than those that would be uncovered by the routine operation of the plans we suggest. We have tried where we could to imagine those difficulties; any failure to mention problems rises from our lack of imagination, not from any belief that none exist.

courses are not required, faculty and students usually conspire to "require" them through informal counseling by faculty advisers and older students. However, the formal requirements often work a hardship on students who do badly in one or another of the requirements, although otherwise progressing satisfactorily, and thus provoke difficult problems for the faculty, who are usually not prepared to sacrifice a promising recruit because of one such failure. Our discussion centers on the justification for a mechanism that diffuses the responsibility for course requirements by identifying them as the collective decision of the entire faculty.

We ordinarily justify required courses by referring to a core of sociological knowledge and technique to which every would-be sociologist must be exposed. We cannot, of course, demonstrate the existence of this core, and, indeed, easily available evidence makes its existence unlikely.[5] For example, if there is such a core, why does its content vary so much from one department to the next, and within departments over relatively short periods of time? Perhaps more to the point, we know that there are many distinguished sociologists whose works are widely respected who are incompetent in one or another conventional core area. Some sociologists are superb statisticians but cannot conduct an interview; some are superb field workers who cannot calculate a chi-square; some theorists cannot do research and some researchers know little theory. We deplore such a state of affairs in the abstract, but are pleased to have any such person for a colleague, knowing that people who can do even one thing well are quite rare. In short, it is not necessary to master the core of sociology to be a good and respected sociologist.

Requirements probably serve a number of purposes. They pacify those within a department who want a chance to recruit students to some specialty or technique (thus the push to get requirements into the first year). They make the department and its graduate program "respectable" in the eyes of various audiences: sources of funds, ad hoc standard-setting groups, and subspecialty colleagues. They ease faculty consciences and anxieties, allowing us to feel that "our" students will not make damn fools of themselves in public by revealing an ignorance of Durkheim or whatever else they ought to know. They ease student anxieties by setting a minimum performance level for the first year, during which most students are

[5]Sibley (1963:114–21) hints at this state of affairs by describing a similar situation in psychology.

quite unsure what they are doing, or why, and how much is enough; if a student has passed the requirements he has clearly done enough.

Ordinarily, no one of these purposes commands universal support. Each represents the special desire of some subgroup, assented to by other participants as one of the compromises necessary to the operation of a program. But the requirements create problems, so that the satisfaction of subgroups' desires carries with it some cost. For example, when several factions get their particular courses required, the total burden of requirements may become so great that students are effectively prevented from taking any courses not officially required.

Course requirements create a further problem because they are also requirements for the faculty. What students must take, professors must offer. Problems arise when departments collectively require what no individual wants to or is available to teach. Every department has suffered from the constraints on teaching assignments, hiring, and leaves of absence that result.

Departmental requirement of courses transfers the responsibility for these problems, and any others that may be associated with the requirements, from the subgroup or individual whose demand the requirement satisfies to the faculty collectively. Students cannot blame any particular person for onerous requirements, nor can faculty complain of the problems that arise incident to the requirements, since a collective decision has ratified their necessity vis-à-vis some presumed core of knowledge and distributed the guilt over all equally.

The various purposes discussed above can perhaps be served better if we view as problematic, rather than given, the necessity of a collectively ratified set of requirements. Hence our first proposal:

> *Unilateral Course Requirement Plan.* Any faculty member may unilaterally, without approval by his colleagues, require any course he is currently teaching. No student may graduate without passing all such required courses.

This program accomplishes all the functions discussed above, but it does it without the protection implicit in a departmentally imposed requirement: the faculty member who imposes the requirement is structurally prevented from arguing that this is the consensus of his colleagues. He must on his own justify the requirement to whoever wants to have it justified.

This program will have many advantages and disadvantages. Many faculty members will be relieved no longer to have to justify to students requirements they themselves do not believe in. The plan will also relieve departments of the need to find staff for courses they have required as being good for students but which no one wants to teach. Lengthy discussions of revisions in the requirements will be unnecessary, freeing faculty time for other pursuits.

On the other hand, the plan might be grossly abused. One can imagine a department in which everyone requires everything, so that students are burdened with an intolerable amount of work. Assume, however, that faculty members share a general human responsiveness to the feelings of others, a capacity to feel shame over the arbitrary use of authority, such that they would refrain from excessively cruel actions if they were taxed with them by students or colleagues. Under this plan, inhibiting sentiments would operate extremely effectively, for those discomfited by the requirement know exactly whom to complain to and the offender cannot take advantage of a diffusion of responsibility to anesthetize that responsiveness and capacity.

But our assumptions about human nature may mistake its beneficence. For those who feel this danger keenly, the plan may be revised to require students to take, *but not necessarily pass,* all required courses, thus ensuring their exposure to the desired material. Another variation might allow professors to require any course they want (their own or someone else's) as a prerequisite to allowing students to work further with them. A student who did not meet one professor's requirements would be penalized to the extent that he wanted to work with that man, and this might constitute a powerful incentive to gain the required knowledge.

Some students may feel lost without the direction provided by a list of requirements. For them, a suggested menu guaranteed to provide a conventionally well-balanced meal could be provided. Other students could be allowed to treat course offerings as a smorgasbord, constructing their own idiosyncratic specialty (what D. T. Campbell [1969] has referred to as a "fish scale") out of what is available within and outside the department.

Examinations

Departments habitually examine students before admitting them to candidacy for the Ph.D., a requirement usually imposed by graduate-school regulations but one that few faculty members protest as unreasonable. Departments may give an oral examination, a written examination, or both. They may examine once, twice, or even more frequently during the student's career, at the end of the first, second, or third year, or any combination of these. "Prelims" or "comps" are usually lengthy affairs, running four to six hours each (when they are written) in several fields.

We often justify general exams by asserting the necessity of some test of general competence. We conceive that a student may be able to do well in individual courses but lack the ability to integrate specific items of information into an overall sophistication about the field. We conceive that he may make that integration in his dissertation but be unable to extend it beyond the narrow technical and topical demands of the one piece of research. General exams presumably measure that desired breadth. In addition, we sometimes justify exams by saying that the broad and detailed preparation they require produces the very sophistication they are supposed to measure.

Graduate education should produce a sociologist of wide sophistication. But agreeing to that proposition does not necessarily entail agreeing either that students need to be formally examined to see whether sophistication has been achieved or that, if an assessment is wanted, conventional examinations provide a reliable enough estimate given their educational cost.

We believe that the costs of prelims are considerable. The time students spend preparing for examinations varies among students, among cohorts, and among departments. Students who devote a major block of time (in some cases, this may amount to a year or even longer) to preparation for exams become relatively unavailable for such other experiences as independent pre-dissertation research attempts or exploration of neighboring fields and ancillary skills (e.g., history, computer technology, literary criticism, specialized language preparation). In addition, while what they study at this time no doubt contributes somewhat to mutually desired goals, they also study with an eye on the file of previously given exams, and a substantial amount of effort is devoted to "psyching out" the faculty, developing "systems" for beating the system, and similar enterprises that do good indirectly, if at all.[6]

These costs might be acceptable if they bought a reliable judgment of student ability. But, although we can cite research on the

---

[6]This phenomenon has been documented in a number of studies (Becker et al. 1961; Becker et al. 1968; Olesen and Whittaker 1968; Orth 1963).

effect of examining systems on behavior *of the student,* we know of no study that relates the results of Ph.D. prelims to *post-school* criterion variables of general interest, such as the quantity or quality of scholarly work produced after graduation or the quantity or quality of teaching done.[7] David Mechanic's study (1962) of the examination process in another field indicates that the ranking of students generated by exams roughly parallels that generated by having faculty rank them before the exams. It is not clear whether this finding should be interpreted to mean that there is no point in giving exams, since we can get the same results with less trouble, or that the exams are in fact reliable. Mechanic's study does show, however, that the results are related to such formally irrelevant matters as the degree of involvement in informal student groupings in the department.

While most students would probably applaud dropping course requirements, many of them appear to approve of examinations, on much the same grounds as the faculty. They say that without the stimulus of the examination they would never try to put the whole field together in some coherent and intelligible way. We agree that the objective is important, but note that it is a problem every sociologist faces throughout his working life and that the first approximation achieved under the threat of exams might be achieved in less annoying and artificially stressful ways.

Unfortunately, discussants ordinarily invoke pedagogical justifications of examinations as an afterthought, a backup defense of the status quo, rather than as a primary goal. As a result, no particular care is taken to maximize the educational benefits of examinations and no consideration is given to whether in the examination setting the two goals of evaluation and education are mutually reinforcing or inhibiting.

As will be seen later, we question in general the wisdom of using assessment procedures in connection with graduate education. In this case, however, a pedagogical benefit is alleged, and we have tried to develop a plan that will preserve it. Our second proposal, therefore, is for a

Voluntary Examination Plan. Each student may petition to be given an examination in any field or fields he desires in which the faculty feels itself competent to examine. The results of the

---

[7]See Meltzer (1949) for an excellent study of scholarly productivity that makes use of many predictors but does not include exam grades among them.

examination will be advisory only, will be revealed to the student alone, and will not be incorporated into any official record.

As a minor variation, faculty members might individually offer exams in fields they thought especially important; students who wished to be motivated to learn that field could sign up for them. Again, one might make taking the exams optional but make the results consequential, if the prospect of a low grade was what proved to have motivational value.

In any case, the examination would obviously serve its pedagogical purpose best if, instead of being graded on a simple pass-fail-honors scale as is now usually done, it received a full-length critique demonstrating where the student had gone wrong, suggesting further reading and exercises, arguing with the student's conceptualization of the field, and in general further deepening the student's sophistication. The degree to which we now fail to do this measures exactly the seriousness of the pedagogical justification. The Voluntary Examination Plan is designed to take seriously that purpose, and no other.

Insofar as the argument from pedagogical effects involves, as it usually does, the notion of a "core" of knowledge that all sociologists must possess, faculty members may feel that they, rather than the students, bear the burden of ensuring that it is learned. This situation is similar to what we found with respect to required courses. We propose a similar solution:

Unilateral Compulsory Examination Plan. Each faculty member may give, and require that all students take, an examination in any field he believes students must be certified in. The form, content, time, and place of examination are left to the discretion of the faculty member giving it. No other examinations are given.

Here again, each faculty member must accept the responsibility for his own judgment; no other professor need make evaluations he does not believe in or deem important. Similarly, we might allow as a variation that each professor could require whatever examinations he thought appropriate before allowing a student to work further with him.

Whatever the arguments about evaluation, if we take the educational value of preparation for general examinations seriously, then it is worth devising improved mechanisms for inducing that preparation, not necessarily tied to any scheme of evaluation or assessment. Some professors and some students object to examinations because they bear no resemblance to the typical situations in professional life to which such learning is actually relevant. A more relevant system might approximate the scholarly features of professional meetings, or of the exchange of papers, lectures, and seminars that make up academic life. The following plan attempts to embody many of these characteristics, and individual components might be usable by themselves:

Sociology Symposium. At the end of the first or the beginning of the second year of graduate study, all students in the cohort receive a list of general questions or issues in major areas of sociology, similar to those ordinarily found on general examinations. Students devote a major part or all of their time to preparing for a performance, a Sociology Symposium, to be given in the spring of the second year. The Symposium (which can take anywhere from a few days to several weeks) consists of a series of public meetings at which students read research reports and theoretical essays, engage in debates and panel discussions, and, in any other way they can devise, address themselves to the topics posed earlier. The results might be embodied in an intramural publication. All faculty and students in other cohorts would attend and would be free to join in discussion and questioning. Outside guests might be invited as well.

Under this system, especially if no grades were given, students would presumably work hard, but not because they feared noncertification. Instead, they would have pride in their own performance, would wish to see how well they could master professional skills, would wish to avoid the shame of giving a bad public performance, and would be aware that their performance would begin the process of development of their professional reputations.

We could expect the resulting work to be better, more cogently presented, and less of a burden to read and hear than current examination performances. In addition, the Symposium might be truly educational for the audience, as examinations seldom are.

The Symposium invites the same kind and amount of student preparation as current examining procedures, minus the more irritating features and with several advantages. Students might become actively and responsibly involved in such departmental affairs as, to take a minor example, inviting outside speakers, and for the same reason the faculty does, that it will help them in their work.

Not least, the Symposium would provide an annual event that would uplift and refresh, rather than bring down and oppress, everyone involved.

Degrees

The reader who has followed us this far may by now be wondering how we propose to weed out unfit students, what means we suggest for ascertaining whether students have learned what they are supposed to learn, how we will go about protecting the rest of the world from unfit sociologists. If we make both courses and examinations optional, only the dissertation is left, and that can presumably be written and rewritten until the student finally gets it right.

These problems seem to raise convincing, indeed crushing, arguments against the previous plans. After all, department chairmen and prospective colleagues will want to know whether a graduate can teach various subjects competently. Directors of research organizations will want to know whether a graduate can be counted on to do creditable and competent research. Readers of the graduate's work will want to know how heavily they may rely on what he has to say, this need presumably being greatest among lay people, who have least basis for independent judgment. If the person holds an advanced degree from a reputable institution whose graduate program contains sufficient requirements and evaluative checkpoints to ensure that the unfit have been weeded out, all such people know that he may be relied upon in all these ways.

To put it that baldly reveals how inadequate and insufficient an indicator of sociological prowess the degree actually is. A new graduate may attain his first position because he has a degree from a respectably "tough" department, but if he does not perform up to the hoped-for or acceptable standard he will not remain; this is true even with respect to personal recommendations, which ordinarily are taken more seriously than mere possession of the degree. In fact, as is well known, degrees and school accomplishments are widely believed to be only crude indicators of competence; everyone can tell stories of the less-than-competent who graduated with him and of the more-than-competent who never finished. More than one eminent sociologist never received the Ph.D., and a number have received it only after lapses of many years during which they made important contributions to the field.

We can put the point this way. Institutions hiring sociologists apply their own tests anyway and use departmentally supplied test results only as a first approximation to be discarded as soon as more recent data become available. The institutionally applied tests rely not on "artificial" measurement devices but on the performance of the person in professionally relevant situations for which in-school measurements stand, at best, as predictors of probably unknown quality. Institutions frequently concern themselves not only with the actual work done but also with the reputation that work achieves within the discipline, and for this, again, in-school tests can at best serve as predictors, to be discarded when more immediate measures are available.

In short, the arguments in favor of requirements and evaluative procedures carry weight only to the extent that we agree that certification of competence is the job of a graduate faculty, and this does not seem to us obvious. It can be argued that, quite the contrary, the graduate faculty has no immediate concern with whether its students know anything, this being exclusively the concern of those persons who later utilize the services or work of the person the department has trained. We have argued further that those people in fact apply their own tests and make use of other tests routinely applied in scientific life. Why then should departments undertake the time-consuming chore of certifying their graduates when the job will only be done again and again and again by employers, colleagues, and the discipline at large?

In answer to this, some will say that, although the argument is true as far as it goes, the department that undertakes various evaluations prior to awarding the degree spares itself the embarrassment of having many of its graduates found wanting and thus earning a bad reputation for itself. We find this argument unconvincing, although we know of no data bearing on the matter. We guess, and it is no more than a guess, that departments are known by their distinguished graduates rather than by their disgraceful failures, though most departments have their share of both. (The paucity of data on all these matters is quite remarkable; it might be a first order of business for all interested parties to begin collecting relevant data.)

Since neither protection of those who hire our graduates nor protection of the departmental reputation seems a sufficient reason to undertake strenuous programs of evaluation before awarding the degree, we suggest the following plan:

Matriculation Degree Award Plan. Every student shall be awarded the Ph.D. on entrance into the program of graduate study. This degree cannot be revoked. Students may remain in residence for three years at maximum, after which they must leave; but they may leave at any time before and need never show up at all.

This plan still awards the degree, in deference to students' need for a credential that can be displayed to administrators and others in need of such documentation. They would get jobs as they do now, on the basis of whatever scholarly work they had done and personal recommendations from faculty members. In order to assure themselves of the latter, we can suppose that many students would probably stay the full three years; and many students, in order to acquire the skills necessary for the former, might take a great many of the courses now required. We could not, of course, be assured of this.

Students may object to this plan. Some will feel that it devalues their degree; "We want our degree to be worth something," they will say. To this, we reply that their degrees will be worth whatever they make them worth by their actual scientific and pedagogical work. They can demonstrate that worth most clearly and unarguably by, for example, assembling a portfolio showing what they can do.[8] Such a portfolio might contain a report of research in published or publishable form, papers or other documents exhibiting theoretical and methodological prowess, a well-worked-out plan for one or more courses, and other artifacts appropriate to individual cases.

Students may also object that a system that does not provide impersonal methods of student evaluation for which the faculty is collectively responsible leaves the personal biases of their teachers free to operate without the constraints furnished by course and exam grades. The danger exists, but we believe that the system of recommendations for jobs operates under constraints that tend to obviate it. Faculty members, when recommending students, find themselves constrained by their very real responsibilities to colleagues elsewhere, by a responsibility to furnish recruits, and by the necessity of answering the complaints that will arise if those recommended are not adequate. Oswald Hall (1948) has analyzed the controls present in sponsorship systems of this kind.

Those of our colleagues who have considered the plan deeply voice a more serious objection. They believe the plan to be exces-

---

[8]We are indebted to Charles Bidwell for the idea of the portfolio.

sively cruel in limiting residence to three years, and believe that many students will overwork themselves, attempting to master everything possible before the time limit and deprived of the approved limits given by a conventional degree program. This is a serious problem, but we must simultaneously keep in mind student tendencies to prolong the comfortable dependency of the student status. Without some time restriction, we should probably find ourselves up to our asses in aging graduate students with Ph.D. degrees. Nevertheless, we are willing to consider some variation in the time limit, perhaps an extension to four years.

Admissions

If the last plan is adopted, we seem to face a particularly severe problem with respect to admission policies. Those who wish to make the degree "mean something" may, even if they accept the basic notion of the plan, attempt to ensure quality of departmental graduates by making admissions standards more demanding. Here again we must point out that present-day admission standards offer little solace. We believe that they do not work well, that they do not in fact produce anything more than a haphazard selection from the pool of applicants with respect to ability or the likelihood of becoming competent or distinguished sociologists. Naturally, we cannot prove this contention; the necessary data are not available. But, by the same token, no one can prove that present-day admissions practices are, in fact, an improvement over some random procedure. Since admissions usually takes a great deal of faculty time and a great deal of poring over uninterpretable scores on the Graduate Record Examination and equally ambiguous undergraduate grade-point averages, we propose the

Random Admissions Plan. A predetermined number of applicants will be selected through the use of a table of random numbers.

For those who feel that various existing procedures have some indefinable something to recommend them, we recommend the more rococo and time-consuming

Multivariate Admissions Plan. One or more students shall be selected from the pool of applicants by each of the criteria proposed by any member of the faculty, up to the predetermined number.

For instance, one or more students might be admitted on the basis of the highest GRE scores submitted, one or more on the basis of the highest cumulative college grade-point average, one or more on the basis of recommendations, and so on. Faculties should consider, for a variety of reasons, also admitting a few students who score lowest on these criteria. One student might be admitted on a sort of decathlon basis, the best overall record across all the criteria used. Some departments may wish to consider bio-social criteria, such as race or physical attractiveness.

As a final alternative, one might consider allowing each faculty member one or more peremptory admissions, choices of prospective students that need not be justified on any ground. This plan could, of course, be combined with either of the two preceding. We ourselves are content with the random plan, since it probably does as well as any of the others and requires least effort.

A Final Plan

Some will feel, with us, that the above plans are too complicated, that they still contain elements that interfere with the development of a community of scholars. For such people we have devised a plan that, though it might be the most difficult to finance and gain acceptance for, has much to recommend it.

The Tree Plan. Each faculty member is assigned a tree, under which he sits at designated times, talking with those individuals or groups who come by.

The important feature of the plan is that *this is it in its entirety.* A number of minor problems may arise, such as traffic congestion in the case of popular faculty. Also, some faculty members may prefer rocks or other features of the landscape to trees[9] or may even, especially in colder climates, wish to interpret the plan metaphorically and continue to use conventional offices.

What would the faculty members and their visitors talk about? Since neither students nor faculty would be coerced into these conversations (faculty would have to be available, but presumably would not have to talk very long to unwanted guests), topics of discussion would be arrived at, as in any voluntary discourse, by mutual consent. Similarly, participants in discussions would decide themselves

[9]This point has been argued to us strongly by Professor Paul Bohannan.

on the length, number, and timing of their conversations. A professor might propose to one or more students that they discuss a topic in theory or methods or in some substantive field until they got tired of it or felt there was nothing further useful to say. Or students might originate a similar proposal. Participants presumably would choose topics in the fields they were expert in or proposed to become expert in, though this would not be required.

The Tree Plan is most radical in doing away with a system of prearranged courses unilaterally decided on and offered by the faculty, courses of fixed length with an officially announced subject. To be sure, the rigidity of the course system breaks down in the later years, when advanced seminars come to have something more of a mutually negotiated character. But faculty and students often find themselves condemned to a semester of dull class meetings neither are interested in; if the college catalog did not require them to go through with what had been officially announced they would all gladly give it up. Or participants find that they have exhausted a subject in six weeks, but have nine more now to go; much worse, they find that they are just getting well into a topic but must stop because the semester is over. All these troubles can be gotten around, but the conventional system of courses creates them to be gotten around.

In one sense, the Tree Plan is nothing new at all, but rather something professors and students have always created for themselves, in the time left over from officially prescribed activities. Every department has known the "informal seminar"—sometimes started by a professor, sometimes by students who invite professors to join them, sometimes carried on by students alone. These seminars have not ordinarily been conceived as anti-faculty, as has been the case with the Free University movement. Rather, they grow up to do something people want done, something the conventional system is not against but simply fails to provide time for. (Professors who have been involved in these seminars typically report that students in them work very hard and that they themselves profit greatly. Once again, we lack sufficient data to say anything less speculative; research on these informal collective educational enterprises should have high priority.)

The Tree Plan, then, calls our attention to the kind of exchange that might take place in the shade of those trees as being what graduate education ought properly to be about, and to the obstacles the conventional system places in the way of that exchange.

Conclusion

Whether or not our disciplinary colleagues ultimately adopt the Tree Plan or any of the less drastic modifications of current practice recommended above, we believe it will be worthwhile to consider these often-discussed problems in the broader contexts we have suggested. Should individual responsibility for course requirements be instituted or evaded? Should examinations be engineered to serve a pedagogical purpose and no other? Should departments undertake to certify the competence of their graduates when that competence will undergo repeated and more realistic tests in the intellectual life of the discipline? Should admissions criteria whose predictive efficacy is unknown continue to be used? Should we allow bureaucratic requirements to interfere with the activity of a disciplinary collegium made up of younger and older, more and less experienced, sociologists?

While we think our plans have merit, we do not suppose that we have exhausted the possibilities, touched on all the problems, or achieved the best solutions. Since graduate programs are continually up for revision, and never more than now, we invite our colleagues to contribute further suggestions and plans.

12

WHAT'S HAPPENING TO SOCIOLOGY?

Sociology has changed so much since the end of World War II that someone who went through graduate school then, as I did, can hardly recognize it. The number of practicing sociologists, measured by membership in the American Sociological Association, increased from 2,364 in 1950 to 15,567 in 1978. The number of departments giving the doctoral degree has likewise increased dramatically. There is no easy way to count the increase in organizations devoted to sociological and related concerns or in the number of journals sociologists read and contribute to, but it is obvious that these numbers have increased even out of proportion to the increase in sociologists.

Fragmentation and Growth

Simultaneously, the field (which Thomas Kuhn once charitably suggested was in a pre-paradigmatic stage) has become increasingly fragmented along theoretical and subject matter lines. Again, there is no easy way to count the increase in theoretical positions and schools of thought, but there are surely many more of them than there used to be, and they are more separated from one another than they used to be. It is harder for their adherents to find common ground.

Finally, the discipline of sociology no longer has easily defined boundaries. Where sociologists once worked almost exclusively as teachers in academic departments of sociology, as many as fifteen percent (and the number increases continually) now work in non-academic positions. As in other disciplines which have experienced this change, sociology has as a result many practitioners whose loyalties and attention are attached to organizations, problems, and styles of work that have very little to do with the traditional view of sociological activity. These people, trained in sociology and still members of the ASA, nevertheless find their real colleagues outside the discipline, and the same is true for many academic sociologists interested in problems that bridge or lie outside traditional sociological subjects and concerns.

Despite all these changes, most sociologists carry around in their heads a picture of their field as something much like it was in 1950: a theoretically coherent, centripetally organized discipline, whose members share a common view of the work to be done and the ideas which should inform it. In this view, sociologists are really all engaged in the same enterprise—the creation of a body of scientific knowledge about society—and share a similar view of how it should be carried on. But sociology no longer resembles that image, and the actions sociologists undertake based on it produce grossly different results from those anticipated. As a result, most sociologists experience in their daily work lives a series of insoluble problems, complications, and vexations which they approach (like any non-sociologist) as practical matters, to be dealt with piecemeal and, usually, with a heavy moral concern. It is, therefore, worth detailing how this growth has changed the experience of members of the discipline and affected the efficacy of traditional solutions to their problems.

Academic Sociology

Consider first, as archetypal, the experience of that part of the profession which still works in universities and colleges, teaching undergraduates and training graduate students. These sociologists are subject to the same career contingencies academic sociologists have always been subject to. Academic success is reckoned and rewarded as it always was: professors succeed by publishing sociological works in scholarly media (journals or books), and they are rewarded in higher salaries, in positions in universities with greater prestige and (as a rule) better working conditions (which allow them to increase the amount of research and publishable work they produce), and in tenure.

Academic sociology has probably always been characterized by a deep division between two or more layers in a stratification system. A small percentage of professors have written the vast majority of the items published. A much larger group published their Ph.D. dissertations and seldom anything more. A network of journals and scholarly publishers served as the outlet for this work, augmented occasionally by journals in related fields and subject matter areas (for example, journals in social psychiatry, geriatrics, or area studies).

The dramatic increase in the number of sociologists had, inevitably, an impact on this more-or-less well adjusted system of training, research, publication, rewards, and promotion. Whereas in 1950 there were only three truly national journals (*American Journal of Sociology, American Sociological Review,* and *Social Forces*) and a handful of regional and specialty journals (for example, *Sociology & Social Research, Social Research, Midwest Sociologist, Sociometry*), by 1978 sociologists were routinely publishing in at least fifty journals, and new ones continue to spring up. Where have all these journals come from?

If you train large cohorts of people to do research and, further, expect them to do it and publish it in order to be promoted to tenure positions in universities and win other rewards, some sizable number will obey these injunctions and produce research and written materials no worse than what has hitherto appeared in the scholarly media. But those media will not be able to accommodate the flood of new materials that, given contemporary standards, deserves publication. If no means for the publication of this work is developed, and if the standards of publication for promotion are maintained, a situation of blatant inequity will exist and everyone involved will so see it.

In fact, the situation was worse than that, because during this same period of growth institutions of higher learning themselves engaged in organizational mobility, trying to raise their scholarly prestige by instituting Ph.D. programs and then trying to upgrade their faculty to demonstrate that they deserved the honor of a doctoral program; they did that, of course, by requiring of their faculties, as they had not previously, publications. So both the new cohorts entering the field, with normal ambitions and a clear understanding of what it would take to fulfill them, and the older cohorts already teaching who had been exempted from such requirements, began to look for publication outlets.

In fact, during those years, one frequently heard that "They" wouldn't publish work of this or that kind, work by people from this or that school of thought. Rampant paranoia, sometimes based in fact, but always fed by the observable and experienced fact that more and more articles were turned down and that publication delays were increasingly long, began to appear in print and especially

in discussions, public and private, at the annual meetings of both
the national and regional societies. The substantial distrust of the
ASA during this period (much of it emanating from the Midwest
Sociological Society, which had more than its share of the Sons of
the Wild Jackass, and from the leftish contingent that participated
in the founding of the Society for the Study of Social Problems)
had its origins in the thought that if the ASA was controlled by a
conservative "eastern" clique, and if they used that control to ap-
point editors of their persuasion, then work of good quality but of
the wrong theoretical and political cast would have difficulty being
published; scarcity of publication space would lead to de facto
censorship.

Conflicting Theories

This fear reflected the growing disagreements within sociology
over theoretical viewpoints, though it would be wrong to ascribe
all the disagreements to that cause. Members of various branches
of the "Chicago School," and especially the second- and third-
generation descendants of the founders, began to find that they
frequently if not invariably saw the standard problems in a different
light than the increasingly important functionalist school based at
Columbia and Harvard. The difference had something, although
again not everything, to do with differences in method, the former
being more inclined to fieldwork and intensive interviewing, the
latter to surveys; those differences, it could be argued, led the former
group to an anti-establishment approach more frequently than their
eastern counterparts. And all of this had something, though not
everything, to do with geography. But, in fact, all these differences
were confounded and confused, and there was a great deal of overlap
in interests and ways of viewing the problems and tasks of sociology.

Nevertheless, the danger of "censorship" by the "eastern clique"
coincided with the growing number of productive sociologists to
create a large number of new journals. The SSSP produced *Social
Problems,* which soon became a national journal, and regional societies upgraded their journals (for example, *Midwest Sociologist* became *Sociological Quarterly*). The number of new sociologists rose
faster than printing costs, so that new journals were economically
feasible. Enough people would subscribe, and cause their university
libraries to subscribe, that quarterly journals could be published and
break even; those that represented organizations with a substantial

membership had no difficulty at all. (Indeed, the SSSP was always embarrassed because, due to a precedent set by Arnold Rose, the society benefited from the royalties from a number of books published under its auspices and thus, even though its dues were very low and it published a quarterly journal, it still accumulated a surplus.) Somewhat later, Sage Publications and other organizations found it "financially feasible" to sponsor the publication of scholarly journals of limited circulation. The ASA took over a number of journals that had originally appeared under other auspices (for example, *Sociometry* and *Sociology of Education*) and marketed them to its members, increasing both their circulation and their financial base.

Organizations proliferated along with journals. These organizations represented interests—theoretical, political, regional, and subject area—which were not given sufficient voice in the official existing organizations (chiefly the ASA and the regional societies). Though the ASA tried to contain these through the device of the section, many groups went ahead and set up on their own, although they all took advantage of the annual ASA meeting as the natural place to hold their own meetings, utilizing where possible such ASA resources as hotel space. These groups included politically oriented caucuses, such minority caucuses as the organizations that later became Sociologists for Women in Society and the Caucus of Black Sociologists, and theoretically distinct groups such as the group that is now the Society for the Study of Symbolic Interaction.

All of these organizations provided a forum for the articulation of submerged interests and, in addition, provided places in which people could hold office and thus simultaneously get their hands on some kind of power to affect the discipline and achieve organizational positions that, listed on a vita, might persuade deans and colleagues that they merited promotion, tenure, and other rewards. In addition to publication outlets through their official journals, the meetings of these organizations also provided occasions for papers to be read, scientific discussion carried on, and further additions to vitas justified.

In short, for a variety of reasons, ranging from career necessities through the desire to avoid the stultifying political and scientific effects of centralization to real differences in paradigms, the amount of scientific publication and organization increased massively. Where, to take one example, there had been one president installed during the annual meeting, there were now many.

Polycentric Discipline

Many people complained about these changes, finding the result an intolerable chaos. Those who looked for order and unanimity in the discipline had their patience and faith strained by the spectacle of people they had never heard of producing organizations and journals and demanding that these upstarts be taken seriously. Further, and worse, many did take them seriously. The new journals were refereed, just like the old ones, and people in charge of promotions for better or worse had to accept work published in them as serious evidence of scholarly merit. In a short time, the old status system—centralized and in the hands of a relative few—gave way to a much larger polycentric system. The old rewards of senior statesmanship meant less as they were swamped in a galaxy of similar rewards. The opportunity to exert decisive power decreased as the discipline became not only polycentric but defiantly and rebelliously so.

So we now have a very different discipline than we did thirty years earlier. What have the consequences been, besides the remaking of the disciplinary status system? What are the consequences for sociology as an intellectual enterprise, as a collective effort to achieve greater understanding of society?

The biggest change, of course, is that it is no longer possible for any sociologist to keep track of what is going on. No one can read all the journals or attend all the meetings in or at which material of interest to their own work and thinking might be found. The most immediate response to this, begun before it was quite necessary but now clearly indispensable, was the publication of *Sociological Abstracts*. At one time, you knew *everything* that was being done in sociology if you read the three major journals and the output of a few scholarly presses—their combined total could not strain anyone's energy or time budget. In fact, people waited breathlessly for a new sociological book, each one an Event. But now you cannot even think of reading all the journals published. If you have an interest in a particular topic, you keep track of it by checking the abstracts.

As an immediate result, people find it less necessary to look at any journal, for they do not keep up with what is interesting and necessary for them to see by looking at journals. They are, therefore, less likely to see things that might interest them if they knew about them, but that are in the wrong subject matter area or are in one way or another mislabeled (hence the concern with mechanical retrieval systems). The serendipity which comes from unrelated materials being side by side in the same issue of a journal is thereby lost.

Sociological readers, in addition to using abstracting services, also keep track of what is going on in their areas of interest by monitoring specialty journals that appeal exactly to their subject matter interest and by heeding the recommendations of personal acquaintances or pen pals, who send each other materials (hence the ballooning of copying expenses) prior to or at the same time as publication.

These developments coincide with another consequence of the increased numbers of sociologists: the increasingly esoteric character of sociological subfields. Not only do people try less to keep up, because of the increased amount of material; they find that, if they want to keep up, they must make a large investment in time and energy because fields quickly produce so much work and so many points of view, so much data and so many methodological advances and variations, that one must devote an enormous amount of time to mastering all this new material. Because so many people are at work, both the amount of material and the amount of change in basic frameworks increase at a very rapid rate.

"Keeping Up"

As a result of both the increasing amount of material and its increasing specialization, it becomes increasingly difficult and then impossible for anyone to know what is going on in sociology. No one can master the entire field, with all its detailed and developed branches, and no one can be the Renaissance sociologist who, knowing all of it, can speak about or on behalf of the discipline as a whole. Presidential addresses tend to be the statement of a subfield of interest, an assessment of its possibilities and prospects, rather than an address to all of the faithful, for there is nothing that would be interesting or intelligible to all of them.

All these difficulties are compounded by the existence of the increasingly larger number of sociologists who work outside academia. For these sociologists have even more reason to be diverted from an overall view of the field. Their work is more tied than that of academicians to a specific problem area, to specific clients who want particular kinds of answers to their questions and have little interest in the development of sociology as an intellectual enterprise. They are, in many cases, consumers of academic sociology, importing into their specialty only those few developments in the field as a whole which have immediate use in their own problems. Their own contributions, which might have great import for academic sociological theorizing, are often buried in confidential reports or bureaucratic memoranda which never reach the bulk of practicing sociologists. In addition, their professional concerns do not get much attention from the sociologists who control the professional associations, so that they are not much inclined to keep in full touch with "the field."

For all these reasons, sociology is fragmented and diverse. But many sociologists (probably most academicians) still accept the notion of the Renaissance sociologist, to some degree (and perhaps especially, as we will see, in relation to graduate training), and feel that they should "keep up." One result is the annual review and the review article, devices intended to summarize a field for the benefit of those outside it. These reviews are probably most important as statements within the subfields in which they occur, as political moves staking out the character of some area in opposition to other ways of staking it out, and are probably not read by many people outside that subfield (with the exception of graduate students studying for exams).

Donald Campbell (1969) has described another result. With the increasing subdivision of major fields, each scientist develops his or her own specialty, consisting of some idiosyncratic combination of material from a number of smaller, specialized fields. No two specialties are alike, but there is enough overlap that, like the scales on a fish, the entire larger area can be covered without gaps. This idealized picture is becoming increasingly realistic. People combine theoretical predilections, methodological habits, topical interests, and area specialties in a mélange that overlaps with the mélanges of others in various ways, but doesn't really coincide with any particular field as currently defined. This development has the positive features Campbell ascribed to it: overall, a vast amount of territory is covered with possibilities (how high the probabilities are is another question) of communication across the entire field. In principle, a scientist working in one area can be in touch with any other area that contains material of interest. But it also means that there is almost nothing one could appeal to as something that every sociologist knows.

20

Most sociologists (and I now speak primarily of academicians) run across this problem as a practical matter of their everyday disciplinary lives. One problem is publication. Having produced an article reporting some research I have done, where can I send it? Some residual feeling exists that publication in the "big journals" brings more prestige in publication than the host of "lesser" journals, but as a matter of fact everyone (including the most prestigious members of the discipline) publishes, when they do, in a variety of media, ranging from the most well known and nationally distributed journals with a large circulation to small, esoteric specialty journals. They do not count on an article's appearance in one or another place affecting who sees and reads it, and instead depend on an informal network of interested colleagues to see that the material gets to the people who need to know about it. So most sociologists find they decide where to submit finished work by turning to journals that have some publicly announced commitment to the area the work deals with. This, of course, increases the centrifugal and decentralizing tendencies already present. (Interestingly enough, it also makes it difficult for journals to change their character. Once they become known as a "home" for a certain kind of work, a vastly disproportionate share of the manuscripts they receive will be of that kind, ensuring that they will publish a disproportionate amount of such work and thus renew the reputation as a home. *Sociometry* [now *Social Psychology*], for instance, has over the years, with each new editor, tried to escape its fate as the home for small-group experimental research, but with very little success.)

Training the Graduate Student

An even more continuous confrontation with the results of disciplinary growth and disorganization occurs in those departments with graduate programs. What shall we teach the graduate students? What shall we require them to know? This question becomes most pressing around the issue of required courses and preliminary examinations. When these matters are discussed, people usually have in mind some notion of the Renaissance sociologist or, more mundanely, the utility infielder. They think the graduates from their program may be called on to do almost anything, that prospective employers will be looking for odd assortments of talents and skills, that a well-trained sociologist knows something about everything going on in sociology, is "well rounded," and that all this is necessary, if for no other reason, so that the graduate can read and judge the literature intelligently.

No one, of course, expects sociologists to know everything any more, but they do have this notion in mind when they talk of requiring basic skills in methods (for methods is now a subject of monumental and ever-changing complexity, a field in itself and one which, as Richard Hill [1969] remarked some years ago, has less and less relevance to the actual work research sociologists do) and theory (another specialty made up of arcane subspecialties). Beyond that, everyone has a notion of what a decently trained and *au courant* sociologist ought to be prepared to talk about literately and intelligently. But few people have the same notion of what that "core" of sociology is. *American Sociologist* demonstrated this conclusively in 1968 by publishing the Ph.D. preliminary examinations given by eighteen of the "top twenty" departments in the United States (fortunately for everyone's nerves, the survey did not cover other countries in which graduate degrees in sociology are given). Simple inspection of those examination questions showed that very little of what students would have to know to answer them successfully was required everywhere and that, while there was some overlap in the material covered from department to department, there was neither anything which every department required nor any departments whose requirements were the same. If sociology has a core, someone better tell the top twenty what it is.

To be specific, departments tended to ask about those things their own faculty specialized in. So North Carolina required students to know a good deal about the statistical methods H. M. Blalock (then on that faculty) was pioneering, while UCLA (then as now the home of Harold Garfinkel) required a knowledge of ethnomethodology. Any honest faculty member will admit that it would be difficult to pass the entire exam set by their own department. In fact, what the exams invariably consist of is some compromise among the different views of sociology and what is important in it held by the members of the current faculty. Especially in graduate training centers, the faculty are quite specialized and in some ways represent the leading edge of the trends we are discussing. So they necessarily have more disparate and disconnected views of the field of sociology than might be held by those at less prestigious centers, teaching a wider variety of materials.

Students trained in these varying departments, then, start professional life with disparate views of what sociology is all about, what constitutes acceptable research, what are reasonable questions for sociologists to ask and reasonable answers to them. This probably is the structural basis (or one of the important ones, to be cautious) of the much-decried paradigm crisis sociology is thought to be experiencing (the people who decry it usually think it a shame and a scandal). In any event, with these disparate views, students then embark on careers of research and writing in specialized areas, reading specialized journals and participating in specialized organizations, knowing more and more about less and less.

Finally, many sociologists find that they have more in common with people in other departments than their own, that the problems they are really interested in working on involve them with people in some other of the social sciences or perhaps with people in biology or philosophy or history or engineering. In some cases, sociologists simply find that people in another discipline are doing what they want to do—they become born-again philosophers or whatever. In other cases, they join with apostates from other fields to work together on topics that have little legitimacy in any of the more established disciplines.

In any event, these groups add even more complications to the lives of disciplinary sociologists and academic departments. It is harder than ever to make judgments about work in these increasingly esoteric fields, harder than ever to do justice to the needs of students for intelligent and knowledgeable advice. Above all, it is harder than ever to think of sociology as one discipline, one organization with one paradigm. The myth dies hard, but the reality disappeared long ago. As sociologists develop increasingly strong and compelling attachments to these smaller organizations, the possibility of one paradigm being known and intelligible to all of them, let alone acceptable, becomes increasingly smaller.

Specialty Subworlds

The overall result is that sociology is now a discipline in name only. To be sure, all the people who go by the name of sociologist meet in the same place once a year, they all receive (probably) a few of the same journals (although not even the *American Sociological Review* is now received by all members of the ASA), and old school ties and other personal relationships create bonds across the specialty lines we have been discussing. Nevertheless, it is not one world in sociology any more. Rather, what we have is a loosely connected network of specialty subworlds, which operate and work together mostly at the departmental level (although, of course, there are other areas of cooperation such as on ASA committees and the like). All the subspecialties subscribe to a common ancestor myth, in whose name they look for the links that bind together their in fact quite different areas of work. They do, however, create such links, even if they cannot discover them as already there, and much of the innovation in theorizing comes from people who have made a specialty of looking for links. (This probably explains the otherwise mysterious concentration on Marx-Durkheim-Weber, the Holy Trinity whose fathomless interconnections, if they were charted, would provide the final word on the integration of the field.)

Where will it all end? Prediction is foolhardy, but I will make a few guesses, based largely on analogy to fields where the process started earlier and has gone on longer. Sociology will fragment into a large number of smaller fields, each with its own status system, organizations, publications, and the like. Academic departments will not fragment so rapidly, but will become federations of loosely connected subgroups. At the most general level, the field will suffer from the parochialism of subgroups, but this will be counterbalanced by the development of new specialties which will introduce the findings in particular fields into the others, so that the benefits of comparative study will not be totally lost. Polycentrism in professional politics will continue and no "school" or department or network will control the entire discipline. I say this not because I think there are not sociologists who would like to see such control exerted, in the name of order and progress, but because the structure of the discipline makes it too difficult for them to achieve it.

PART 4
PHOTOGRAPHY

13

PHOTOGRAPHY AND SOCIOLOGY

Photography and sociology have approximately the same birth date, if you count sociology's birth as the publication of Comte's work which gave it its name, and photography's birth as the date in 1839 when Daguerre made public his method for fixing an image on a metal plate (see Newhall 1964 and Lyons 1966). From the beginning, both worked on a variety of projects. Among these, for both, was the exploration of society.

While sociology has had other ends, moral and metaphysical, sociologists have always wanted to understand how society worked, to map its dimensions and then look into the big sectors and little crannies so mapped. They ordinarily wanted to find things out rigorously and scientifically, and to develop general theories. But some sociologists have made it their main business to describe what has not yet been described, in the style of the ethnographer, to tell the big news, in the style of the journalist, combining these (more or less) with the desire for rigor and general theory.

Sociologists' choice of theories, methods, and topics of research usually reflect the interests and constraints of the intellectual and occupational communities to which they are allied and attached. They often choose research methods, for instance, that appear to have paid off for the natural sciences. They frequently choose research topics which are public concerns of the moment, especially as those are reflected in the allocation of research funds: poverty, drugs, immigration, campus or ghetto disorder, and so on. These faddish tendencies are balanced by a continuing attention to, and respect for, traditional topics and styles of work.

Work on this paper was supported by the Russell Sage Foundation. I am grateful to Marie Czach, Blanche Geer, Walter Klink, Alexander J. Morin, and Clarice Stasz for their useful comments on an earlier version.

The efforts and projects of photographers have been much more various. In order to understand how photographers go about exploring society when they undertake that job, it will be useful to remember the mélange of other jobs photography does. Think of a camera as a machine that records and communicates much as a typewriter does. People use typewriters to do a million different jobs: to write ad copy designed to sell goods, to write newspaper stories, short stories, instruction booklets, lyric poems, biographies and autobiographies, history, scientific papers, letters. . . . The neutral typewriter will do any of these things as well as the skill of its user permits. Because of the persistent myth that the camera simply records whatever is in front of it (about which I will say more below), people often fail to realize that the camera is equally at the disposal of a skilled practitioner and can do any of the above things, in its own way. Photographers have done all of the things suggested above, often in explicit analogue with the verbal model. Different kinds of photographers work in different institutional settings and occupational communities, which affect their product as the institutional settings in which sociologists work affect theirs (Rosenblum 1978).

Photographers have worked to produce advertising illustrations. They have made portraits of the rich and famous, and of ordinary people as well. They have produced pictures for newspapers and magazines. They have produced works of art for galleries, collectors, and museums. The constraints of the settings in which they did their work (Becker 1974, 1982) affected how they went about it, their habits of seeing, the pictures they made, and, when they looked at society, what they saw, what they made of it, and the way they presented their results.

From its beginnings, photography has been used as a tool for the exploration of society, and photographers have taken that as one of their tasks. At first, some photographers used the camera to record far-off societies that their contemporaries would otherwise never see and, later, aspects of their own society their contemporaries had no wish to see. Sometimes they even conceived of what they were doing as sociology, especially around the turn of the century when sociologists and photographers agreed on the necessity of exposing the evils of society through words and pictures. Lewis Hine, for instance, was supported by the Russell Sage Foundation in connection with the early surveys of urban life (Gutman

1. *Lewis Hine, "Girl Working in Cotton Mill." Hine, one of the early documentary photographers, collaborated with sociologists and other reformers in the investigation of such social problems as child labor. (© Art Institute of Chicago.)*

1967). The *American Journal of Sociology* routinely ran photographs in connection with its muckraking reformist articles for at least the first fifteen years of its existence (Oberschall 1972:215).

Another kind of social exploration grew out of the use of photographs to report the news and to record important social events. Mathew Brady (Horan 1955) and his staff, which included Timothy H. O'Sullivan (Horan 1966) and Alexander Gardner (1959), photographed the Civil War, and Roger Fenton the Crimean War. But it was not until the 1920s that the development of the illustrated weekly in Europe produced a group of photographers who made the *photoreportage* or photoessay into an instrument of social analysis (Alfred Eisenstaedt and Erich Salomon are among the best-known graduates of these journals) (Gidal 1973). Later, the *Picture Post* in England and *Time, Life,* and *Fortune* in the United

2a and b. Dorothea Lange, "Street Meeting; San Francisco" (above) and Russell Lee, "Trying on a pair of shoes, St. Augustine, Texas, 1939" (right). Photographers working for the Farm Security Administration during the 1930s produced a vast archive of ethnographic images of American life. (Courtesy of the Library of Congress.)

States provided outlets for serious photojournalists who worked with the photoessay form: Margaret Bourke-White, Walker Evans, W. Eugene Smith, Robert Capa.

The impulse to photographic social exploration found another expression in the work produced by the photographers Roy Stryker assembled for the photographic unit of the Farm Security Administration during the 1930s (Hurley 1972, 1973; Stryker and Wood 1973). Dorothea Lange, Walker Evans, Russell Lee, Arthur Rothstein, and others made it their business to record the poverty and hard times of Depression America, their work very much informed by social science theories of various kinds.

More recently, political involvement has had a hand in shaping the use of photography to explore society. Photographers participated actively in the civil rights movement of the 1960s and brought back photographs which effectively stirred people just as Lewis Hine's photographs of child laborers had. They then used those skills in somewhat less immediately political kinds of essays—exploring communities, occupations, subcultures, institutions—that

*3a and b. Dorothea Lange, "Plantation owner; near Clarksdale, Mississippi, 1936"
(above) and "Abandoned farmhouse on large mechanized cotton farm; Texas, 1938"
(right). Lange's photographs of poverty and hard times in Depression America were
informed by a social science perspective. She saw and recorded the facts of social stratification
in the South, and of the replacement of the family farm by agribusiness. (Courtesy of
the Library of Congress.)*

have a sociological intent. These essays combine a journalistic and
ethnographic style with a self-conscious and deliberate artistic
purpose.

Photography from the beginning strove toward art just as it did
toward social exploration. To be sure, earlier photographers in this
tradition understood that what they did had an artistic component.
They worked hard to produce images that measured up as art. But

the artistic element of photography was held at a substantial distance from photography carried on for more mundane purposes, including journalism. Such influential photographers as Edward Weston conceived of their work as something more like painting—they produced for galleries, museums, and private collectors as much as they could—and did very little that could be interpreted in any direct way as an exploration of society.

Art and social exploration describe two ways of working, not two kinds of photographers. Many photographers do both kinds of work in the course of their careers. And even this is an oversimplification, since many photographs made by someone whose work is predominantly of one kind have strong overtones of the other. Paul Strand is clearly an art photographer; but his pictures of peasants around the world embody political ideas, and any number of socially concerned photographers do work that is personally expressive and aesthetically interesting quite apart from its subject matter—as, for instance, in Danny Lyon's *The Destruction of Lower Manhattan* (1969) and Larry Clark's *Tulsa* (1971).

Photography has thus, like sociology, displayed a shifting variety of characteristic emphases, depending on the currents of interest in the worlds of art, commerce, and journalism to which it has been attached. One continuing emphasis has been the exploration of society in ways more or less connected with somewhat similar explorations undertaken by academic sociologists. As sociology became more scientific and less openly political, photography became more personal, more artistic, and continued to be engaged politically. Not surprisingly, then, the two modes of social exploration have ceased to have very much to do with one another.

Sociologists today know little of the work of social documentary photographers and its relevance to what they do. They seldom use photographs as a way of gathering, recording, or presenting data and conclusions. I want to acquaint them with this tradition and show them how they can make use of the styles of work and techniques common in photography. Many social scientists have already been active photographically, and what I say will not be news to them (Barndt 1974).

Many photographers have undertaken projects which produce results that parallel those of sociology, and make claims that in some ways parallel the claims to truth and representativeness of sociology. Insofar as their work has this character, I intend to show them how a knowledge of some of the ideas and techniques of academic sociology can be of help to them.

I do not want to make photographers of social scientists or impose a social science imperialism on photographers (not that there is any chance such attempts would be successful). Many sociologists will find the work and methods I describe hopelessly unscientific, although I hope that this discussion will cause them to reconsider their own methods. Many photographers will find my suggestions academically arrogant; satisfied with the way they now work, they will see no advantage in alien ideas and procedures.

What I say is most directly addressed to those social scientists and photographers who are sufficiently dissatisfied with what they are doing to want to try something new, who find difficulties in their present procedures and are interested in seeing whether people in other fields know something that might help. Ideally, it is directed to the growing number of people, whatever their professional background, who are concerned with producing photographic explorations of society.

In addition, I have tried to show how even those sociologists who have no interest in photographic work can learn something from the light shed on conventional research methods by a comparison with photographic methods. Some generic problems of social exploration profit from the light the comparison generates.

I will not be concerned with every aspect of the use of visual materials in social science in this paper. Specifically, I will not consider three major areas of work to which social scientists have devoted themselves: (1) the use of film to preserve nonverbal data for later analysis, as in the analyses of gesture and body movement by such scholars as Birdwhistell, Ekman, Hall, and Lennard; (2) the analysis of the visual productions of "native seers" for their cultural and social meanings, as in the Worth-Adair study (1972) of Navaho filmmakers; (3) the use of photographs as historical documents, whether they have been taken by artless amateurs and preserved in family albums, as in Richard Chalfen's work, or by professional photographers, as in Michael Lesy's *Wisconsin Death Trip* (1973). All three are interesting and important areas of work, but differ from the use of photographs to study organizations, institutions, and communities that I have in mind. There is considerable overlap, of course, and I do not insist on the distinction.

Anyone who gets into a new field must pay some dues. Photographers who want to pursue the matter further will have to read some social science prose, and many will probably find that too steep a price; some will find a viable solution in a working partnership with a social scientist (as in the fruitful collaboration of Euan Duff and Dennis Marsden in their study of unemployed men and their families in Britain [1972]).

The price to social scientists is less painful. They must acquaint themselves with the extensive photographic literature; I have reproduced some examples here and will provide a brief guide to more. In addition, they will have to learn to look at photographs more attentively than they ordinarily do. Laymen learn to read photographs the way they do headlines, skipping over them quickly to get the gist of what is being said. Photographers, on the other hand, study them with the care and attention to detail one might give to a difficult scientific paper or a complicated poem. Every part of the photographic image carries some information that contributes to its total statement; the viewer's responsibility is to *see*, in the most literal way, everything that is there and respond to it. To put it another way, the statement the image makes—not just what it shows you, but the mood, moral evaluation, and causal connections it suggests—is built up from those details. A proper "reading" of a photograph sees and responds to them consciously.

Photographers learn to interpret photographs in that technical way because they want to understand and use that "language" themselves (just as musicians learn a more technical musical language than the layman needs). Social scientists who want to work with visual materials will have to learn to approach them in this more studious and time-consuming way. The following exercise, taught to me by Philip Perkis, is a way of seeing what is involved:

> Take some genuinely good picture; the ones reproduced in this article will do. Using a watch with a second hand, look at the photograph intently for two minutes. Don't stare and thus stop looking; look actively. It will be hard to do, and you'll find it useful to take up the time by naming everything in the picture to yourself: this is a man, this is his arm, this is the finger on his hand, this is the shadow his hand makes, this is the cloth of his sleeve, and so on. Once you have done this for two minutes, build it up to five, following the naming of things with a period of fantasy, telling yourself a story about the people and things in the picture. The story needn't be true; it's just a device for externalizing and making clear to yourself the emotion and mood the picture has evoked, both part of its statement.

When you have done this exercise many times, a more careful way of looking will become habitual. Two things result. You will realize that ordinarily you have not consciously seen most of what is in an image even though you have been responding to it. You will also find that you can now remember the photographs you have studied much as you can remember a book you have taken careful notes on. They become part of a mental collection available for further work. (When you do this exercise a number of times you will acquire new habits of seeing and won't have to spend as much time looking at a new print.)

I hope this does not sound mystical. Black-and-white still photographs use visual conventions that everyone brought up in a world of illustrated newspapers and magazines learns just as they learn to talk. We are not ordinarily aware of the grammar and syntax of these conventions, though we use them, just as we may not know the grammar and syntax of our verbal language though we speak and understand it. We can learn that language through study and analysis, just as we can learn to understand music and poetry by making technical analyses of harmony and counterpoint or of prosody. We don't have a large amount of such photographic analysis available, especially as it relates to the concerns of social scientists. But it is absolutely prerequisite to any analysis and discussion that you practice looking at photographs long and hard, so that you have something to analyze.

The Photographic Literature

TOPICS OF STUDY

One reason sociologists should be interested in the work of social documentary photographers is that photographers have covered many of the subjects that are persistent foci of sociological concern. Some have done their work for the government, some on assignment, or speculatively, for magazines and newspapers, some supported by foundations, some as the "private" work they do between paying jobs, or as a hobby. Describing the variety of topics photographers share with sociologists will provide the opportunity to acquaint those unfamiliar with the photographic literature with some of the most interesting and important work.

In dealing with the topics they share with sociologists, photographers say what they have to say in many ways. Without giving many examples, or offering an extended description of the various forms of photographic statements, I'll simply suggest the following as among the possibilities now in use. A photographer may make his statement in the form of an aphorism or witticism, a photographic one-liner that may be no more than a joke (in the case of Elliot Erwitt 1972, for example) or may be of considerable depth (as in the work of André Kertész 1972). He may produce slogans. He may be saying "Look at that!" in wonder at some natural phenomenon (Ansel Adams's pictures of Yosemite seem to say that), or in revulsion from some disgusting work of man (McCullin 1973). He may tell a story, or, finally, he may produce something that implicitly or explicitly offers an analysis of a person, an artifact, an activity, or a society. It stretches ordinary usage to speak of these projects as "studies," as though they were sociological research projects; but the exaggeration emphasizes, as I want to, the continuity between the two kinds of work.

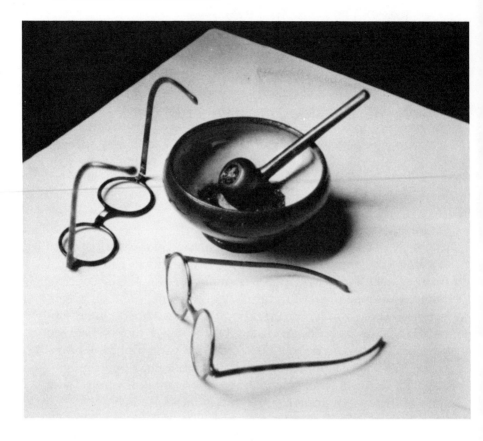

4. *André Kertész, "Mondrian's pipe and glasses, Paris," 1926. Photographers sometimes communicate their analyses in the form of witty visual aphorisms. (© Art Institute of Chicago.)*

Both photographers and sociologists have described communities. There is nothing in photography quite like such major works of social science as W. Lloyd Warner's Yankee City Series, Robert and Helen Lynd's *Middletown* and *Middletown in Transition,* and Everett C. Hughes's *French Canada in Transition.* Photographers have recently produced more modest efforts, such as Bill Owens's *Suburbia* (1973) and George Tice's *Paterson* (1972), both describing smaller communities through a hundred or so images of buildings, houses, natural features, public scenes, and (in Owens's book) family life. A number of photographers have accumulated massive numbers of negatives of one city, as Eugéne Atget (Abbott 1964) did in his attempt to record all of Paris or Berenice Abbott (1973) or Weegee

(1945), the great news photographer, did, each in their way, of New York; but only small selections from the larger body of work are available, and we usually see only a few of the images at a time.

Like sociologists, photographers have been interested in contemporary social problems: immigration, poverty, race, social unrest. In that great photographic tradition, one typically describes in order to expose evils and call for action to correct them. Lewis Hine, who called himself a sociologist, put his credo succinctly: "I want to photograph what needs to be appreciated; I want to photograph what needs to be corrected." His greatest project showed conditions of child labor in the United States in a way that is thought to have helped the passage of remedial legislation. Before the turn of the century, Jacob Riis, a reporter, photographed the slums of New York and exhibited the results in *How the Other Half Lives* (1971). I have already mentioned the photographs of rural poverty by the members of Stryker's FSA photographic unit and might add to that the collaboration of Bourke-White and Erskine Caldwell (1937) in *You Have Seen Their Faces*. Life in black ghettoes has been photographed, from the inside, by men like James Van Der Zee (DeCock and McGhee 1973) (among other things the official photographer for Marcus Garvey) and Roy de Carava (de Carava and Hughes 1967); from the outside, by Bruce Davidson (1970) and many others. Dramatic confrontations of the races make news, and many photographers have covered such stories (Hansberry 1964) and gone on to more extended explorations of the matter. W. Eugene and Aileen Smith recently published a major essay on pollution, its victims, and the politics surrounding it in Japan (1974, 1975).

Other photographic work deals with less controversial problems, in the style of the sociological ethnography. Sociologists have studied occupations and the related institutions of work, and photographers have too: Smith (1969) did major essays on a country doctor and a black midwife; Wendy Snyder (1970) has a book on Boston's produce market; and Geoff Winningham (1971) produced a book-length study of professional wrestling. Photographers have also investigated social movements, as in Paul Fusco's book (1970) on Cesar Chavez and the United Farm Workers, Marion Palfi's work on civil rights (1973), or Smith's classic essay on the Ku Klux Klan (1969). They have shared with sociologists an interest in exotic subcultures: Danny Lyon's work on motorcycle gangs (1968) and Brassaï's studies of the Parisian demimonde (Museum of Modern Art 1968), for instance.

5. Danny Lyon, "Route 12, Wisconsin," 1963. Lyon made his images of motorcycle gangs, a visual parallel to sociological studies of deviant subcultures, by participating fully in the life of the gang, as this image shows. (From The Bikeriders, *© Art Institute of Chicago.)*

Photographers have been as alert as sociologists and cultural commentators to call attention to the rise of new social classes or to forgotten groups in society. Alwyn Scott Turner's *Photographs of the Detroit People* (1970) concentrates on the working class, in front of their homes, in the parks, streets, and churches, at parades and rallies. Enrico Natali's *New American People* (1972) does something similar for the rising middle class.

Many photographers have worked at depicting the ambience of urban life in a way reminiscent of the long tradition of theorizing about cities by sociologists from Simmel to Goffman. Walker Evans's *Many Are Called* (1966) consists of portraits made on the New York subway with a hidden camera. Lee Friedlander, Garry Winogrand (Lyons 1966), and a host of others have photographed "behavior in public places," creating in the mood of their images a sense of alienation and strain, maybe even a little anomie. Euan

Duff's *How We Are* (1971) systematically covers major aspects of urban British life.

In addition to these relatively conventional analogues of socio-logical investigation, photographers have also been concerned with the discovery of cultural themes, modal personalities, social types, and the ambience of characteristic social situations. Thus, Robert Frank's enormously influential *The Americans* (1969) is in ways reminiscent both of Tocqueville's analysis of American institutions and of the analysis of cultural themes by Margaret Mead and Ruth Benedict. Frank presents photographs made in scattered places around the country, returning again and again to such themes as the flag, the automobile, restaurants, race—eventually turning those artifacts, by the weight of the associations in which he embeds them, into profound and meaningful symbols of American culture.

The long tradition of the photographic portrait has led photog-raphers to attempt, in a way sociologists have seldom tried (despite the tradition of the life-history document), to depict societies and cultures by portraits of representative types. The most systematic attempt must be August Sander's *Men without Masks* (1973), which characterizes Germany in hundreds of portraits of Germans of every social class, occupation, ethnic, regional, and religious group. Paul Strand's portraits (1971) of peasants from France, Egypt, Ghana, Morocco, Canada, and elsewhere, though surrounded by other im-ages of places and artifacts, attempt the same thing, as do Elaine Mayes's portraits (1970) from the Haight-Ashbury.

Photographers have seldom, constrained as they are by time lim-itations built into the institutions they work in, attempted longi-tudinal studies. One recent project of this kind suggests how it can happen. Larry Clark's *Tulsa* (1971) tells the story of a group of young men in that city who began using intravenous amphetamine. It follows them from an idyllic hunting-and-fishing youth into drugs, police trouble, and death. Clark was one of the group and visited his old friends periodically as the story unfolded, thus producing a unique inside view of an exotic subculture.

Photographers like to capsulize their understanding of people, situations, even countries, in one compelling image. Henri Cartier-Bresson (1952) coined the phrase "the decisive moment" to refer to that moment when things fall into place in the viewfinder in such a way as to tell the story just right. It sounds mystical, but many of his pictures accomplish just that.

MODES OF PRESENTATION

Photographers present the results of their explorations of society in a variety of ways, using varying quantities of images to make different kinds of statements. One might, at one extreme, present a single image, capturing in it all that needs to be shown about something from some point of view. Alfred Stieglitz's "The Steerage," for instance, seems to make a self-sufficient statement about the experience of European immigrants, showing both the masses Emma Lazarus wrote about, crowded onto the deck of the ship, but also a brilliantly lit gangway that seems to lead to better things. (Ironically, the ship was actually headed *east,* to Europe.)

Usually, however, photographers exploring society give us more than one striking image. They explore a topic more thoroughly, sometimes in one concentrated burst of attention and activity, sometimes (on a timetable more like that of the social scientist) over a period of a few years, sometimes as the preoccupation of a lifetime. The concentrated burst occurs when the conditions of work—a magazine assignment, for instance—make it unlikely that you will be able to return to the subject again.[1] It may occur when circumstances make a brief visit possible to an ordinarily inaccessible place (Bourke-White's visit to Russia). Photographers can seldom get the support for more long-term projects, certainly not on a routine basis, so a great deal of important work has been done in this concentrated way and many prized photographic skills consist of doing good work despite the lack of sufficient time.

Probably because of the connection with magazine work, such photographic studies typically saw publication as a photoessay. The form, pioneered in Europe, reached maturity in *Fortune* and *Life*. Bourke-White, Smith, and others developed a form in which a few to as many as thirty photographs, spread with an accompanying text over four to eight or ten pages, explored a subject in some detail, giving more space and attention to a subject than a conventional journalistic treatment allowed. Photoessays often, like good sociological studies, showed the great variety of people and situations involved in the subject under study. Of course, magazine editors played a decisive part in the selection and arrangement of the materials, and photographers frequently objected to their interference. Gene Smith resigned from *Life* over this issue.

[1]See, for instance, the quote from Bresson in Lyons (1966:41), and the descriptions of magazine work in Bourke-White (1972).

6. Alfred Stieglitz, "The Steerage," 1907. A single image can express the photographer's understanding of a situation. (© Art Institute of Chicago.)

When a photographer finds it possible to pursue a subject for a longer time—a year or more—he may accumulate sufficient material for a more extended presentation. Guggenheim grants and other fellowship and foundation funds have supported many such projects (Bruce Davidson's *East 100th Street* [1970], many of Marion Palfi's studies [e.g., 1973], Smith's work on Pittsburgh [1969]). The government has supported others: the FSA projects, Hine's exposés of child labor. Or the project may be the photographer's private affair, supported by work of an entirely different kind.

In any event, photographers who work over a more extended period accumulate a large pool of images from which they can choose those that best express their understanding of their topic. Choices are made from that pool of images for specific uses, often in consultation with or entirely by others: editors, curators, and the like. The selection so made may have more or less organization and coherence. The work of the FSA photographers, for instance, typically appears simply as a collection of variable size and made up of a variety of combinations from the entire body of work they produced.

Larger selections of work usually appear either as books, museum exhibits, or both. They may contain anywhere from thirty to four or five hundred prints. Especially when they appear as books, the projects often take on a more organized and sequential format. Such formats allow, and almost require, a more analytic stance than a simple collection, and suggest statements that overlap considerably with those found in sociological ethnography.

The function of text in a photographic book is not clear. Photographic books may contain no text at all (e.g., Davidson's *East 100th Street*). In others, photographs are presented with a brief identifying label, often no more than a place and date, as in Frank's *The Americans*. Some contain a paragraph or so of commentary on many of the images, as in Leonard Freed's *Made in Germany* (1970). Still others contain large chunks of independent text—as in Danny Lyon's *Bikeriders* (1968) or *Conversations with the Dead* (1971) or Winningham's studies of wrestlers (1971) and rodeos (1972)— taken from extant documents or tape-recorded interviews. Finally, as in Smith's essay on pollution in Minamata, the photographer may include an extensive explanatory and analytic text.

Theory in Photography

Close study of the work of social documentary photographers provokes a double reaction. At first, you find that they call attention to a wealth of detail from which an interested sociologist could develop useful ideas about whose meaning he could spin interesting speculations. A collection of photographs on the same topic—a photographic essay or book—seems to explore the subject completely. Greater familiarity leads to a scaling down of admiration. While the photographs do have those virtues, they also tend to restrict themselves to a few reiterated simple statements. Rhetorically important as a strategy of proof, the repetition leads to work that is intellectually and analytically thin.

Many sociologists and photographers will find those judgments irrelevant. Some sociologists work with equally simple ideas; but those who are responsive to the tradition of ethnographic fieldwork will want photographic explorations to provide results as rich and interesting as their own descriptions. Some photographers are content to produce a few compelling images. But many of the booklength projects just described aspire to more than that, whether they make the aspiration explicit or not. Their authors are sensitive to the currents of thought and interest in the larger cultural community, and want to do work that is thought of as more than a beautiful illustration. Photographers and sociologists who don't share these traditions and sensitivities will find what follows of little use.

The problem, then, is why photographic exploration of society is so often intellectually thin. A subsidiary question of interest to photographers and to sociologists who may take a photographic approach to their work is: what can be done to make that work intellectually denser?

The answer to these questions lies in understanding the role of theory in making photographs of social phenomena. Most sociologists accept the folk notion that the camera records objectively what is there for it to record, no matter what the ideas of the person who pushes the button. Laymen may believe this, but photographers know better. To be sure, something *real* has to emit light rays in order to produce an image on film or paper, and whatever is real that is emitting light rays where they can go through the lens will make some kind of image. That constraint exists, so that John Collier, Jr., is right to say that "the camera constantly trips up the artist by loyally going on being a recorder of reality" (Friends of Photography 1972:49).

Nevertheless, the photographer exerts enormous control over the final image and the information and message it contains. The choice of film, development and paper, of lens and camera, of exposure and framing, of moment and relation with subjects—all of these, directly under the photographer's control, shape the end product.

The way he controls it—what he decides to make it into—depends in the first instance on professional traditions and conditions of work. The kind of photograph he has learned to value and the possibilities for making them provided by the institutions he works in influence his decisions in general. Thus, for example, the short time-periods magazine editors allotted to projects meant that photographers could not produce pictures that require lengthy acquaintance with the subject. Newspaper photographers do not, as a rule, make pictures that contain large blurred areas, because editors prefer pictures sharp enough to look good in newspaper reproduction (Rosenblum 1978).

A second influence on the image the photographer produces is his theory about what he is looking at, his understanding of what he is investigating. Saul Warkov says: "The camera is a wonderful mechanism. It will reproduce, exactly, what is going on inside of your head." That is, it will make the picture (given a modicum of technique) look just the way the photographer thinks it should look. Think of it this way: as you look through the viewfinder you wait until what you see "looks right," until the composition and the moment make sense, until you see something that corresponds to your conception of what's going on. Similarly, when prior to making the exposure you choose a lens and film, an f-stop and a shutter speed, you do so with the same considerations in mind. If you make exposures that look some other way than what makes sense to you, you probably will not choose them for printing or exhibition. Thus, what you expect to see and what, even if you did not expect it, you can understand and make sense of—your theory— shape the images you finally produce.

Since the skilled photographer can make the image look as he wants it to, and knows he can, photographers should be aware of the social content of their photographs and be able to talk about it at length. As a rule, they are not. One of the foremost recorders of the urban scene, Lee Friedlander, asked to verbalize the explicit social criticism his pictures seem to make, answered by saying, "I was taught that one picture was worth a thousand words, weren't you?" (Friends of Photography 1972:10). (And the recorder of the exchange adds that the audience of photographers and photography buffs burst into applause.) It is as though the criticism is there, but the photographer doesn't want to verbalize it directly, preferring to rely on intuition. Friedlander's attitude, while not universal, is very common.

If the above remarks are accurate, then when social documentary photography is not analytically dense the reason may be that photographers use theories that are overly simple. They do not acquire a deep, differentiated, and sophisticated knowledge of the people and activities they investigate. Conversely, when their work gives a satisfyingly complex understanding of a subject, it is because they have acquired a sufficiently elaborate theory to alert them to the visual manifestations of that complexity. In short, the way to change and improve photographic images lies less in technical considerations than in improving your comprehension of what you are photographing—your theory. For photographic projects concerned with exploring society it means learning to understand society better. Insofar as sociology possesses some understanding of society (a very large if), then a knowledge of sociology, its theories, and the way they can be applied to specific situations might improve the work of both photographers and photographic sociologists.

A sociological theory, whether large-scale abstract theory or a specific theory about some empirical phenomenon, is a set of ideas with which you can make sense of a situation while you photograph it. The theory tells you when an image contains information of value, when it communicates something worth communicating. It furnishes the criteria by which worthwhile data and statements can be separated from those that contain nothing of value, that do not increase our knowledge of society.

The work of social documentary photographers suffers then from its failure to use explicit theories, such as might be found in social science. This does not, of course, mean that their work embodies no theory at all. If they had no theory, they would have no basis on which to make the choices through which they produce their images. They have a theory, one which, because it is not explicit, is not available to them for conscious use, criticism, or development. Since they do not make explicit use of a theory designed to explore the phenomena they are interested in, they end up relying implicitly on some other kind of theory. The arguments that have attended the publication of some of the major works of obvious social import (e.g., Davidson's *East 100th Street*) indicate that the theories photographers rely on are, not surprisingly, lay theories, the commonplaces of everyday life in the intellectual and artistic circles they move in. Since photographers, for all their public inarticulateness, tend to be in touch (via their connections in journalism and art, and increasingly, through their location in academia), with contem-

244/Doing Things Together

porary cultural currents, they use the ideas and attitudes that are making the rounds in order to organize their own seeing.

That is probably overly harsh, since often enough photographers contribute images that help to shape those attitudes. Nevertheless, photographs of Harlem residents tend to revolve around such ideas as "Look how these people suffer" and "Look how noble these people are in the face of their suffering" (it might be argued that the latter was the twist Davidson relied on for the originality of his work). It is not that these things are incorrect or that for any reason they should not be said. But they are not sufficiently complex to sustain the weight of a real exploration of society, which will inevitably show that things are more complicated. In fact, the complications provide a great deal of the interest and points of active growth for social science thinking.

Training in social science, which presumably fills your head with social science theories, will not necessarily improve the social science content of your photographs. Knowledge does not automatically shape what you do, but works only when it is deliberately put to work, when it is consciously brought into play. Jay Ruby (1972) argues that the pictures anthropologists take in the field are really vacation pictures, no different from the ones they take on any other vacation or that nonanthropologist vacationers take, focusing on what seems exotic and out of the way. Anthropological thinking does not affect the pictures. Photographic sophistication does. An unsophisticated photographer will produce a lot of isolated images while a sophisticated one will go after sequences of action.

Sociologists are probably like anthropologists. As they become more photographically sophisticated they will produce more interesting images, but not necessarily ones that have sociological content. Similarly, giving photographers a course in sociology or a list of suggested readings will not make their pictures sociologically more sophisticated. Learning some of what sociologists know will be necessary for improving the sociological content of their work, but it will not be sufficient.

How can sociological ideas and theory be brought to bear, in a practical way, on photographic explorations of society? The example of sociological fieldwork, as that has been described by a number of writers (e.g., Lofland 1970; Schatzman and Strauss 1973), provides a useful model in the procedure of sequential analysis. I'm not referring to anything very esoteric, just to the procedure which allows you to make use of what you learn one day in your data-gathering the next day.

In some social science and photographic styles of work, you defer analysis until all the materials have been gathered. In a large-scale survey or experiment, the researcher can seldom change the way he gathers his data once he has begun; the inability to apply knowledge gained to the gaining of more knowledge is the price of standardized precision. (To be sure, one can apply the lessons of one survey or experiment to the next one, and workers in these styles usually do.) Photographers' failure to apply the lessons they learn at the beginning of a project to its later phases is more likely due to the photojournalistic emphasis on short intense trips to places one would not otherwise ordinarily be in, or getting the shooting done as rapidly as possible to cut down on expenses, and the great value placed on personal intuition, all of which have been elevated in some versions of photographic work to operating norms. (Like sociologists, photographers of course bring what they have learned in previous projects to bear on the next one.) Working in this style, photographers take advantage of their temporary presence in a situation to shoot a great deal, waiting until they have left the field to develop film, make contact sheets, and edit their results.

Fieldworkers work differently, in a way immediately adaptable to photographic projects. As they write up the descriptions and verbatim accounts that constitute their field notes, they simultaneously or shortly thereafter make preliminary analyses of that information (Lofland 1970; Schatzman and Strauss 1973). What is there in what they have recorded that they don't understand? How can they find out more about it? What ideas does it suggest about the organization they are studying and the people's experience in it? What patterns of interaction, of cause and effect, of interrelationship are suggested by what they now know? If the rest of what they observe is like this, what generalizations will they be able to make? Where should they look to find evidence that these preliminary ideas are wrong (or right)? In short, they develop tentative hypotheses about the object of their study, setting it in a context of theories and other data, and then orient their next day's observations and interviews along the lines suggested by the analysis. They try out different observable indicators of various sociological concepts. The concepts, embedded in theories, suggest links with other concepts and hence with other events observable in the situation, which can then be searched for, to provide both confirming and disconfirming evidence relevant to these provisional ideas. The analysis is continuous and contemporaneous with the data-gathering.

The photographer can do the same thing. To do so requires a longer time perspective than many photographic projects envision: certainly as much as the two years Davidson spent in Harlem, probably more than the seven months Winningham spent with wrestlers, or the couple of weeks that are even more common. To spend that much time requires establishing relationships with the people being photographed of a different order than those that photojournalists usually establish; it requires something akin to the research bargain sociologists make with the people they study. It means that the photographer has to find some way to support the long-term effort he is going to undertake.

Supposing that all this has been taken care of, let us consider how a sociologist photographer might go about such a sequentially organized project. He could begin by shooting almost anything he sees in the situation (the community, organization, or group), trying to cover whatever seems in a commonsense way to be worth looking at. The result is likely to be incoherent, visually as well as cognitively. The investigator will be learning how to work in the spatial arrangements and light situations in which what he is studying occurs. He will also be learning what is occurring, who the people are, what they are doing, why they are doing it. He learns the first by intensive study of his contact sheets and work prints; he should make plenty of work prints, in order to have something to study and hypothesize about. He learns the second in part in the same way. He looks at his work prints in a careful, detailed way, asking who all those people are and what they are up to. (Photographers tend to be satisfied with quick answers to these questions, and I think sociologists who would otherwise know better are just as likely to do that when they start working with a camera.) He should pay careful attention to details that don't make sense. For example, if people seem to be dressed in several distinctive ways, it pays to find out what status differences that marks, and then to ask in what other ways those groups differ. If people get into an argument which makes for a visually exciting image, it pays to find out why they are arguing. What is worth arguing about in that organization? What breach of expectations led to this argument? Do those circumstances occur frequently? If not, why not? Bourke-White, on photographing Gandhi, notes: "If you want to photograph a man

7. *Margaret Bourke-White, "Gandhi Spinning," 1946. Photographers make good images when they understand the social meaning of what they photograph. (© Art Institute of Chicago.)*

spinning, give some thought to why he spins. Understanding is as important for a photographer as the equipment he uses. In the case of Gandhi, the spinning wheel is laden with meaning. For millions of Indians, it was the symbol of their fight for independence" (1972:26).

The photographer pursues these questions with his camera, but also by asking people about what he has seen and by observing closely and listening carefully as the everyday activities of the group go on around him. He should not keep away from the people he is working with, shooting from a distance with a long lens, but rather should get up close and establish a working relationship with them, such that they expect him to be there and accept that he has some sort of right to be there which he will probably exercise most of the time. (Aside from the visual considerations, photographers doing this kind of research might want to use a wide-angle lens, perhaps 35mm, as standard equipment, because it will force them up close where they ought to be.)

The photographer can also get more data by showing people the pictures he has already taken. He probably will have no choice, because people will want to see what he's up to. This will give him the chance to use the photo elicitation technique Collier (1967) describes so well: showing the pictures to people who know the situations under study and letting them talk about them, answer questions, suggest other things that need to be photographed, and so on.

If the photographer has some sociological ideas available, he can apply them to these more or less commonsense questions and answers. Much of what I've described so far is only what any reasonably curious person might want to know. Nevertheless, basic sociological theory is involved, one compatible with most varieties of sociology in current use. Let me put it in the form of a list of questions to be answered in the field, cautioning that the answers don't come all at once, but through a process of progressive refinement and constant testing against new information. This formulation of the questions a sociological-photographic study could usefully orient itself to is not original; it has been heavily influenced by Everett Hughes (1971).

1. What are the different kinds of people in the situation? They may or may not look different; they will certainly be called by different names.
2. What expectations does each kind of person—members of each status group—have about how members of other groups ought to behave? What are the recurring situations around which such expectations grow up?
3. What are the typical breaches of those expectations? What kinds of gripes and complaints do people have? (A complaint is a sign of a violated expectation; "He's supposed to do X and he hasn't.")
4. What happens when expectations are violated? What can people do to those who do the violating? Is there a standard way of settling these conflicts?

These questions put in a commonsense way ideas integral to almost any sociological analysis. Question 1 refers to what a sociologist might call status groups; 2 to norms, rules, or common understandings; 3 to deviance or rule violations; 4 to sanctions and conflict resolution. The advantage of the translation is that these concepts are linked in such a way that if you identify something you have seen as an instance of one of them you then know that you ought to look for other things that will embody the ideas it is connected to in the theory. If, for instance, you see someone reward or punish someone else, the theory directs you to look for the expectations that have been violated in this case, and for the status groups to whom those expectations apply. Anyone exploring society photographically can ask these questions, both visually and verbally. Each day's data provide some provisional answers and some new questions, both discovered by careful inspection and analysis of the material.

The photographic investigator can supplement his visual material with a running verbal record. Depending on his intentions, this might be a full set of field notes such as a sociologist doing a conventional field study would keep, complete with verbatim conversations, or a record of a few outstanding thoughts and remarks. Some photographers (e.g., Winningham and Lyon) have tape-recorded interviews with the people they photograph. Some (e.g., Owens) have recorded the responses of people to their photographs.

As the work progresses the photographer will be alert for visual embodiments of his ideas, for images that contain and communicate the understanding he is developing. That doesn't mean that he will let his theories dominate his vision, especially at the moment of shooting, but rather that his theories will inform his vision and influence what he finds interesting and worth making pictures of. His theories will help him to photograph what he might otherwise have ignored. Simultaneously he will let what he finds in his photographs direct his theory-building, the pictures and ideas becoming closer and closer approximations of one another. Like the sociological fieldworker, who finds much of his later understanding latent in his early data (Geer 1964), he will probably find that his early contact sheets, as he looks back through them, contain the basic ideas that now need to be stated more precisely.

The photographer, like the sociologist who builds more and more comprehensive models of what he is studying (Diesing 1971), will arrange the visual material into the patterns and sequences that are the visual analogue of propositions and causal statements. He will consider the problems of convincing other people that his under-

standing is not idiosyncratic but rather represents a believable like-
ness of that aspect of the world he has chosen to explore, a reasonable answer to the questions he has asked about it.

Some Common Problems

Whether they start as sociologists or photographers, anyone who
undertakes the kind of project I have just described will run into
certain problems, which are common both in being frequent and
ubiquitous and in being shared by the two vocations. In some cases,
sociologists have ways of dealing with problems that photographers
might find useful; in others, the way photographers deal with those
problems will throw a new light on sociologists' troubles.

TRUTH AND PROOF

Insofar as a photograph or group of them purports to be "true,"
the particular meaning of that ambiguous claim needs to be specified. Once we know the kind of truth a picture claims, we can
assess how far we accept the claim and how much of the statement
it makes we want to believe.

Photographs (barring those that have been obviously manipulated to produce multiple images and the like) minimally claim to
be true in that what they show actually existed in front of the camera
for at least the time necessary to make the exposure. Photographs
in the social documentary style claim more than that, presenting
themselves as pictures of something that was not done just for the
photographer's benefit, but rather as something that occurs routinely as part of the ordinary course of events. Or the photograph
suggests that what we see is, if not ordinary, characteristic in some
deeper sense, portraying some essential feature of the phenomenon
photographed. When people speak of a photograph having "captured" something, they generally mean that it displays some such
characteristic feature. Frequently, though not always, the photograph suggests that what it shows, while characteristic, is ordinarily
hidden from view, so that we might never know its particular truth
if the photographer did not show it to us.

Many photographers make no such claims, at least explicitly,
preferring to avoid the responsibilities that accompany the claims
by describing their pictures as containing only the truth of "how
it felt to me." This makes the photograph the visual analogue of
something like a lyric poem, its author's sole responsibility to have

rendered honestly his own feelings and responses. Such work can be interesting and moving; we often feel that, because we trust and feel some empathy with the lyricist's sensibility, we have learned something about the world from his response to it. The lyric poem or photograph need not give us that bonus, however, and its maker needn't satisfy any requirements of truth or objectivity.

Photographers frequently find themselves troubled because, after they have shown us some way of seeing a part of society, someone else accuses them of not having told the truth. Perhaps the photographs are not what they claim to be: though they appear to be "candid" portrayals of everyday events, the people or objects in the picture never really appeared that way, and only did so at the time of the photograph because the photographer posed them (as in the case of the flag-raising at Iwo Jima or the controversy over Arthur Rothstein's picture of a skull on parched Dust Bowl earth [Hurley 1972:86–92], where opponents said he had made an old skull appear to be the product of the recent drought). Photographers often feel the accusation that they set up a shot, rather than photographing something that occurred naturally, to be damaging. When they do, they reveal the degree to which they are claiming something more than subjective truth for their work.

In a commonsense way, people make judgments about that threat to the validity of a photograph (to paraphrase Donald Campbell's useful notion of the threat to the validity of a hypothesis). We may base the judgment on evidence contained in the photograph, recognizing that we have seen similar things elsewhere, so that their existence is not in question; the photographer has simply called our attention to something we already know. The photograph may have been made in a place so public and accessible to independent checks that we reason the photographer would not fake something whose phoniness could so easily be discovered. We may rely on the established reputation of the journal the photograph appears in, being sure that *Life* would not risk its reputation for accuracy just for the sake of this one picture. How we establish the credibility of a photograph is a problem in commonsense reasoning I won't pursue further here.

When the validity of the individual photographs is not in doubt, a more serious question about the "truth" of a presentation remains. Couldn't someone else have photographed the same people, places, or events and produced a quite different statement about that social reality? Any collection of photographs is a selection from a much larger population of photographs that have been or could be taken, and the answer to the question is necessarily yes, that reality could have been presented in another way. I don't know why photographers are as sensitive as they are about this, since they have a simple counter available to the accusation of "bias." The answer lies in distinguishing between the statement that X is true about something and the statement that X is all that is true about something. Thus, Neal Slavin's photographs of Portugal (1972) prompted one critic to complain that he couldn't believe that, as this portfolio suggested, no one ever smiled in Portugal. If photographs indicate that other phenomena, even though not central to the statement being made, exist, much of this difficulty could be avoided. Sociologists typically plaster their work with such caveats. Statements so qualified lose something in dramatic impact, but they gain in credibility over the long run; you can choose which you'd like, but you can seldom have both.

SAMPLING

Another version of the same problem arises when, having assured ourselves that the photographs are valid and that, while they claim to be true, they do not claim to be the whole truth, we ask: if we had gathered our data at some other time, or from some other part of the universe our assertion applies to, would we get essentially the same result? Put it another way: if I know what I do about these people and places at this time, what else can I be reasonably sure I know about? Sampling problems have two aspects: (1) what procedures shall I follow to maximize the generality of my findings? and (2) how can I convince others that my findings have that generality? The first question is procedural, the second rhetorical. Social scientists often deal with the two questions simultaneously. They use a certified technique whose logic is well known; by asserting that the appropriate procedure has been used, they assure readers that their conclusions follow logically. For photographers, the two questions more frequently arise separately.

Social scientists deal with threats to the generality of their propositions by a variety of sampling techniques. If they are concerned with whether certain quantitative distributions or relationships found among those they have observed approximate those in the larger universe from which their observations were drawn, they may use some version of probability sampling. If they want to make sure they have covered all the major aspects of a group's activities or of a social organization, they may rely on what Barney Glaser and Anselm Strauss (1967) have called theoretical sampling, choosing units for observation because some theory suggests they would be strategic.

Photographers are seldom concerned with quantitative generalizations, or with covering some theoretical map adequately. But they often present their material in a way that suggests they believe that what they show us applies to a far wider area and population than the one they have covered, that were we to look at a different part of the same whole, we would see more of the same. I don't know what procedures photographers use to assure themselves about these matters. Sociological fieldworkers use some simple procedures that would serve the double function of maximizing generality and thus responding to such queries, and simultaneously enlarging the possibility of getting unanticipated and possibly exciting material (both sociologically and visually). Following some of these suggestions might produce a lot of dull pictures, but so do most procedures; exciting and informative photographs are always hard to come by.

Fieldworkers may use crude time-sampling devices: checking up on someone or someplace every half-hour, or on different days of the week, or different times of the year. Some avoid "leaving things out" by attaching themselves to one person at a time and following that person through his entire daily (and nightly) round. They may ask people under study who else they ought to talk to or observe. As they become aware of categories or situations that deserve special study, they can systematically choose some to observe or they can observe all of them. Fieldworkers follow the discipline of recording everything they see and hear while making these observations.

Photographers could do all of these things, but they would need to observe some discipline equivalent to incorporating everything into the field notes, for a photographer's data do not exist unless they expose some film. In following someone around for a day, they might for instance adopt some such convention as exposing at least one roll of film every hour or so, adapting the time period to the character of what they were observing. They would thus avoid waiting until "something interesting" happened, and increase the chance that things that don't as yet fit into the photographer's developing understanding would nevertheless get into the record. They might similarly photograph certain activities or places on some schedule that interferes with their tendency not to shoot what does not seem visually interesting. Any theory of the kind discussed earlier would likewise direct the photographer to things his intuition and visual sense might not call to his attention. Remember that theory is itself a sampling device, specifying what must be incorporated into a full description.

Shooting what seems interesting usually satisfies the photographer's need for a method. However, they often realize, if they are sensitive to their own work, that they are producing essentially the same pictures in a variety of settings, because their notion of what is visually interesting has become divorced from the social reality they are working in. If they are not sensitive to that possibility, others might point it out. A technique that breaks up their established visual habits guards against this. In addition, photographers often find that they are slow to discover and shoot things they later realize they need for a more complete visual understanding. The same techniques of randomized and theoretically informed sampling may help. The object of all this is not to turn photographers into sociologists or enslave them in mad sociological rituals, but rather to suggest how sociological tricks might solve problems of photographic exploration.

Sociologists try to convince their readers that generalizations from findings are legitimate by indicating that they have used a conventionally approved technique. The scientific community has already inspected the logic of that technique, so it is sufficient to indicate that it has been appropriately used. Readers who accept that convention are automatically convinced.

No photographer uses such standardized devices, and I'm sure that none would be interested in pursuing such techniques as probability sampling. They have their own devices, however, worth exploring because these produce conviction in the viewers of photographic work similar to that produced by sampling designs in sociological readers. Since sociological procedures are, to quote Campbell again, "radically under-justified," it is worth considering photographers' methods, even though they may appear even more under-justified to sociological readers.

The chief device photographers use is to identify their photographs by place and sometimes by date. The photographs in Frank's *The Americans* are identified simply by a generic organizational type and a town: "Bar—Gallup, New Mexico," "Elevator—Miami Beach," "Bank—Houston, Texas." Dennis Stock's *California Trip* (1970) identifies the individual images by town and/or neighborhood:

"Sunset Strip," or "North Beach, San Francisco." These labels, coupled with a reiteration of themes, so that one sees the same kind of place or thing or person from half a dozen widely scattered places in the country, imply the conclusion that if you can find it in that many places, it is really very widespread. Thus, when Frank shows you luncheonettes, diners, and coffee shops from Indianapolis, Detroit, San Francisco, Hollywood, Butte, and Columbia, South Carolina, all of which share a gritty plastic impersonality, you are prepared to accept that image as something that must be incorporated into your view of American culture. The logic of this deserves further analysis, since it is convincing (there are other such devices which need to be described and analyzed).

REACTIVITY

The problem of the reactivity of data-gathering procedures is very similar in ethnographic and photographic work. Does the sample of behavior observed and recorded accurately reflect how people ordinarily act or is it largely a response to the observer's presence and activities? Both sociologists and photographers frequently deal with this by cultivating the art of being unobtrusive. Many people know how to manipulate their bodies and expressions so that, in the absence of any reason to pay special attention to them, the people they are observing ignore them; how they actually do this is not explicitly known, and deserves investigation. It is probably easier to be unobtrusive in public places where you are not known as an investigator, and it may or may not be easier if you are carrying a camera. In many situations carrying a camera validates your right to be there; as a tourist, as a member of the group recording the scene for their purposes, or as a representative of the media. Under many circumstances, observing or photographing is commonplace and expected; many other people are doing it. Your presence does not change anyone's behavior since observers and photographers are part of the situation. You should, of course, include their presence in your observations and photographs.

In many situations the people being observed are engaged in activities of considerable importance to them and cannot change what they are doing for an observer's benefit even if they would like to. Reactivity depends on the freedom of those observed to respond to the observer's (or photographer's) presence. If they are enmeshed in the constraints of the social structure in which they carry on their normal activities, they will have to carry on as they

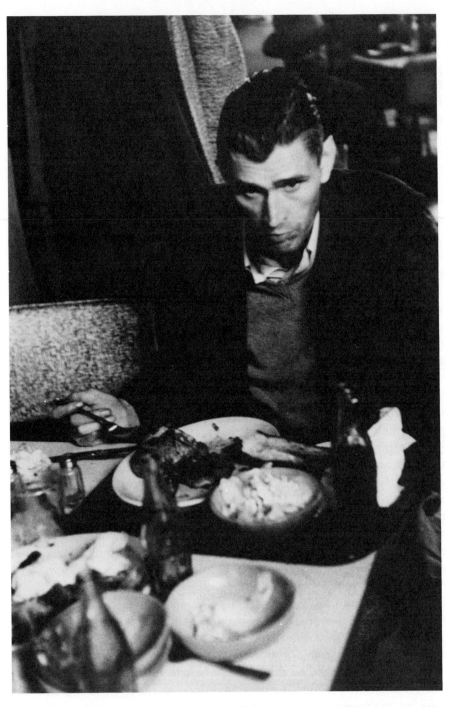

*8a and b. Robert Frank, "Cafeteria, San Francisco" (above) and "Drug Store, Detroit,"
1958 (right). By making photographs embodying the same observation—in this case,*

*that Americans eat in an uncivilized way—in a number of places, Frank demonstrated
the generality of his observations.* (*From* The Americans, © *Art Institute of Chicago.*)

ordinarily do for whatever reasons cause them to do that ordinarily (Becker 1970d). They may be well aware that they are being observed or photographed, but not be free to change what they do. Photographers routinely make use of this possibility. I once watched Michael Alexander photograph a woman fighting with her small child in a playground. Alexander was practically on top of her, but the child was kicking and screaming and, though she had no idea who he was, she felt she had no choice but to deal with her child despite the unwelcome recording going on.

A third solution recognizes that the reactivity often reflects fears about what will be done with the information or photographs. If the observer gives evidence that these will not be used to harm the people he is observing, they may decide to ignore him, or to cooperate, for instance, by pointing out things that need to be investigated or photographed, or by keeping him up to date on things that have happened while he was not around.

Photographers make use of a fourth possibility that sociologists seldom employ, though it is the chief element in studies of experimenter bias and similar problems. They encourage reactivity and make it the basis of their exploration of people and events. The photographs become a record of their relationship with the people they photograph, and the reaction of the people to being photographed becomes the chief evidence used in analyzing them. Sociologists make use of this possibility when they look at the difficulties of gaining access as revelatory of the social structure to which access is sought (e.g., Gardner and Whyte 1946).

GETTING ACCESS

Sociologists have increasingly worried about the conditions under which they will be allowed to gather data and then make their research results public. Science requires that data and operations be open to public inspection and independent verification. Unconstrained, scientists would (and should) make all their data public. But they are constrained by both legal and moral considerations from doing so, and ordinarily take substantial precautions to avoid harming anyone by revealing who furnished information for or are the subjects of research. They may simply change the names of people, organizations, and places, or use elaborate coding procedures to preserve the anonymity of survey respondents.

People sociologists write about seldom sue them (though my colleagues and I were once threatened with a libel action by the administrator of an organization we studied). Consequently, they worry more about ethical than legal problems. Though a substantial literature debating these problems has grown up, the situation is confused, and sociologists do not agree on procedures or relevant ethical principles. They tend to agree on generalities—"We should not do harm to the subjects of our research"—but not on the application of such crucial terms as "harm." To take one example: Are organizations, especially such public ones as governmental agencies or schools, entitled to the same privacy as individuals, or is not social science research part of the public review to which they are necessarily subject? Another: Where do you draw the line between inconvenience or embarrassment and substantial harm?

Photographers have been considerably more interested in legal problems. When they make simplified analyses of the problems they explore, they can take an equally simplified view of the ethical problems. Having no trouble telling the good guys from the bad guys, they have not had to worry so much about ethical questions. If their work hurts the bad guys on behalf of the good guys—well, that was the point. But they have had to worry about being sued for invasion of privacy and for libel. The law here seems to be as ambiguous as the ethical standards of sociologists. Photographers know they can be sued and often take the ritual precaution of having people sign standard release forms, though these may not be as useful as supposed.[2] They also try to maintain friendly relations with the people they photograph, in much the same spirit as the advice I heard given to medical students: if you are good friends with your patients they won't sue you for malpractice. Alternatively, they rely on this being a large, differentiated society in which it is relatively unlikely that anyone will see the picture of him you put in a book or exhibit.

Everett Hughes's idea of the research bargain (1971) provides the terms for a useful comparison. What bargain do investigator and investigated make? In both photographic and sociological investigations, it is fair to say, the people investigated probably do not know what they are getting into. They may give their consent, but it is not an informed consent. From an ethical and perhaps a legal point of view, the bargain is not fully valid. Sociologists are generally very cautious about this, at least in public discussions, and

[2]Boccioletti (1972) deals with a number of common photographic, legal problems and refers to *Photography and the Law* by G. Chernoff and H. Sarbin (Amphoto: n.d.), which I have not seen.

I think they might consider seriously a view more common among photographers: people can and should take care of their own interests, and once the investigator has honestly described his intentions he has fulfilled his obligations. I don't propose that we accept this view uncritically, but we might think hard about why we should not. Journalists have long operated with a different ethic, and there is perhaps as much reason to adopt their practice as that of physicians, which has tended to be the one sociologists orient themselves to.

Photographers have probably taken a tougher line because they can't use some of the devices sociologists do. Unless you block out faces and other identifying marks, everyone in a photograph is identifiable and there is no possibility of preserving anonymity. That is the strength of the medium, and no one would sacrifice it for ethical considerations. The strength of photographic work may not depend on the people and organizations studied being identified specifically, since the implicit argument is that what you see is characteristic of a large class; so the people in the individual prints are in effect anonymous, though they might be known to some who see the pictures and others could conceivably find out who they are if it seemed important. (But see Alwyn Scott Turner's *Photographs of the Detroit People*, in which a great many people photographed are not only named but their approximate addresses are given, too.)

The other aspect of the photographer's situation that leads him not to worry so much about ethical considerations is that, when he is not photographing anonymous people who will be made to stand for some more general aspect of the human condition, he is usually photographing people who, because they are public figures, expect to be photographed and only complain when it is grotesquely overdone, as in the case of Jacqueline Onassis. These people epitomize the rationale I mentioned earlier: perfectly capable of defending their own interests, they accept their photographic burden as one of the costs of being a public figure, whether they like it or not.

Both these strategies offer-possibilities for social researchers. Sociologists frequently disguise names of people and organizations without thinking why, and might often be able to identify them, particularly when what they have said or done is no more than ordinarily discreditable and when (as is inevitable in social research) a long time elapses between getting the information and putting it into print. Studs Terkel has done that in his books on Chicago and on the Depression to good effect and without doing anyone harm.

Similarly, we might treat public figures as just that, justifying our observations, interviews, and quotations on the grounds that we are entitled to them as citizens and need no special social science warrant for our actions. A good example appears in a study by a combined legal and social science research staff of public access to information (Northwestern University Law Review 1973). As part of an elaborate experiment, researchers visited a number of public offices in search of information to which their access was guaranteed by law. Information holders often refused them or evaded their requests with transparent devices; the researchers, in providing evidence for their conclusions, described their encounters with public officials, *identified by name and office*. I see no reason why that device should not be used more often than it is.

CONCEPTS AND INDICATORS, OR IDEAS AND IMAGES

Sociologists tend to deal in large, abstract ideas and move from them (if they do) to specific observable phenomena that can be seen as embodiments, indicators, or indices of those ideas. Photographers, conversely, work with specific images and move from them (if they do) to somewhat larger ideas. Both movements involve the same operation of connecting an idea with something observable, but where you start makes a difference. Granting, and even insisting as I already have, on the conceptual element in photographs, it still is quite different to start with something immediately observed and try to bend ideas to fit it than to start with an idea and try to find or create something observable that embodies it. Sociologists have something to learn from photography's inextricable connection with specific imagery.

Many sociological concepts, whose meaning seems intuitively clear, would be very hard to portray visually. Consider the notion of status integration. Defined as a congruence (or lack of it) between two or more indicators of social rank (education and income, for instance), its human meaning seems obvious. A man who made $100,000 a year but had never finished grade school would, we can imagine, have troubles another man with the same income who had completed college would never know. Does it have a visual counterpart? Can we imagine what a person in either of those states would look like, what we might see him doing, what his possessions and environment would consist of? The answer, to both questions, is probably no.

We cannot imagine the visual counterpart of status integration, I think, because the concept has been defined by the rules for calculating a status integration score from numerical indicators of specific ranks. The human meaning of the concept has been left to be evoked intuitively from the label applied to the results of that operation. As a result, no one can be sure what an instance of status integration would look like and thus no one can photograph it.

Obviously, every sociological idea need not be connectable to a visual image to be valid or useful. On the other hand, consider this. Some sociologists describe a basic problem of empirical research as one of finding empirical indicators (things observable in real life) to measure a concept whose meaning they have already decided. A sizable literature discusses the logic by which the two can be defensibly connected. But, as the example of status integration suggests, a third element is involved: the basic imagery we intuitively supply to fill out the meaning of an abstract concept operationally defined. We seldom consider the logic by which we connect concepts and indicators to that basic imagery, or the procedures by which we can develop that imagery explicitly and connect it defensibly to concepts and indicators. While, to repeat, sociological ideas needn't evoke a clear visual image to be defensible, considering the processes by which photographic imagery arises may help us understand what is involved.

The gap that develops between concept and indicator, on the one hand, and basic underlying imagery, on the other, is nicely illustrated by a device Blanche Geer uses in teaching fieldwork to graduate students. They are given to talking in rather grand theoretical terms when asked to describe what they have seen, and she counters this by asking if any of them have observed a status (or norm or social structure or whatever). When someone claims to have observed such a thing, she asks what it looked like, what it said, how it acted. She thus hopes to make students understand that such terms are shorthand for a class of observable phenomena that can be described, and have no more reality or meaning than they get from the collection of phenomena so described and the resemblances among them.

The imagery underlying a sociological concept implies, if it does not state explicitly, a picture of people acting together. It may picture them engaged in familiar forms of social interaction, or it may imply a more mechanistic vision (as when people are conceptualized as members of an aggregate rather than an interactive group, in which case the imagery may be of something like social molecules engaged in an analogue of Brownian movement). In either case, the concept and its indicators evoke (even when they use the language of operationally defined variables) an image of social life. The fidelity of that imagery to the realities of social life is, as Herbert Blumer (1969) has emphasized, an important issue in assessing the utility of a concept.

When the imagery underlying a concept is explicit, it can more easily be criticized and revised. Émile Durkheim (1951), for example, gives very explicit and vivid descriptions of the collective and individual states which he defines abstractly as embodying the theoretically defined quality of anomie. We can easily judge for ourselves how well the abstract concept and the empirical indicators mesh with the imagery. Where the underlying imagery is left implicit, the reader invents his own and the critical assessment of that relationship tends not to occur.

We might expect, as a result, more dispute over the meaning of theoretical concepts than there is, because differing underlying images lead to a different understanding of a concept's meaning, use, and appropriate measure. One reason for the lack of dispute is the sociologist's tendency to discuss concepts in a purely verbal and logical way divorced from any close relation to empirical materials. When they do that they play on the underlying imagery without taking responsibility for it. Several generations of psychologists have played that game with the concept of intelligence, defining it operationally, saying "Well, let's call it X" when its validity was questioned, but never calling it X because they would then lose the meaning imparted by the imagery associated with "intelligence." (They thus paved the way for the excesses of Jensen, Herrnstein, and Shockley.) If we cannot imagine or discover a visual image that embodies our understanding of a concept, we might take that as a warning that the concept is not explicitly related to its underlying imagery. Looking for an appropriate visual image might help clarify the relationship.

Photographers, of course, do not have this problem. They work in the opposite direction, needing to find concepts that adequately convey what is important in what they give us to see, the explicit conceptualization working for both photographers and viewers to provide a framework for their joint work of making sense of what they see. I've already discussed how the failure to use explicit concepts and theories hampers the development of photographic analyses and how sociological ideas might be brought to bear on the development of photographic projects. What photographers do very well, however, is to refine over a period of time the image they create of something. They may photograph people, places, and situations again and again, seeking to make the resulting image express more clearly, concisely, and unambiguously their basic understanding of those things. They tend to approach this task visually, stripping away extraneous elements so that the statement the image makes communicates its substance efficiently and emphatically to the viewer.

Sociologists might well work at the job of continuously refining not only their concepts and measures but also their basic imagery, relying on that refinement more than they have to to clear up theoretical and technical muddles. Blumer has often recommended something like this, though he hasn't been very explicit about what is involved, so his advice sounds mystical. I don't at this time have any less mystical and more specific suggestions. The basic idea, however, is to clarify how you think things really are, using the imagery you develop as a touchstone against which to test concepts and indicators as these develop.

BOUNDARIES, LIMITS, AND FRAMING

No intellectual or artistic enterprise can include everything. Scientific studies tend to make clear that they have a limited area of responsibility, that they are only studying *these* phenomena, *this* area, the relationship between *these* variables and *those*; while other things may be important too, they will be left out, since you can't study everything at once. Scientists often contrast their practice in this respect with that of artists or novelists whom they caricature as striving to include "everything" in their works, as though most artists were superrealists or as though even superrealists actually included "everything" or thought they did. In fact, artists leave things out too. But their selectivity is more conscious, and they often use as an artistic resource the necessity to choose between what will be included and excluded. They make the selection itself an artistic act. They rely on the viewer's tendency to supply in imagination what is not present to make allusion work in the total statement, so that what lies beyond the frame becomes an integral part of the work. For photographers, "framing"—choosing what will go inside the bright line of the viewfinder—is one of the key decisions.

The choice of the boundaries of a study has an enormous effect on the results. For social science, it has among other things a strong political effect. What we choose not to study becomes a given in our research. We rule out the possibility of taking its variations into account (though we can of course focus on them in some other study, so the tendency I am talking about is only a tendency, not a rigid constraint). We may thus come to regard what we choose to see as fixed as being in fact unchanging. We see this tendency at work, for instance, in any statement which suggests that an organization must do some particular thing (e.g., satisfy some particular need or requirement) if it is to survive. The statement is misleading unless we interpret it as shorthand for the cumbersome proposition that it will change from its present form of organization and level of performance in various ways if the particular need or requirement is met at some other level or in some other way than that specified. When we put it that way, we recognize that survival, which the simpler statement treats as a given, can be made problematic and variable. The political effect comes about when we take what we have defined, for scientific convenience, as unchanging, as in fact unchangeable. We thus, implicitly or explicitly, suggest to those who think that some particular change is the way to solve a pressing problem, that their solution is utopian and unworkable. What we are really saying, in such a case, is that the phenomenon in question can only be affected by changing something so difficult to change that only extraordinary effort and power can accomplish the feat. The mobilization of effort and power might be accomplished, if only in a way that the analyst might think unlikely or distasteful (e.g., violent revolution).

Likewise, when sociologists fail to consider some people and some aspects of a situation and do not gather data about them, they forgo the possibility of finding out that some things said by or about those people are not true, that their informants' descriptions of their own actions may be self-servingly misleading. For social scientists, this choice usually results in studying subordinate echelons in an organization or community, while taking the descriptions by superiors of their own activities as adequate and trustworthy and therefore not needing any investigation. This lack of scientific skepticism is a political choice and has political consequences (Becker 1967a; Blumer 1967; Becker and Horowitz 1972).

Since photographers seldom produce explicit analyses of social problems, they are less likely to confront this problem directly. But their idea of who should be photographed and who should not may have the same consequences as the sociologist's decision about who is to be studied, the photographer thereby giving us great informational detail about some people, and suggesting that others either do not exist or can be filled in from the viewer's imagination. How, for instance, would Hine's documentation of the problem of child labor have been affected had he included among his portraits of exploited children portraits of the men and women who owned the factories, profited from that exploited labor, and lived in extravagant luxury on the profits? It might have given a more damning indictment of the entire system, though it is questionable that his work would then have had greater effect. One could also argue that the machines and factory buildings present in his pictures convincingly evoke the owners and their power (though not the luxury of their lives), or that other photographers provided that material (e.g., Edward Steichen's portrait of J. P. Morgan [1963:31]).

Another aspect of framing is that we can either include all of what we do show within the picture's frame, and thus indicate that it is self-contained, or include parts of things that extend beyond the frame and thus evoke the world into which they extend, or things that stand for and evoke worlds and situations which lie beyond. Portraits, for instance, can contain all of the person's body and thus indicate that it is not necessary to know more, or they can contain only parts and thus indicate that there are other parts the viewer must supply from his imagination. Likewise, a portrait can contain some chunk of the person's ordinary environment—an artist's studio, a scientist's laboratory—which evokes a world of activity not pictured, but there. Or it may simply show some setting (home or whatever) in such a way as to suggest more about the person. André Kertész (1972:118–19), for instance, has a portrait of Mondrian that faces a picture of Mondrian's house, which arguably conveys a more Mondrianish spirit than the portrait of the artist himself.

In any event, photographers do understand and use what lies beyond the portion of reality they actually show. In this they differ from social scientists, who prefer not to discuss explicitly what they cannot claim to have studied scientifically. In that sense, social scientists make themselves ignorant about matters that lie beyond their frame, ignoring even what they do know by casual observation or in some other informal way. Instead of building such partial knowledge into their analyses, they rely on time-honored verbal formulae (e.g., "all other things being equal") to limit and frame their analyses. These formulae, like legal formulae, have been revised and refined so as to say exactly what is meant, what is defensible, and no more. A large number of these conventions exist, part of the rhetoric of contemporary science.

In any event, when social scientists fail to deal with the reality that lies beyond the frame they placed around their study, they do not get rid of it. The reader, as with photographs, fills in what is hinted at but not described with his own knowledge and stereotypes, attaching these to whatever cues he can find in the information given. Since readers will do this, whatever verbal formulae are used to attempt to evade the consequences, sociologists might as well understand the process and control it, rather than being its victims.

PERSONAL EXPRESSION AND STYLE

Sociologists like to think of science as impersonal. However, they recognize that people work differently, that some have easily recognizable styles of work, that some work has an elegance missing in other research. In short, they recognize a personally expressive component in sociological research and writing. They seldom discuss that component (I suppose because it contradicts the imagery of impersonal science). When they do discuss it, they usually describe it as a flaw. For instance, critics frequently complain of Erving Goffman's jaundiced view of the world, of modern society, and especially of personal relationships. They characterize that view as overly calculating, as cynical and even as paranoid. Similarly, some critics of so-called labeling theory criticize it for being overly skeptical about established organizations, their operations and records.

Both Goffman and labeling theorists have the elements these criticisms single out. So does every other theory and style of work. The critical analysis errs only in suggesting that some theories and studies have such components while others are properly impersonal, as befits scientific activity. But Peter Blau and Otis Duncan's study of the occupational structure of the United States (1967), to take a random example, likewise contains a personally expressive element, both in its view of the nature of people and society and in the way it handles and presents data, even if we see that element minimally, as a non-sharing of the Goffman view. The style of scientific impersonality is also a style.

9a, b, and c. Paul Strand, "Man, Tenancingo," 1933 (above). (© Art Institute of Chicago.) Frank Cancian, "Untitled" (right and following). (From Another Place, courtesy of Frank Cancian.) Strand and Cancian use the stylistic possibilities of photography to express different degrees of respect and familiarity.

Photographers typically accept responsibility for the personally expressive component in their work as a natural accompaniment of its status as art. Accepting that status also allows them the quasi-mystical retreat from analyzing the social components of their work and the emphasis on intuitive inarticulateness I criticized earlier.

Nevertheless, they understand something sociologists need to learn more about, so they can work with it consciously and control it.

We can approach the serious analysis of the personal component in sociological work by looking at specific devices through which it is expressed. There is a dictionary of the expressive language of photography yet to be compiled; at present, I can only find occasional ad hoc discussions.

Here is an example of the stylistic devices that express the personal component in photographs. Paul Strand (1971) is famous for his

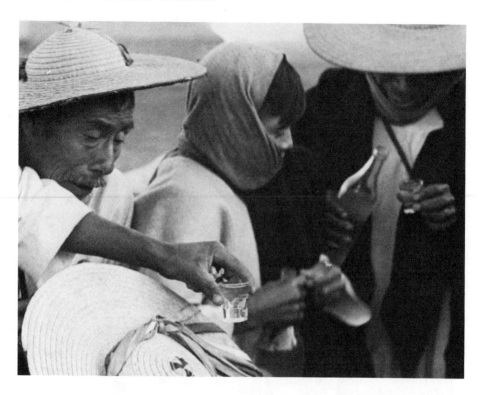

portraits of peasants from all over the world: Mexico, Morocco, Egypt, Romania, the Gaspé, the Hebrides. The portraits overwhelmingly convey an attitude of respect for the people portrayed, describing them as strong, sturdy, enduring, good people who have the traditional virtues despite the difficult circumstances of their lives. This is quite a different description from that of ethnographers as various as Sol Tax (1941) and Edward C. Banfield (1967), who depict people who are meaner, more cunning, more spiteful. Strand has chosen to portray them that way. He has not simply conveyed the reality of peasant life. He conveys his view by habitually photographing his subjects at eye level, directly facing the camera, thus treating them as equals. He does not suggest that he has caught them in an unguarded moment; on the contrary, he has allowed them to compose themselves for the occasion, to put their best foot forward. The stability implied in their formal postures, the honesty suggested by the openness with which they gaze into the camera, all help to suggest peasant virtues. Likewise, by photographing them in natural light and utilizing a wide tonal range, Strand conveys an attitude that respects their reality, that makes them look fully human.

Frank Cancian's photographs of Mexican peasants (1971) use different devices to convey a view of peasants which is (not surprisingly, since Cancian is himself an anthropologist) much more like that of earlier ethnographic descriptions. His Zinacantecos occasionally show the nobility Strand emphasizes, but more frequently seem less noble and more human. They grin, smile slyly, bargain shrewdly, drink hard. The photographs view them from a variety of angles, show them in blurred motion, in a variety of light conditions, all of which express somewhat less respectful distance and somewhat more knowledgeable familiarity than Strand's pictures. The difference in knowledge of and attitude toward the people being photographed is conveyed by the choice of topics too, of course, but the stylistic elements play an important role.

I'm not sure where we might find the expressive devices characteristic of sociological work. One place is in the use of adjectives. Sociologists frequently, perhaps in an attempt to achieve a little literary grace, apply adjectives to the people and organizations they write about, these adjectives implying judgments and generalizations not justified by the data they present or required for the scientific points they are making. A variety of other devices known to literary analysts likewise convey attitudes and moral evaluations. Goffman, for instance, often achieves ironic effects by using perspective by incongruity, and many people use a Veblenesque deadpan translation of evaluative statements into mock-objective academese to the same end.

Sociologists use a variety of devices, interestingly, to hide the personal attitudes, evaluations, and other components in their work. Chief among these are the incessant use of the passive voice and the first-person plural to blur recognition of what is obvious: that one person is in fact responsible for the research and results being reported. Even more interesting to me is how do various styles of handling quantitative data contribute to a rhetorical effect of impersonal fact? What are the aesthetics of tabular presentation? These questions, to which I have no answers, lay out an area of work still to be done.

DO PHOTOGRAPHS TELL
THE TRUTH?

Do photographs tell the truth? Social scientists and photographers are equally concerned with the question, though they come to it by different routes. "Visual sociology" and "visual anthropology" are small but growing movements within those disciplines, and historians (Michael Lesy [1973, 1976] being the most obvious example) are toying with more imaginative and extensive use of photographs than had been customary. If we are going to use photographs as evidence for social science assertions, we need to know whether they can be trusted as evidence, whether and how they "tell the truth."

Photographers have a much more ambivalent concern with the truth of photographs, and often adopt a strategy that attempts to have it both ways, presenting photographs in a way that intimates, without quite saying, that they convey some important or essential truth about the matter they picture. But the photographers know perfectly well that the pictures represent a small and highly selected sample of the real world about which they are supposed to be conveying some truth. They know that their selection of times, places, and people, of distance and angle, of framing and tonality, have all combined to produce an effect quite different from the one a different selection from the same reality would produce. They worry that, because someone else could have photographed the same subject differently, they will be accused of bias. With that worry in mind, they think defensively and assert before they can be accused of it that their pictures are only a personal view, "just the way it looked to me," that any other personal view would be just as "valid." But they never really mean the disclaimers, either about their own pictures or about any other pictures that have any claim to documentary veracity.

You can easily prove to yourself the uselessness of the "it's-only-personal" disclaimer. Take some photograph that has a strong element of seeming to report on the truth about society or some

14 📷

portion thereof—the well-known photographs made by Dorothea Lange, Walker Evans, and others under the auspices of the New Deal Farm Security Administration (FSA) are good for the purpose, although they needn't be classics (I often use the photographs my students make). Now tell yourself, or some friends, or anyone who will listen, that you have just discovered that this picture was not made where it appears to have been made or where its caption says it was, or that the people in them are not who they seem to be or are not doing "naturally" what the picture shows them doing. I once upset a class by telling them that the pictures one student had made were phony in that, while they were photographed at O'Hare Field, every person in them was an extra he had hired and whose movements he had choreographed. The response to such an assertion is interesting. I have never known anyone to respond in any way other than to say, "It's not true!"—even people who a moment earlier were asserting stoutly that the picture represented a personal view whose truth didn't matter. If we refuse to believe that a photograph does not have the warrant of reality we have assumed it did, we must see that part of our response to it was a response to it as evidence of something about the real world and the photographer in it.

Not every photograph will produce such a response, of course. Whole genres simply do not raise the issue of truth. No one knows or cares where a construction by Jerry Uelsmann originated, and if Duane Michals uses models, so what? On the other hand, it would make a great deal of difference to us if we thought that even such obviously "personal" work as Diane Arbus's or Robert Frank's was not shot where it purports to have been or that the people who appear in those images were hired models; and the case is stronger when we think of photographs by W. Eugene Smith or the FSA photographers. Anyone whose response to photographs never includes this reaction need not read further.

Most of us, then, do worry about whether the pictures we make and look at are "true" and can be seen to be true by others who look at them. I want to suggest some ways of thinking about this question that are less confusing than the approaches we commonly take. In doing so, I will rely on some ideas more or less well known to social scientists and will probably violate some photographic sensibilities, but that is the price of escaping the traps we get ourselves into.

What I will propose is not necessarily the best or the only or even a terribly important way of evaluating photographs, nor must all photographs be evaluated by the standards I will describe. But if truth is a factor in our response to a photograph, then these standards are relevant to our understanding and judgment of it, and to our aesthetic experience of it as well.

What's True?

A first clarification requires us to give up the question "Is it true?" In that simple form it is unanswerable, meaningless, and therefore foolish. Every photograph, because it begins with the light rays something emits hitting film, must in some obvious sense be true; and because it could always have been made differently than it was, it cannot be the whole truth and in that obvious sense is false.

To talk about the question more sensibly, we have to refine it. To begin, we can ask, "Is this photograph telling the truth about *what?*" Pictures ordinarily contain enough information that we can use them to give us evidence about more than one topic. Are Brassaï's pictures (in *The Secret Paris of the Thirties* [1976]) telling us the truth about Paris, or about Paris in the 1930s, or about the Parisian demimonde, or about that sort of demimonde in general, or . . . ? Are Bill Owens's photographs (in *Suburbia* [1973]) telling the truth about suburbia in general, Livermore, Calif., in particular, about sex roles in modern America, about housekeeping practices, about American children, or . . . ? So we must first specify what we are getting the truth about.

Even that is not enough. If we know the topic, we still don't know what is being asserted about it. We sometimes feel that the assertions a photograph makes—its "statement"—are so subtle and ineffable that they cannot be reduced to words. No doubt the entire statement cannot be reduced in that way. Much of it is made in a visual language that we don't have any workable rules for translating into words. Further, it contains so much material that reducing it to words would take more work than it is worth. Still, we do not usually feel that we can say nothing at all about the content of the picture. So we need a way of extracting from the image some verbal statements that will help us decide what, if anything, the picture is telling us the truth about, and what that truth is.

10. Bill Owens, "Untitled [pantry shelves]." (From Suburbia, courtesy of Bill Owens.)
In classic ethnographic style, Owens's photographs of suburbia record the details of everyday
life.

Here is a way to proceed. For any picture, ask yourself what
question or questions it *might* be answering. Since the picture could
answer many questions, we can decide what question we are interested in. The picture will, of course, suggest that some questions
are likely to find answers in it. For instance, Owens's pictures of

pantries and refrigerators clearly suggest that they will answer questions about what kinds of food the inhabitants of the houses store and presumably eat, while other pictures in *Suburbia* suggest that they will answer other questions about the housekeeping arrangements of these people. Walker Evans's photographs of sharecroppers' kitchens don't contain such detailed information about food and cannot be used to answer such questions; their content suggests that they will answer questions about the kind of household furnishings sharecroppers had to live with. In the same way, some of Brassäi's photographs, like the image of a whore sitting on the bidet while her customer bends over to tie his shoes (1976), clearly answer questions about how Parisian whores did business, while Danny Lyon's pictures (in *The Bikeriders* [1968]) answer some of our questions about how members of motorcycle gangs spend their leisure time.

We needn't restrict ourselves to questions the photographs suggest. We can also use them to answer questions the photographer did not have in mind and that are not obviously suggested by the picture. Thus, Lesy (in *Real Life* [1976]) uses photographs from Caulfield and Shook's commercial studio to investigate how participants in the social life of Louisville in the twenties purposely altered reality, a question their pictures were meant to keep from awareness. We can thus avoid interminable, unresolvable, and irrelevant questions about the photographer's intent, for, whatever the intent, we can use the photograph to answer questions we want to raise and still not do violence to the work of artist-photographers.

In either case, we choose a question we think the photograph might enable us to answer. We may approach the photograph with the question already in mind, or it may come to us as we inspect the image. Either way, we go over the image systematically to see what kind of answer it can give. We may find that it doesn't really answer the question very well, but will answer some other question more satisfactorily, leaving less margin for doubt. The job is to find a question and answer which fit each other, the answer being the answer for that question and vice versa.

The most obvious questions that photographs answer are the most specific. What did those people have on their pantry shelves? What kind of jackets did the members of Lyon's motorcycle gang wear? But we are only interested in such specific information if the subjects of the photograph are celebrities of some kind or intimates of ours, or if the photographs are to be used in a legal proceeding.

Normally, we find photographs interesting because they answer questions about something larger than the immediate subject, and photographers usually give us to understand that their images have such broad meaning. Thus, Owens does not call his book *Livermore,* he calls it *Suburbia,* and in so doing intimates (presumably purposefully) that the photographs answer questions about the suburban way of life generally, not just about one suburb. If it were only about that one suburb, we would find the photographs less interesting; few people (other than those who live there) have a deep interest in Livermore, Calif. Books of documentary photographs often have titles that imply that kind of interesting generalization (think of *The Americans* [1969], *American Photographs* [1975], or *You Have Seen Their Faces* [1937]). But even without such help, we quickly jump to such generalizations, for without them the photographs would never command our attention at all.

So we usually inspect this kind of photograph with an eye to answering some general question about social arrangements or processes. The kinds of questions that concern us are often those social scientists ask. For instance, what are the main themes of the culture of this society? That is the kind of question Ruth Benedict raised in *Patterns of Culture* (1934) and *The Chrysanthemum and the Sword* (1946), and I think it a fair way to characterize Robert Frank's book to say that *The Americans* (1969) is a kind of answer to such questions about the United States. The list of themes his book gives as an answer, if we should put that question to it, includes (and my list is not exhaustive) such themes as these:

1. The automobile dominates American society. Americans revere their automobiles and practically live in them.
2. They similarly revere the flag, or at least display it everywhere, in so many and such varied places as to devalue and degrade it.
3. Religious symbolism is likewise omnipresent and thereby meaningless and degraded. Only among blacks is it a living force.
4. Some males—white, upper middle class, middle-aged, or Westerners—are powerful, inspiring fear and deference. Older men are devalued, ignored, and badly treated, as are poor people and members of ethnic minorities.
5. Women are powerless, and get by only on looks and an attachment to a powerful male.

This is not the place for a full analysis of *The Americans*. But the nature of cultural themes is at least one order of question to which it gives answers.

Other photographic work characterizes the way of life of some social stratum, occupational group, or social area by detailing major forms of association among the group's members and placing them in relation to some set of environing forces. Danny Lyon's work does that. Other photographers answer questions that amount to some version of: can such things be? That is, they verify that certain phenomena have actually occurred or existed, so that we know that future talk and theorizing will have to take their existence into account. Insofar as Diane Arbus's published photographs tell us about something beyond herself, they serve that purpose, pointing to the existence of a population of freaks and weirdos ordinarily conveniently forgotten by more "normal" members of American society, a population ignored by both lay and professional theories of how the society works. Or take this question: would small-town American men, farmers and similar working-class people, perform cunnilingus in public on women who are total strangers to them? Most writers about American society would find that unlikely, but a few photographs in Susan Meiselas's *Carnival Strippers* (1976), plus the supporting text, show us that they have, at least often enough for her to photograph it; on the testimony of her informants, the event is commonplace.

Further examples are unnecessary. We can read out of these photographs answers to such questions. The answers, both specific and general, that we find in the photograph can be taken as the propositions whose truth the photograph asserts. Thus, we no longer have to ask such unanswerable questions as "Is Smith's essay on the Spanish village a 'true' picture of life there?" Instead, we can ask specific questions about that life—do the villagers take religious rituals very seriously?—and use the material in the pictures to answer them. The first step in deciding whether pictures tell the truth, then, is to decide what truth they assert by seeing what answers we can extract from them to questions either we or they have suggested. (This way of looking at things emphasizes that pictures do not simply make assertions, but rather that we interact with them in order to arrive at conclusions—in short, that we play an active role in the process, as Dewey long ago argued and a host of other people have reiterated since.)

Threats to Validity

Once we know what we think a picture asserts, or can be made to assert, we can ask: is the assertion true? Before I suggest a way of dealing with this problem I want to make a few preliminary remarks.

1. The truth need not be the *whole* truth. It is irrelevant to criticize the assertion we have extracted from a picture because there is some other assertion it will also support, *unless* the two assertions are contradictory. Since pictures often contain a wealth of information, it is not surprising that more than one true thing can be said on the basis of a single image. When this happens, it only means that we are asking different questions, which deserve and get different answers.

2. The truth will ordinarily not be verified by a single photographic image and usually not by any number of photographic images taken by themselves. Photographers and others have fallen into the habit of discussing the question of truth as though it had to be settled with reference to one picture—what can we assert for sure on the basis of this one picture? The answer is usually nothing at all. We generally decide important questions on the basis of an assessment of all kinds of evidence, balancing all the fragments of fact we can assemble to arrive at the best judgment we can make about a proposition. Those fragments will ordinarily include other photographs besides the one we are working with, *and* a variety of textual materials: documents, interviews, and so on.

3. We can never be absolutely sure of the truth of an assertion. Our knowledge is always partial and therefore fallible; we may find a new piece of evidence tomorrow which will show us that the assertion we thought true is, after all, false. Thus, recent investigation (Scherer 1976) of the circumstances of the making of many of the early photographs of American Indians shows that they are grossly inaccurate, because the photographers clothed and posed their subjects according to the way they thought Indians ought to look rather than investigating their lives sufficiently to be able to photograph them as they did look in ordinary life. This and similar cases show how new information can shift our ideas about the validity of an assertion and thus the degree to which those ideas rest on more than the internal evidence deducible from one photograph.

4. No single standard of proof is acceptable for all social groups and all purposes. Some groups are more skeptical than others, in part because of professional biases (i.e., psychologists are probably more skeptical than anthropologists) and in part depending on whose ox is being gored (proof of something that damages some cause of mine is going to have to be very convincing proof, much more so than in the opposite case). Further, we demand a higher standard of proof if we are going to base some important action on our conclusion. (One reason we are less skeptical about photographic materials may be that we seldom take any important action on their basis.)

With those qualifications, we can think about how to tell whether the assertion we have drawn from a photograph is true. The idea of *threats to the validity* of a proposition was first proposed and much elaborated by Donald Campbell, a psychologist and philosopher of science, and a number of his collaborators. The idea is simple enough. We decide whether a proposition is true (or, perhaps better, whether we ought to believe it) by thinking explicitly of all the reasons we might have to doubt it, and then seeing whether the available evidence requires us to take those doubts seriously. If the evidence suggests that we need not entertain these doubts, that these threats to the validity of our idea are not sound, then we can accept the proposition as true.[1]

Campbell and his collaborators have listed a large number of threats to the validity of hypotheses or assertions. Many of them have special reference to the situation of the laboratory experiment; others are more generally applicable. I don't intend to go through their entire list, but rather to generate the beginnings of a similar list applicable to assertions based on photographic materials. We now have available many photographic monographs and essays which make some sort of statement about social life. Inspecting a variety of these works, we can see what doubts we have about them; generalizing those doubts, we can see what the general categories of threats to the validity of photographically derived assertions might be. (Campbell has revised his list several times since its first publication, and the list I will give is likewise provisional, to be extended on the basis of how it works in practice.) When we understand the

---

[1]The original statement of the approach is Campbell and Stanley 1966. Some important revisions are suggested in Campbell 1969.

11a and b. Caulfield and Shook, unretouched photograph of a factory worker (top); the same photograph retouched (below). The danger of such manipulation causes many scientists to doubt the usefulness of photographic evidence, but retouched photographs become evidence for the investigation of just such manipulative practices. (Courtesy of the University of Louisville Photographic Archives, Caulfield and Shook Collection.)

threats to the validity of our assertion we can also see what kinds of material will deal with the threat. In short, we can compile a catalog of problems and solutions. Here are some of them.

1. The most obvious threat to the validity of a conclusion based on photographic evidence is the suspicion that the photograph was faked in some way. It might have been retouched; Lesy shows some gross examples of filthy factories, worthy of Lewis Hine, magically turned into spacious, sunlit, healthful places of work. The print might be a composite of a number of negatives, showing people together who in fact never met. The people and things in the picture might have been specially arranged by the photographer, or by someone else (with or without the photographer's knowledge and consent), as in the case of Arthur Rothstein's "skull" picture. Rothstein photographed a bleached steer skull sitting on some parched earth in South Dakota. He had found the skull nearby and moved it around the square of bare dirt and some nearby grass, looking for the best light and angle. Republican politicians, in an effort to embarrass the Democrats and Franklin Roosevelt, charged that the picture was faked, that the skull had never actually been where Rothstein photographed it. They intimated that he carted the skull around with him looking for likely places to put it so as to dramatize the drought. What they objected to was the implied conclusion that the drought was so bad that cows were simply dying and rotting on the open range.[2]

The Rothstein story illustrates several points. Whether the picture is "true" depends on what conclusion we draw from it. If we take it as evidence that South Dakota cows were dying of thirst, it is probably not true. If we take it as symbolizing a condition of drought, illustrating its severity, then it probably was true. The story also indicates what is required for a picture to be taken as unassailably "true." If we suspect that it has been covertly interfered with by someone so that it does not picture what would have been there without such interference, its value as evidence diminishes. Thus, we may not trust Irving Penn's pictures of Peruvian peasants (1974) to tell us what kind of people they are, because Penn tells us that he arranged their poses himself, moving arms, legs, and torsos as he did with fashion models. Whatever we might conclude about peasant life and culture from the way they held themselves before the camera is now suspect, since it might only be Penn's idea of

[2]The story is told in Hurley 1972.

12. *Arthur Rothstein, "Skull, Pennington, South Dakota, 1936." (Courtesy of the Library of Congress.) Did Rothstein, by moving this skull a short distance, mislead viewers?*

peasants that we see. Conversely, when a picture openly displays the visible signs of having been "doctored," we find no fault with it; no one is trying to fool us and we know that we must make any inferences with the doctoring in mind (cf. Ades 1976).

2. The Rothstein story suggests a second threat to the validity of assertions based on photographs. Photography has an ambiguous status in relation to high art, and many photographers whose work is unabashedly commercial or journalistic also would like it to be taken as "artistic." They are encouraged in this by the overseers of

the art photography world who periodically discover artistic merit in work of that kind, so that photojournalists like Henri Cartier-Bresson and W. Eugene Smith are recognized as artists, their work hung in museums, bought and sold by dealers and collectors. No genre of photography seems immune to this. A strong move to take fashion photographs seriously has been launched, and even aerial reconnaissance photographs made under Edward Steichen's direction during World War I have received such treatment.[3]

I don't want to debate the rights and wrongs of this practice here. Some of the people and photographs so ennobled deserve it; many do not. In any event, because photographers, whatever kind of work they are doing, may want to be recognized as artists, we sometimes suspect that they have made their pictures to fit into currently fashionable artistic styles, either technically and compositionally, or with respect to mood and subject matter. Thus, some years ago, Pirkle Jones and Ruth-Marion Boruch mounted an exhibition of photographs of a dying California town: boarded-up stores, deserted streets, a closed bank. The show received a respectful review from Margery Mann, who, some months later, wrote an aggrieved letter to the editor in which she announced that she had since been to that town and discovered that not a block away from the dying downtown was a brand-new thriving downtown, with a new branch of the bank that had closed, two auto dealers, and other signs of prosperity.[4] The photographers seemed to have succumbed to an "artistic" desire for nostalgic stories of the death of the Old West. None of this is a criticism of the photographs or an assertion that they are untrue, only a statement that you cannot conclude from them that the town was dying; the photographers could be faulted only insofar as they had suggested that you could.

The desire to make "art" may, then, lead photographers to suppress details that interfere with their artistic conception, a conception that might be perfectly valid in its own right, but that unsuits the photographs for use as evidence for certain kinds of conclusions. Many social scientists have just this fear about photographs. It is a justified fear, but one relevant not only to photographs or to those photographs made with some artistic intention. Insofar as the artistic intention interferes with the photograph's evidentiary use, it does so by affecting the selection and presentation of details, so

[3]See the discussion in Sekula 1975: 26–35.
[4]Mann's review appeared in the May 1964 issue of *Artforum*, her letter in the September 1964 issue.

that some things are not shown, some details are emphasized at the expense of others and thus suggest relationships and conclusions without actually giving good cause for believing them, and by presenting details in such a way (through manipulation of lighting or the style of printing, for instance) as to suggest one mood rather than another. Since every way of making a photograph, whether for artistic purposes or for presentation as evidence in a courtroom, does all of these things, there is a problem, but it is one every user of photographs has. Further, every form of verbal material poses the same problems, for writing and oral testimony are likewise shaped with some audience in mind and must be interpreted and understood accordingly. So, knowing that the photographer had some artistic intentions does not invalidate the work as evidence; we can still decide that some conclusion is true. Knowing that, however, we will be alerted to certain threats to the validity of our assertions. These threats are not easily summed up, for they depend on whatever artistic conventions and fashions were current when the photograph was made. Knowing that, we can look especially for those kinds of sampling and presentational omissions or biases that might be associated with those conventions.

3. We may suspect that the photographer has inadequately sampled the events that might have been photographed, failing to see all the things relevant to the question and answer we are interested in, or having seen them, failing to photograph them. One of the chief problems here is access. Can we get access to the full range of relevant activities, and, if we can, on what terms can that access be negotiated? What do we have to give in return? When we look at photographs as evidence, we want to know about access and terms. Photographers usually give us information on these points, either explicitly (as in Bruce Davidson's introduction to *East 100th Street* [1970] or W. Eugene Smith's lengthy text in *Minamata* [1975]) or implicitly, by the evidence of the pictures themselves. It's often said that a photograph records, among other things, the relation of the photographer to the people in the picture, whether that be intimate, friendly, hostile, or voyeuristic. We can see, for instance, that Danny Lyon (1968) and Larry Clark (in *Tulsa* [1971]) must have been intimately involved with the people whose bike riding and drug taking they photographed, while Robert Frank was a stranger to those he photographed; that Jill Freedman (1975) was a friendly acquaintance of the circus people she photographed, that Bill Owens knew some people in Livermore better than others

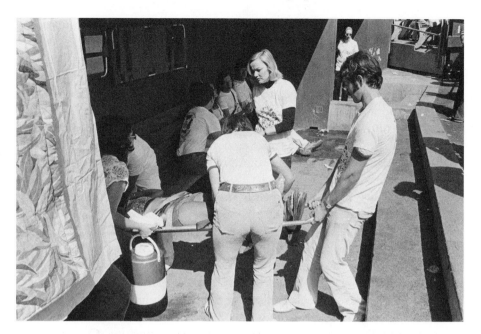

13. Howard S. Becker, "Untitled" (from Rock Medicine Series). I agreed to hide the faces of the emergency medics' patients, in return for permission to photograph in the rock medicine setting.

but knew the area comprehensively, the way a reporter would. Part of our concern is always to know how much time the photographer spent; we trust the sample more if we know it was a long time. A week is one thing, a year or two or ten is something else.

Getting permission or freedom to make photographs of people can profitably be viewed as a negotiation between them and the photographer. Each gives something and gets something. Most photographers have developed some way of handling this problem, but it is seldom discussed frankly or at length. What did the photographer trade for permission to do the work? For instance, I have spent two years photographing the people who provide emergency medical services for large outdoor rock concerts in the San Francisco Bay Area. The one rule I had to accept in order to get access with a camera to large parts of the operation was never to photograph, or use a photograph of, a patient's face; the reason is clear and understandable, and I accepted the prohibition as the price of doing the project at all. Nevertheless, people who see the work now cannot answer questions about what kinds of people the patients are or how they feel about the service they are getting, because of the rule I accepted during that negotiation.

A second problem is the photographer's theory. We don't photograph what is uninteresting to us or what has no meaning. What can have meaning and be interesting is a function of the theory we have about what we are investigating. We can usually get an idea of the photographer's theory by investigating both the pictures themselves and the accompanying text. We may decide that the theory has blinded the photographer to things we need to know to decide whether a particular assertion is true. We criticize here, insofar as we make a criticism, not the photographs but the theory or idea that lay behind their making.

In any event, an inadequate sample, however it came about, can lead us to feel a serious threat to the validity of the assertion we want to make based on the photographs.

4. Finally, we may suspect that some form of censorship has prevented us from seeing all the pictures we might have seen, and that the ones that have been withheld would have changed our view substantially and perhaps even altered our conclusions. Censorship may be imposed by the state or some subdivision thereof, by a general cultural atmosphere that makes certain photographs unseemly or distasteful, or by photographers themselves out of some personal or political conviction.

Contemporary standards have loosened up so much with respect to "moral" issues that we now see photographs that would not have been made public only a few years ago. A striking example of this is Brassaï's 1976 version of his Parisian photographs, which includes many well-known images plus many other photographs made at the same time but presumably considered too raunchy for public exhibition or distribution then, but not now. So we now see the gay bars we didn't see before, the whores and their customers in private, and so on. None of this contradicts what we saw before; it extends and amplifies it just as we might have imagined, without being quite sure we were right, even though our worldly wisdom told us we probably were.

But because we now see these pictures doesn't mean that we don't still have to consider the possibility of censorship. In particular, keep in mind that sex is only one topic which may be censored. There are many others. Anything people don't want known about, and there are millions of such things, may be censored if those who want the matter covered up have the power to do it. In fact, preventing things from being made public is one element of the practice of public relations, and businesses and communities, in particular, often try to keep "unfavorable" material, including photographs, from being made public. Though carried on by private parties rather than the government, and not the result of some general cultural standard, this too has the effect of limiting what we see.

The photographer may similarly limit what we see. In this case, of course, there is a nicer name and a rationale for what is done. We often speak of editing, meaning the weeding out of a small pile of superior pictures from the larger mass of all the photographs. It is unlikely that we would want to see all that material, although it is not, for instance, ridiculous to suggest that proof sheets might be available for independent checking—everyone has found it extremely interesting to see the full range of negatives Walker Evans produced for the FSA. We will frequently find that seeing the larger body of work will not change our ability to make various assertions or the warrant for those assertions. But it might, and we might want to know about that before accepting the answer to some question.

Photographers may also censor their work for reasons of ideology or ethics, as I have done with the faces of rock medicine patients. Without being required to by circumstances, they may decide that they don't wish to show everything, that some things are no one's business or disrespectful to the people being photographed. It is instructive to compare the work of Bill Owens and Roslyn Banish in this respect. Banish (in *City Families* [1976]) has treated a somewhat similar subject matter to that Owens worked with (the only difference being that she is interested in the domestic life of city dwellers instead of suburbanites) in a quite different way. Instead of Owens's "candid snapshots," with the one short, snappy statement by the subject appended, she made formal family portraits, to which are appended lengthy interviews, filled with details about the families' lives and aspirations. The much more respectful photographs present the families in a dignified, sober way that emphasizes their respectability and dignity. Owens does not let his people stay so buttoned up; he persuaded them to show a less dignified, more comic side to the camera, and at the same time has not allowed them to speak for themselves at such length. Owens's photographs give us much more information about a variety of topics (what goes on behind the neat walls of these suburban cottages? Disorder, drinking, bad taste, sloth, and mess?) and much less about a variety

14a and b. Roslyn Banish, "The Entwistle Family" (above). (From City Families, *courtesy of Roslyn Banish.) Bill Owens, "Andrew doesn't like to go to the bathroom by himself" (right). (From* Suburbia, *courtesy of Bill Owens.) Banish, respectful of her subjects, shows less of their lives than Owens. But Owens quotes no more than a line of what his subjects say while Banish, quoting hers at length, gives more of their perspective.*

of other topics (hopes, dreams, and aspirations). If I had my choice of a basis for understanding families-in-an-environment, I'd like to have both; I can answer more questions more completely from the combination than with either one taken alone. I don't know if it's fair to call Banish's respectful photographic editing or Owens's severe editing of his subjects' words censorship; probably not, but the effect is the same and in each case means that we can have less confidence in the conclusions we draw from the material presented than we might otherwise have.

There will always be reasons good enough for some people not to present all the material they might, whether the reasons are matters of ethics, politics, or just good taste. In seeing what we can conclude, what questions we can answer plausibly, we must take into account whatever we know or suspect about the degree to which this kind of selection occurred. We must recognize that others will regard whatever signs of such selection they discover as weak-

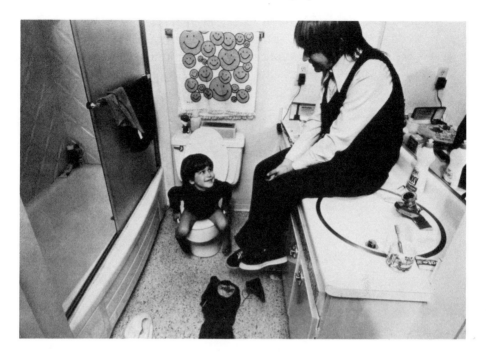

nesses in the argument we are presenting, and thus we will want to avoid such biases, hide their signs, or explain what they are and why they are present.

One final point. Insofar as we take some particular way of doing things as evidence that a suspected threat to the validity of some answer we are drawing from a photograph is not operating, we must be watchful for the possibility that the sign of authenticity itself has been faked. Many photographers now print their photographs with a heavy black line around the border of the print. Among other things, the line indicates that the negative has not been cropped, that all its evidence has been openly and honestly presented to us. But, of course, black lines can be made around parts of a negative. And, more to the point, the device obscures a more serious threat: any ordinarily skillful photographer can frame an image so as to leave out the unwanted details a less skillful person would have had to crop.

Conclusion

To repeat, my purpose here has been to begin the discussion, not to conclude it. The list of threats is sketchy, the suggestions for means of dealing with them hardly even suggestive. The way to proceed, I think, is to continue to investigate successful practice—works that convince and succeed in overcoming doubt—in both social science and photography, learning from and generalizing from experiences in both areas.

15

AESTHETICS AND TRUTH

Begin with these premises:
1. Every photograph can be interpreted as the answer to one or more questions.
2. We care whether the answer the photograph gives to our questions is true.
3. Every question we ask of a photograph can be put, and therefore answered, in more than one way.
4. Different questions are not the right or wrong way to ask (or answer); they are just different.

These premises need some discussion. In saying that we can interpret photographs as answers to questions, I don't mean that we always do, only that we often do, that in principle we always can, and that it is a useful way to think about photographs. The question we ask may be very simple and descriptive: What does Yosemite look like? What does the Republican candidate for President look like? How did our family and friends look in 1957? Sometimes the questions are historical or cultural: How did people take pictures in 1905? How do they take them in Yorubaland? What did the battlefield at Gettysburg look like? Sometimes they are scientific: Is this lung tuberculous? If I bombard an atomic nucleus in a certain way, what will happen? Sometimes they are psychological: What is the true character of the Republican candidate for President? Sometimes they ask for an abstraction: What is the essence of virginal innocence or Mexican peasant life or the urban experience?

Different people can ask different questions of the same photograph, not always the question the photographer had in mind. Some questions interest many people, who share the same way of asking it. News photographs are like that. Scientific photographs are like that too, although a narrower community shares the interest in the questions they answer; the community's members ask the same questions and find the same answer in a photograph offered as evidence.

Other questions interest a very small circle, because they ask about personal relations and personally experienced events of no concern to most people. A photograph of me in front of the Eiffel Tower only interests me and mine. But pictures that once had only personal interest can, under other circumstances, become answers to questions interesting to a larger audience: childhood snapshots of people who later become famous or places in which events of general interest later took place.

We care about the truth of many, if not all, photographs, especially those which so much as hint at, let alone state explicitly, something about the nature of society. To exercise that care, we have to understand the phrase "the truth of a photograph" to refer specifically to whether the answer we find in a photograph to the question we have asked is credible. That means that there is no general answer to the question of whether a photograph is true: we can only say that the answer it gives to a particular question is more or less believable, keeping in mind that different questions may be asked of the same image.

When we interpret a photograph as saying something about a country or situation or way of life or social conflict or historical event—whenever we explain what we see in a photograph in that way we raise the question of truth, because we suggest an answer to a question that might in fact have a different answer. Because the questions arouse strong interests and emotions, people may disagree about whether the answers are correct, often suggesting that they are not because the photographs are biased, misleading, subjective, or an unfair sampling.

Many problems arise over an ambiguity: a series of photographs suggests something is true; we don't deny it but think that something else is true too. The question is whether the photographs suggest that X *and only* X is true, or allow for the possibility that, while X is true, Y is too. Specifically: many people think that Robert Frank's *The Americans* (1969) says that American life is bleak, nasty, uncultured, and materialistic—and that that is all it is. Without becoming an apologist for "The American Way of Life," it is possible to cite images by other photographers giving a different view. Does Frank's book suggest that this is *all* there is to American life? The book's length, long enough to allow for the inclusion of a greater variety of imagery, prompts that interpretation. If it does suggest

15. W. Eugene Smith, "Untitled [Three Soldiers]," from the essay Spanish Village. (Courtesy of Time-Life, Inc.) Smith's stylistic choices express a generalization about Spanish society.

that this is all there is, we might want to say the statement is wrong because other kinds of evidence can be found.

Though we may be interested in questions the picture-maker did not have in mind, photographs capable of a "social" interpretation usually have been made to be interpreted that way, so we can ask how they are made and how the different ways of making them affect our response. In making a picture, every small choice we make emphasizes some things and obscures others, asserts some relations between objects and people, generates a distinct mood. These emphases and choices create the assertions which in turn make us wonder whether other assertions might not also be made, and whether the single assertion standing alone does not give a false answer to the question the image implicitly poses.

Angles, framing, and lighting, for instance, cooperate to make W. Eugene Smith's photograph of three Spanish soldiers a strong statement about their brutality and, by extension, the brutality of the regime they worked for. If we ask the question "What kind of men are these?" the photograph tells us that they are brutal. We know, of course, that Smith created that answer by photographing them at the height of the day, when the bright sun would cast harsh shadows and make them squint, by filling the frame with the crude forms of their heads outlined in that light, by photographing them when they had not shaved. That does not make his answer wrong. But it makes us wonder whether another statement about them, created by photographing them from a greater distance, at dusk, when they had shaved, would not also be true. We might decide that Smith's image gives a correct answer to the question "Were these men capable of brutality?" but an incorrect one to the question, should we or anyone else ask it, "Is brutality the only relevant attribute of their characters?" It is not that Smith was wrong, but that his stylistic choices (you might say that the harsh blacks and whites embody an equally black-and-white moral judgment) answer one of many possible questions, and answer it in a particular way.

Even stylistic choices conventionalized to the degree that much scientific picture making (e.g., X-rays) is are a choice from a much wider range of stylistic possibilities, all reasonable ways of arriving at an answer to a question, each perhaps to different questions. There is no neutral, standard, regular way of getting these answers which does not constitute a choice among possibilities.

People who write and think about photography typically distinguish between informational and expressive photographs, between science and art, between photographs mainly intended to answer questions and those intended to engage us in an aesthetic and emotional experience. Most photographic practitioners want to keep that difference clear. I want to muddy it as much as I can, and say that every photograph has some of both, and that that has consequences for the way we look at, experience, think about, and judge photographs of all kinds.

The Science in Art

Artists want the statements they make to be unique, the expression of their own experience and vision, even though made within the limits of a communal agreement on the conventions of making such statements (and that is true even though the conventions change as continually as the membership of the community that agrees on them).

Many photographs, however, depend for the strength of their statement and emotional effect on viewers believing that what they see in the image is "real" or "true," that they could have seen and photographed the same thing had they been there at the same time with the same question in mind. Not that any artist would want to do that; but people do want to believe that what they see was there to see, if you just looked at it that way.

What kind of photographs produce this response? The common term "document" suggests an answer. "Documents" provide evidence, display some of the facts that would justify one answer or another to a question. "Facts" are items of evidence which could be verified by someone else. A photograph documents something by showing us facts on which conclusions might be based; it is documentary because it contains those facts.

Documentary photographs in the art tradition are photographs we understand (ordinarily made to be so understood) as giving us facts which allow us to answer questions about the way the world is and works. Most definitions of documentary are narrower than this, emphasizing (e.g., Stott 1973) that documentary shows us the facts of human experience in an oppressed group in such a way that we can empathize with its members. This indicates the political reformism of much documentary, but ignores work concerned with social facts that is not political in that way.

The emotional and artistic impact of such work comes not only from the artful way the photograph is composed, the space handled, the tonalities rendered, but also from the way these formal elements are put to work to make some facts obvious and thereby suggest answers to questions, some of which we may not even have recognized as questions before. The artistic achievement of such photographs lies as much in the quality of the questions and answers offered as in the formal rendering.

Consider a literary analogy. Dickens's prose is magnificent, his plots complicated and engrossing, his characters memorable. Yet an important part of the effect of his later novels lies in our belief that they tell us the truth, however caricatured, about Victorian institutions. Imagine, as an experiment, that historians, working with masses of court records, have discovered that law suits did not drag on for years, like *Jarndyce v. Jarndyce* in *Bleak House,* until the lawyers had gobbled up all the money involved in fees. I think we would feel differently about the novel, regard it as a fantasy, and probably judge it a smaller achievement. We could not take what we read there as fact of some kind on which to base a response to social conditions, we could not answer questions about Victorian institutions credibly, and we would not find the plot and characters so affecting. It would be a different book, even though the words were all the same.

Similarly with photographs. When we believe they tell us something we didn't know before about some aspect of society, our response to the photograph includes something of our concern with that aspect of society. If we are interested in the life of the demimonde, or the culture of the poor, or British society, or . . . , we can look to some photographs for answers to our questions, and we want those answers to be, in some sense, true.

That puts a strong constraint on the makers of those images. They have to say a true thing in an original way. Their reward for an attention to truth is that a wider audience will be interested than if their concerns were private, and that they can tap a different kind of response than we have to purely formal beauty (if there is such a thing). They become part of the ongoing dialogue about public issues. William Stott (1973) has shown how *Let Us Now Praise Famous Men* (Agee and Evans 1960) was part of a long national discussion of the Depression and the nature of American capitalism. Bill Owens's *Suburbia* (1973) grew out of a similarly long discussion about suburban life and the changing American class system which began shortly after World War II, and a number of recent books have their context in the movements for black and women's rights.

Wanting to give a unique answer to a uniquely phrased question leads artist-photographers to be concerned with style, with differences in the way the image looks. That may cause viewers, in turn, to be wary, fearing that the quest for originality may have led to a concomitant indifference to truth.

The Art in Science

When people make or use photographs for scientific or scholarly purposes, they do not strive for unique visions or personal styles. Instead, they want material that helps them answer a question taken seriously in an established community concerned with questions like that. Such photographs are frequently made in a standardized fashion, so accepted in the user community that its members think it the only way such pictures can be made.

But every choice embodied in those images—of framing, lens, lighting, printing—is a choice that could have been made differently, with a different photographic result. The different ways of making the photograph—the elements they include or leave out, what they emphasize or play down, the mood they generate—produce an aesthetic result as well as answers to scholarly questions. Mike Mandel and Larry Sultan's *Evidence* (1977) demonstrates this effectively by divorcing pictures made for informational reasons from their captions. Cut off from the questions that generated them, the images provoke all sorts of moods. Many could easily be mistaken for contemporary art photographs.

The effect of the technical choices made in the photographing shows up when scholars and scientists use photographs to test their theories, especially in the social sciences, where there has never been any agreement on how such pictures should be made. The different stylistic possibilities provoke confusion. Margaret Mead and Gregory Bateson (1978) had a wonderful exchange on this point (over film rather than still photography, but the point is the same). Mead thought the only safe way to make pictures for anthropological purposes was to put the camera on a tripod and not touch it. The minute you touched it the individual biases of the investigator would inevitably take over. Bateson argued that you had to move the camera to follow what you were interested in. Mead seemed not to see that putting the camera in one place and leaving it there also represented the investigator's bias.

Any choice is a bias because it excludes some material that might be evidence about the question you are interested in and thus it affects your conclusion. The users of any stylistically distinct method think, of course, that they have the best way of getting the evidence they need to answer their questions. By recognizing that these are choices, we recognize the stylistic components in all photographs made to supply evidence. When those photographs all look alike, it is because people want pretty much the same kind of answers to the same kinds of questions. An interesting example is a stylistic feature common to medical, police, and pornographic photographs; all three are brightly lit from all sides so that every feature of the operative site, scene of the crime, or sexual activity is plainly visible. The reason is that such pictures are made to answer all possible questions that might be asked of them. There is no telling what a medical scientist, police investigator, or dirty-book reader might find interesting, so it all has to be shown clearly.

"Scientific" or "scholarly," then, is a style, one of many that might answer the questions one has in mind. The possible styles have to be chosen among. Suppose that I want to photograph social interaction. If I choose a long lens, I can work from a distance but will not be able to get many people, or their entire bodies, into the frame. If I use a wide-angle lens, I can get all of everyone, and their surroundings too, but they will certainly know that I am there. What do I want, and why? Stylistic features—this is just one of the dozens we might discuss—suggest relationships between the elements in the picture and between them and other things not shown. They suggest relative importance, directions of causality, networks of reciprocal influence, hierarchy, classification. Anyone who wants to make photographs scientifically or objectively and does not accept this point will make all these choices unintentionally and in an uncontrolled way. The resulting image will not answer the questions it was supposed to answer, for it will not, except by accident, contain the material needed to answer them.

Styles project moods as well, in scholarly as well as art photographs, and moods implicitly assert both facts and judgments, as in the Smith photograph. Artists create mood deliberately, scholars by accident. Scholars like Mead, trying to avoid style, unwittingly choose a "scientific" style, which intimates impersonality, objectivity, and noninterference by the picture-maker. But the intimation is necessarily false, because you cannot make a picture without making the choices that constitute interference.

These remarks apply equally to photographs not made by scholars, but found by them and used for scholarly purposes. Many people have used photographs for historical purposes; Erving Goffman used advertising photographs to study the gestures which express and maintain hierarchical relations between males and females. Scholars should keep in mind that even found materials were made by *someone* to answer questions *they* had in a style that suited *them*. Found materials do not report reality any more directly than an artist's documentary photograph. But they can, if one is properly critical of them, understanding what the stylistic choices they embody allow them to be used for, answer questions we are interested in.

Implications

If information and expression cannot be separated, then scholars and artists who want one or the other more or less exclusively cannot have their way. Scholars have style, its burdens and possibilities, to contend with and will have to learn to work with it rather than ignore it. Photographs do not record reality neutrally. We can make them for scholarly purposes best if we understand how to make stylistic choices meaningfully, so that the result contains the information that will answer our questions, appropriately arranged and related.

Artists have the burden of the photograph as evidence to deal with. If our aesthetic response to photographic art depends in part on our assessment of it as truthful evidence about something, artists will have to be serious about what they are saying. That means, briefly, that they ought to devote more time and attention than is customary to learning about the social phenomena they photograph, and ought to think about ways of verifying what they think they know. Many photographers already do these things, but they are not codified as common practice. That confuses students and people who don't make pictures themselves.

For all of us, the lesson is not to worry too much about the distinctions between information and expression, scholarship and art, for all photographs contain elements of both, depending on the interests of those who look at them. They are all answers to our questions, and, though they do not change, our questions do.

16

INSIDE STATE STREET:
Photographs of Building Interiors by Kathleen Collins

Photographers make photographs of interiors as a manner of exploring the way of life of a people or community. They photograph the rooms in a house—how the people who live there have furnished them and utilized the space—and let these rooms stand for everything else they intuit and want to say about a culture.

Kathleen Collins has used this method to investigate and report on the city of Chicago. An exhibit of her work entitled Inside State Street: Color Photographs of Building Interiors By Kathleen Collins opened at the Chicago Historical Society on August 15, 1982. She photographed one of the city's longest streets, State Street, from its beginnings in the Gold Coast through the business areas of the Loop to the housing projects of the South Side. In these diverse settings, she recorded the interiors of the buildings, the rooms in which people live, work, play, and survive. To understand what Collins's work offers us, it helps to compare her method with the similar strategy photographers employ in portraiture.

Photographers often make portraits of people they think of as representative of a way of life. In most portraits, they let a part stand for the whole person—usually the face, but sometimes the hands (as in Alfred Stieglitz's portraits of Georgia O'Keeffe) or the back (as in Dorothea Lange's studies of farm workers). Whatever part a photographer chooses to stand for the person, he or she is employing a strategy that relies upon a theory and a method. This strategy depends on an assumption that the experiences of life are recorded in faces, that the life a person has lived leaves physical marks.

Photographers, accordingly, choose faces, details of faces, and moments in their histories which, recorded on film and printed on paper, allow viewers to deduce what they don't see but want to know about. Portraits often contain a wealth of detail, so that careful study allows us to make complex and subtle readings of the character of the person and of the life-in-society of that person. Looking at

16. Dorothea Lange, "Spring plowing, Guadalupe, California. Cauliflower fields." Photographers who use portraits to investigate social organization require the reader to substitute the part for the whole. (Reproduction courtesy of the Library of Congress.)

the lines on a face, viewers may conclude that these were baked in during a life of hard work in the sun. From those same lines, they can infer wisdom produced by hard work and age or, alternatively, senility and decay. To make any of these conclusions a viewer must bring to bear on the image one of several possible theories of facial lines.

Having made an interpretation of a person from an image of his or her face, viewers can then go on to make some deductions about the community in which this person lives. This requires another theory, specifying the relationship between faces and the information they carry and the society in which they exist. In what kind of world could a person accumulate and use the kind of power we see in Edward Steichen's famous portrait of J. P. Morgan? What went on between Stieglitz and O'Keeffe to create the still, uncommunicative look on her face as he photographed her? What makes the people Bruce Davidson photographed on East 100th Street look so serious and dignified? Because we have further theories about the way life-in-society and faces are related, we can infer answers to these questions, deciding, for instance, that American society at the time Steichen photographed Morgan allowed men to gather enormous power and to feel that they could exercise it as they liked.

Photographers are typically not very clear about what inferences they want us to make. They seem to say that interpretation is the viewer's responsibility and privilege; the viewer must decide what he or she wants to know and then find answers, and evidence for the answers, in the photographs. Of course, photographers who adopt that attitude are being disingenuous, for the photographer's method *is* the selection and arrangement of details in a way that coerces the viewer into drawing certain conclusions and not others.

Portraits, in showing a way of life, leave out a lot. This part-whole strategy makes what each photograph *does* contain carry enormous weight. Photographers, as anyone with sophisticated knowledge of photographs knows, recognize this weight and take advantage of it. They know that they can highlight the wrinkles on a face or hide them. They know that the moment they choose to make the exposure will make the subject look wise or foolish, happy or sad, even though that expression may have been fleeting and uncharacteristic. They know that the details they exclude might make us drastically revise the conclusions we draw from the image.

So photographers lead us to make inferences by manipulating details. They can do that because they know that our interpretations rely on conventions of photography that "everyone" knows, whether we are aware that we know them or not. Photographers focus our attention on what they themselves think important and want us to think important by making it bigger or lighter or darker, different in some way from other things in the frame, by manipulating how we ordinarily look at things to make us look *there* rather than somewhere else. They lead us to think that things are mysterious or clear, good or bad, or one of any other pair of adjectives, by manipulating the visual language in which photographs conventionally signify those meanings.

In just this way, photographers rely upon and viewers accept a theory of photographing interiors. Let me make its premises explicit. People make buildings and lay out and furnish the interior spaces. The way they construct those buildings and the way they furnish and decorate the interiors reveal both the intent of the makers and furnishers and their resources. And, over time, the rooms change and age; people leave physical marks. Whatever the original intention for the rooms, they come to show how people actually have used them. By photographing such interiors, highlighting their details, a photographer can tell us who lived there, what kind of people they were, how they lived—all crucial elements in understanding a society and its culture.

When people build, they build both what they want and what they can use. So a structure and its rooms reflect the makers' purpose. What kind of family life did they want to go on in their house? What kinds of economic activities did they expect to carry on there? Contemporary city dwellers find it hard to understand rural buildings which had rooms for the family's cows, sheep, and goats, as well as its own members, but such a house tells us that those people saw their animals as members of the family unit.

Not all purposes for building are so directly utilitarian. Many people intend to create something beautiful. Some want to display their wealth and impress their neighbors; others want the most space at the least cost. They may wish to preserve a traditional way of life, or to provide the material basis for an untraditional one.

People may think they know what they want in their buildings, may even be able to afford their desires, and still not get what they had in mind. Present-day city dwellers seldom design and build their own living quarters. Instead, they hire architects and contractors who, like all professionals, must deal with their own standards and professional exigencies. Most of us have even less control, and can only choose from what architects and builders have created in hope of attracting buyers. The customer's desires are filtered through demands of utility, economy, professional standards, and contemporary trends. With all these provisos, the look of a building's interior can be taken as an accurate indicator of both taste and social relations.

Take taste first. We know what we like, what looks good to us and our peers, what we feel comfortable with. We have, however implicit and unformulated, a standard of taste. Thorstein Veblen described the Gilded Age's standard of taste as pecuniary; objects were in good taste when they showed that hours and days of a skilled worker's valuable time had been put to no useful purpose, thus displaying the owner's ability to dispose of others' time without realizing any material advantage from it. In this way, Veblen explained his contemporaries' fondness for highly ornamented silverware and furniture. According to his principle of conspicuous waste, this understanding shaped the prevalent conception of beauty. One can infer a pecuniary standard of taste and the body of values and social practices that lay behind it by looking at interiors cluttered with highly ornamented furniture.

Similarly, we can see something about social relations in a family and in a society by looking at the arrangement of the houses people lived in and by seeing what kinds of relationships were possible in rooms like that. To take a common and obvious example, the rooms in older houses have doors on them. People who lived in such houses could attain privacy more easily than people who live in contemporary ranch houses with a "living-dining-kitchen space." Father could go into his den and lock the door in the older house; he might have to retreat to the garage now. This difference suggests the change in conceptions of privacy and in the role of the father in the last thirty or forty years.

We can learn about the conditions of labor in the same way by looking at the interiors of workplaces. Most workplaces show, in the allocation of space, privacy, and fixtures, the workers' status and what privileges and powers they have. Executives, presumably, work in ornate private offices with deep leather chairs and heavy wooden desks. Clerks sit at banks of gunmetal grey desks, on plain serviceable chairs—no more comfortable than necessary, one on top of the other. Production workers don't have a desk drawer to put things in, and no chair at all (since their work requires them to stand, they should *never* sit down). One needn't be a sociologist to infer the hierarchy of power and privilege that arrangement embodies.

In some workplaces the product dominates all else. The workshops where craft objects are made, and the factory floors where everything and everyone are subordinated to the machines, exemplify that possibility. Other workplaces are so devoid of any physical trace of the work done there that it is difficult to determine what

17. Walker Evans, "Washroom and dining area of Floyd Burroughs's home; Hale County, Alabama, 1936." Photographers substitute images of the environment for a full description of a culture or society. (Courtesy of the Library of Congress.)

the workers there really do. The blank surface of the executive's desk in one of Kathleen Collins's photographs raises that question.

Because interiors betray so much about people and their way of life—if we are willing to make the inferential leaps this theory of interiors demands—photographs of interiors can provide a wonderful source of knowledge about culture. So we look at Walker Evans's photographs of sharecroppers' homes and infer from them, by the method just described, the meagerness of these families' resources, the poverty of their lives, and the economic system that made their lives that way. (It took a greater inferential leap—a more complex theory—to get to the economic system than to the particulars of sharecropper life.)

Prison interiors give us a quite different sense, as in the photographs made by Danny Lyon, Bruce Jackson (1977), and others. There is a total lack of privacy in a prison, where inmates are deprived of the props that free people use to signify who they are, to themselves and to other people. The inmates' pitiful attempts at decoration heighten our awareness of the meagerness and horror of their lives, because (as the theory of interiors insists) the furnishings of your living quarters in fact tell the world who you are.

In a common variant, photographers make pictures of people in their houses, combining the theory of portraits and the theory of interiors in one image. Consequently, the details of both sorts of image amplify and comment on each other. We understand the Lake Forest residents Mary Lloyd Estrin portrays in *To the Manor Born* (1979) in part because we see their spacious homes filled with expensive furnishings. Roslyn Banish, in *City Families* (1976), adds a third dimension by letting the people photographed in their homes in London's Pimlico and Chicago's Lincoln Park comment on the pictures. Many of the subjects say that a viewer might get a false impression of them from the image because they are all dressed up, or because the house is neater than usual. Bruce Davidson's East Harlem portraits (1970) give us the data for conflicting interpretations, the people's faces and bodies suggesting dignity, power, and autonomy, while their surroundings suggest that none of these positive qualities has much impact on circumstances of their daily lives.

Looking at these photographs, however, we realize that we are seeing the results of a very selective process, that the photographer might have made a very different picture of the same material, that the picture we see embodies a concern with something beyond an "accurate" portrayal of a way of life. We are also looking at a personal vision, shaped by the photographer's personality; aesthetic, political, and ideological commitments; and his ability to penetrate alien worlds. Every way of photographing interiors is a choice among possibilities.

When photographing the interior of a house, store, or factory, should the photographer include the usual inhabitants or not? By leaving them out, he can more easily compose an image that points to crucial details from which taste and social arrangements might be inferred. By including people in the photograph, however, he can use the increased richness of detail to strengthen the viewer's understanding of his subject.

If he includes the people who are usually there, should he photograph them doing what they usually do there, or should he ask them to pose for a more formal portrait? The former allows him to make an image that includes some characteristic activity, thereby giving added depth to the viewer's understanding of the way of life that is being presented. Bill Owens's photographs of the interiors of suburban homes (1973) give us more insight into suburban lifestyles by showing the daily activities that go on there.

If the photographer includes the people who are usually there, which ones should he include? We conventionally see only a handful of the people who inhabit a space. The others are socially, if not physically, invisible, as in G. K. Chesterton's story about Father Brown, who solved an impossible murder—someone had been killed in an empty house which no one had entered or left—by observing that the letter carrier had been there. None of the neighbors saw him because everyone takes the postman's presence so much for granted as to make him invisible. Servants are often socially invisible to their employers and, by extension, to anyone who adopts (as it is easy to do) the employer's attitude. Robert Frank (1969) made some of his most compelling images in office buildings after work hours, when no one was there but the janitors. A bank occupied only by a janitor pushing a mop looks different from one filled with bankers on the phone. Similarly, Bill Brandt's deservedly famous pictures of the maids in upper-class British houses in the 1930s show us a side of that hierarchical style of life we would miss if we saw only the masters and mistresses.

Given this wide variety of options, Kathleen Collins decided to photograph a great number of interior spaces in Chicago's State Street, which extends for many miles across the city. She thus used

18. Kathleen Collins, "Stateway Gardens, CHA Public Housing Development, 3651 S. Federal Street." Originally in color. (Courtesy of the Chicago Historical Society.)

19. Kathleen Collins, "Playboy Mansion, 1340 N. State Parkway. Hugh Hefner's office which is kept undisturbed for occasional use since transfer of his main business office to his permanent California residence." Originally in color. (Courtesy of the Chicago Historical Society.)

20. *Kathleen Collins, "Medinah Barber Shop, 605 N. State Street." Originally in color. (Courtesy of the Chicago Historical Society.)*

21. *Kathleen Collins, "Bridgeview Restaurant, 431 N. State Street. Sandwich shop which has been closed because the building it occupied will be taken down to make way for a new office building." Originally in color. (Courtesy of the Chicago Historical Society.)*

22. Kathleen Collins, "Condominium apartment, 1440 N. State Parkway. Bedroom of teenage daughter of apartment owner, Mrs. S. Dreyfus." Originally in color. (Courtesy of the Chicago Historical Society.)

23. Kathleen Collins, "Marshall Field and Company, 111 N. State Street. Candy factory, 13th floor, showing Thin Mint table in center." Originally in color. (Courtesy of the Chicago Historical Society.)

24. Kathleen Collins, "Pacific Garden Mission, 646 S. State Street. Men's dining hall with stand-up tables set for breakfast." Originally in color. (Courtesy of the Chicago Historical Society.)

25. Kathleen Collins, "Dearborn Park Apartments, 901 S. State Street. Living room in Chester Shelby's apartment." Originally in color. (Courtesy of the Chicago Historical Society.)

26. *Kathleen Collins, "IBM Building, 1 IBM Plaza. Office of a middle management executive, 28th floor." Originally in color. (Courtesy of the Chicago Historical Society.)*

27. *Kathleen Collins, "Musicians Pawn Shop, 424 S. State Street. Musical instruments on display inside store at street level." Originally in color. (Courtesy of the Chicago Historical Society.)*

a primitive sampling device—something like an oceanographer taking a core sample from the ocean floor—to include everything from the posh milieu of the remnants of the Gold Coast, through the working world of the Loop, the industrial South Loop, and some of the public housing of the South Side. By taking such a slice of the city, she has extended the theory of interiors to the point where it becomes a theory of the city seen in its interiors.

What choices has Collins made? She has, first of all, photographed interiors without anyone in them. That deprives her of some resources for telling us about the city. It would be far easier to communicate ideas about Chicago as a social entity by showing Hugh Hefner entertaining in his palatial living room than by showing us the empty living room. Similarly, it would be easier for us to understand life in Chicago's Robert Taylor Homes if we saw the residents using the dangerous elevators and halls.

Nevertheless, choosing to photograph interiors without their inhabitants has given Collins a corresponding advantage. Without the distraction of people acting unpredictably in front of her camera, she made more carefully composed images than she otherwise could have. Her photographs have a thoughtfulness and formal balance that pictures made in the hurry of real-time interaction seldom achieve. We see just what she intends us to see, in the light she wants us to see it in, with all the details given the importance she thinks due them, and with all the resulting implications for our interpretation. We must be as thoughtful in interpreting these images as she has been in making them.

Collins has also overcome the disadvantage of the absence of people by photographing moments in the lives of these rooms which most fully indicate what usually goes on in them. We see the dining room of the Pacific Garden Mission with all the plates set out and the English muffins beside them, waiting for the mission's clientele to come and eat. We see the room where Marshall Field's employees make candy, just after the chocolate has been poured out to cool, at the moment between two crucial stages of candy making; we know the workers will soon be back to do the next step.

Further, she shows us a wide range of rooms, thus invoking a variety that characterizes the city, and makes us aware, however subliminally, of the array of activities that characterizes city life. Seeing the courtroom in the police headquarters at 11th and State reminds us that some of the men who sleep at the mission on some nights will be in that courtroom at other times, to be sentenced to spend the night in the drunk tank. We see all sorts of workplaces, from the boardrooms of major corporations to the studios in which craftsmen produce such rare artifacts as stained-glass windows or such commonplaces as the television weather report.

As a whole, these photographs emphasize the highly varied and interdependent character of city life. We are led to think, viewing such a collection of images, of what connects a major corporation with a small craft operation, what connects the apartments in the projects with those on the Gold Coast. We don't see the middle-aged black women leaving their own apartments in the housing projects and arriving on North State Parkway where they will spend the day cleaning someone else's infinitely more luxurious house, but seeing images of each apartment separately reminds us how many women make that trip, day after day and year after year.

Collins's images force some other reflections on us. We realize how the city changes. In one striking picture, we see the ornate lobby of the Chicago Theatre, in its heyday an up-to-date palace of oriental luxury. Now it is littered with tacky arcade video games. Simultaneously we remember that some things change faster than others. Lobbies of older Gold Coast apartment buildings look just as they did years ago, proving that a great preservative is wealth.

Even more striking is the way apartments in the South Side housing projects have come to resemble those of the Gold Coast. A trickle-down theory of fashion could explain this, but it is still difficult to tell the location of the apartment by simply looking at the furnishings. This ambiguity, created by our knowledge of the role of the photographer in creating such impressions, makes one pause to question. The apartments, photographed similarly and looking at least superficially alike, are still very different places and their inhabitants live very different lives.

Every photographic strategy lets you say some things at the cost of not saying others. These sacrifices are a small, and necessary, price to pay for learning as much as Collins teaches us. We leave her explorations of State Street with a deepened understanding of urban complexity, a fuller appreciation of the connections between the city's diverse elements, and a more detailed knowledge of what has happened and is still happening in Chicago.

References

Abbott, Berenice. 1964. *The World of Atget*. New York: Horizon.
———. 1973 (1939). *New York in the Thirties*. New York: Dover.
Aberle, David F. 1966. *The Peyote Religion among the Navaho*. Chicago: Aldine.
Ades, Dawn. 1976. *Photomontage*. New York: Pantheon.
Agee, James, and Walker Evans. 1960. *Let Us Now Praise Famous Men*. Boston: Houghton Mifflin.
Astin, Alexander W. 1968. Undergraduate Achievement and Institutional "Excellence." *Science* 161: 661–68.
Ball, Donald. 1967. An Abortion Clinic Ethnography. *Social Problems* 14: 293–301.
Banfield, Edward C. 1967. *The Moral Basis of a Backward Society*. New York: Free Press.
Banish, Roslyn. 1976. *City Families*. New York: Pantheon.
Barndt, Deborah. 1974. Toward a Visual Study of Society. Technical Report, College of Social Science, Michigan State University.
Baron, Harold M. 1968. Black Powerlessness in Chicago. *Transaction* 6 (November): 27–33.
Bazerman, Charles. 1981. What Written Knowledge Does: Three Examples of Academic Discourse. *Philosophy of Social Science* 11: 36–87.
Beck, Bernard and Howard S. Becker. 1969. Modest Proposals for Graduate Programs in Sociology. *American Sociologist* 4: 227–34. (Reprinted in this volume.)
Becker, Howard S. 1951. The Professional Dance Musician and His Audience. *American Journal of Sociology* 57: 136–44.
———. 1953a. Some Contingencies of the Professional Dance Musician's Career. *Human Organization* 12: 212–16.
———. 1953b. Becoming a Marihuana User. *American Journal of Sociology* 59: 235–43.
———. 1963. *Outsiders: Studies in the Sociology of Deviance*. New York: Free Press.

———. 1967a. Whose Side Are We On? *Social Problems* 14: 239–48.

———. 1967b. History, Culture and Subjective Experience. *Journal of Health and Social Behavior* 8: 163–76.

———. 1970a. *Sociological Work: Method and Substance.* Chicago: Aldine.

———. 1970b. The Struggle for Power on the Campus. In *Campus Power Struggle*, ed. Howard S. Becker. New Brunswick: Trans-action, Inc.

———. 1970c. Introduction: The Struggle for Power on Campus. In *Campus Power Struggle*, ed. Howard S. Becker. New Brunswick: Trans-action, Inc.

———. 1970d. Field Work Evidence. In Becker 1970a: 39–62.

———. 1974. Art as Collective Action. *American Sociological Review* 39: 767–76.

———. 1974. Photography and Sociology. *Studies in the Anthropology of Visual Communication* 1: 3–26. (Reprinted in this volume.)

———. 1982. *Art Worlds.* Berkeley: University of California Press.

———. 1985. *Writing for Social Scientists.* Chicago: University of Chicago Press.

———, and James W. Carper. 1956. The Elements of Identification with an Occupation. *American Sociological Review* 21: 341–48.

———. 1956. The Development of Identification with an Occupation. *American Journal of Sociology* 61: 281–98.

———. 1957. Adjustments to Conflicting Expectations in the Development of Identification with an Occupation. *Social Forces* 36: 51–56.

———, and Blanche Geer. 1957. Participant Observation and Interviewing: A Comparison. *Human Organization* 16: 28–32.

———, and Irving Louis Horowitz. 1972. Radical Politics and Sociological Research: Observations on Methodology and Ideology. *American Journal of Sociology* 78: 48–66. (Reprinted in this volume.)

———, et al. 1961. *Boys in White: Student Culture in Medical School.* Chicago: University of Chicago Press.

———, et al. 1968. *Making the Grade: The Academic Side of College Life.* New York: John Wiley and Sons.

Benedict, Ruth. 1934. *Patterns of Culture.* Boston: Houghton Mifflin.

————. 1946. *The Chrysanthemum and the Sword*. New York: New American Library.

Bennett, James. n.d. Unpublished.

Biderman, Albert D., and Albert J. Reiss. 1967. On Exploring the "Dark Figure" of Crime. *Annals of the American Academy of Political and Social Science.*

Black, Donald J., and Maureen Mileski. 1967. Passing as Deviant: Methodological Problems and Tactics. Ann Arbor: Center for Research on Social Organization, University of Michigan (mimeo).

Blalock, H. M., Jr. 1969. On Graduate Methodology Training. *American Sociologist* 4: 5–6.

Blau, Peter M., and Otis Dudley Duncan. 1967. *The American Occupational Structure*. New York: Wiley.

Blum, Richard, et al. 1964. *Utopiates*. New York: Atherton.

Blumer, Herbert. 1967. Threats from Agency-Determined Research: The Case of Camelot. In *The Rise and Fall of Project Camelot*, ed. Irving L. Horowitz. Cambridge: MIT Press.

————. 1969. *Symbolic Interactionism*. Englewood Cliffs: Prentice-Hall.

Boccioletti, Lauro. 1972. Photography, the Law and You. *Freelance Photo News* 7: 1–6.

Borgatta, E. F. 1969. Some Notes on Graduate Education, with Special Reference to Sociology. *American Sociologist* 4: 6–12.

Bourdieu, Pierre, et al. 1965. *Un art moyen: Essai sur les usages sociaux de la photographie*. Paris: Les Editions de Minuit.

Bourke-White, Margaret. 1972. *The Photographs of Margaret Bourke-White*. Greenwich: New York Graphic Society.

————, and Erskine Caldwell. 1937. *You Have Seen Their Faces*. New York: Viking.

Brassaï. 1976. *The Secret Paris of the Thirties*. New York: Pantheon.

Bryan, James H. 1965. Apprenticeships in Prostitution. *Social Problems* 12: 287–97.

————. 1966. Occupational Ideologies and Individual Attitudes of Call Girls. *Social Problems* 13: 441–50.

Buckner, H. Taylor. 1964. Deviant Group Organizations. Unpublished master's thesis, University of California, Berkeley.

Cameron, Mary Owen. 1964. *The Booster and the Snitch*. New York: Free Press.

Campbell, Donald C. 1969. The Ethnocentrism of Disciplines and the Fishscale Model of Omniscience. In *Interdisciplinary Rela-*

tionships in the Social Sciences, ed. Muzafer Sherif. Chicago: Aldine.

———. 1969. Prospective: Artifact and Control. In *Artifact in Behavioral Research*, ed. R. Rosenthal and R. L. Rosnow. New York: Academic Press.

———, and J. C. Stanley. 1966. *Experimental and Quasi-Experimental Designs for Research*. Chicago: Rand McNally.

Cancian, Frank. 1974. *Another Place*. San Francisco: Scrimshaw.

Cartier-Bresson, Henri. 1952. *The Decisive Moment*. New York: Simon and Schuster.

Castaneda, Carlos. 1968. *The Teachings of Don Juan*. Berkeley: University of California Press.

Cavan, Sherri. 1966. *Liquor License: An Ethnography of Bar Behavior*. Chicago: Aldine.

Cayton, Horace, and St. Clair Drake. 1945. *Black Metropolis*. New York: Harcourt, Brace, and Co.

Cicourel, Aaron. 1967. *The Social Organization of Juvenile Justice*. New York: John Wiley and Sons.

Clark, Larry. 1971. *Tulsa*. New York: Lustrum Press.

Clifford, James. 1983. On Anthropological Authority. *Representations* 1: 118–46.

Clute, K. F. 1963. *The General Practitioner: A Study of Medical Education and Practice in Ontario and Nova Scotia*. Toronto: University of Toronto Press.

Cohen, Patricia Cline. 1982. *A Calculating People: The Spread of Numeracy in Early America*. Chicago: University of Chicago Press.

Coleman, James S., Elihu Katz, and Herbert Menzel. 1966. *Medical Innovation*. Indianapolis: Bobbs-Merrill.

Collier, John, Jr. 1967. *Visual Anthropology: Photography as a Research Method*. New York: Holt, Rinehart and Winston.

Cressey, Donald R. 1953. *Other People's Money*. New York: Free Press.

Dahl, Robert. 1961. *Who Governs?* New Haven: Yale University Press.

Davidson, Bruce. 1970. *East 100th Street*. Cambridge: Harvard University Press.

Davis, Allison. 1950. *Social Class Influences upon Learning*. Cambridge: Harvard University Press.

Davis, Kingsley, and Wilbert Moore. 1945. Some Principles of Stratification. *American Sociological Review* 10 (April): 242–249.

de Carava, Roy, and Langston Hughes. 1967 (1955). *The Sweet Flypaper of Life*. New York: Hill and Wang.

De Cock, Liliane, and Reginald McGhee. 1973. *James Van Der Zee*. Hastings-on-Hudson: Morgan and Morgan.

Diesing, Paul. 1971. *Patterns of Discovery in the Social Sciences*. Chicago: Aldine-Atherton.

Dolby, James, and Nancy Clark. n.d. Unpublished.

Domhoff, G. William. 1970. *The Higher Circles: The Governing Class in America*. New York: Vintage Books.

————. 1974. *The Bohemian Grove and Other Retreats: A Study in Ruling Class Cohesiveness*. New York: Harper and Row.

Duff, Euan. 1971. *How We Are*. London: Allen Lane, The Penguin Press.

————, and Dennis Marsden. 1975. *Workless*. London: Penguin.

Dumont, L. 1969. Caste, Racism, and Stratification: Reflections of a Social Anthropologist. In *Social Inequality: Selected Readings*, ed. André Béteille. Baltimore: Penguin.

Durkheim, Émile. 1951. *Suicide*. Glencoe: Free Press.

Dye, Thomas R., Eugene R. De Clerq, and John W. Pickering. 1973. Concentration, Specialization, and Interlocking among Institutional Elites. *Social Science Quarterly* 54 (June): 8–28.

Eells, Kenneth, et al. 1951. *Intelligence and Cultural Differences*. Chicago: University of Chicago Press.

Emerson, Richard M. 1966. Mount Everest: A Case Study of Communication Feedback and Sustained Group Goal-Striving. *Sociometry* 29: 64–70.

Erikson, Kai T. 1962. Notes on the Sociology of Deviance. *Social Problems* 9: 307–14.

Erwitt, Elliott. 1972. *Photographs and Anti-Photographs*. Greenwich: New York Graphic Society.

Estrin, Mary Lloyd. 1979. *To the Manor Born*. Boston: New York Graphic Society.

Etzioni, Amitai. 1968. Confessions of a Professor Caught in a Revolution. *New York Times Magazine* (Sept. 15).

Evans, Walker. 1966. *Many Are Called*. Boston: Houghton Mifflin.

————. 1975 (1938). *American Photographs*. New York: East River Press.

Evans-Pritchard, E. E. 1940. *The Nuer*. New York: Oxford University Press.

Feuer, Lewis. 1969. *The Conflict of Generations*. New York: Basic.

Forsyth, S., and P. M. Kolenda. 1966. Competition, Cooperation and Group Cohesion in the Ballet Company. *Psychiatry* 29: 123–45.

Frank, Robert. 1969 (1959). *The Americans*. New York: Aperture.

Freed, Leonard. 1970. *Made in Germany*. New York: Grossman.

Freedman, Jill. 1975. *Circus Days*. New York: Harmony Books.

Freidson, Eliot L. 1961. *Patients' Views of Medical Practice*. New York: Russell Sage Foundation.

———. 1970a. *The Profession of Medicine*. New York: Dodd, Mead.

———. 1970b. *Professional Dominance*. Chicago: Aldine-Atherton.

Friends of Photography. 1972. *Untitled 2 and 3*. Carmel: Friends of Photography.

Fry, Edward. 1972. The Post-Liberal Artist. *Art and Artists* (February): 33–34.

Fusco, Paul, and George D. Horowitz. 1970. *La Causa*. New York: Collier.

Gardner, Alexander. 1959 (1866). *Gardner's Photographic Sketchbook of the Civil War*. New York: Dover.

Gardner, Burleigh, and William F. Whyte. 1946. Methods for the Study of Human Relations in Industry. *American Sociological Review* 11: 506–12.

Geer, Blanche. 1964. First Days in the Field. In *Sociologists at Work*, ed. Phillip Hammond. New York: Basic.

———. 1968. Teaching. In *International Encyclopedia of the Social Sciences*, Vol. 15, 560–65. New York: Macmillan and the Free Press.

———. 1972. *Learning to Work*. Beverly Hills: Sage Publications.

Geertz, Clifford. 1983. Slide-show: Evans-Pritchard's African Transparencies. *Raritan* 3: 62–80.

Gibbs, Jack P. 1966. Conceptions of Deviant Behavior: New and Old. *Pacific Sociological Review* 9: 9–14.

Gidal, Tim N. 1973. *Modern Photojournalism: Origin and Evolution, 1910–1933*. New York: Collier.

Ginger, Ray. 1949. *The Bending Cross*. New Brunswick: Rutgers University Press.

Gitlin, Todd. 1980. *The Whole World Is Watching*. Berkeley: University of California Press.

Glaser, Barney G., and Anselm L. Strauss. 1967. *The Discovery of Grounded Theory*. Chicago: Aldine.

Goffman, Erving. 1961. *Asylums*. Garden City: Doubleday.

———. 1971. *Relations in Public: Microstudies of the Public Order*. New York: Basic.

————. 1983. The Interaction Order. *American Sociological Review* 48: 1–17.

Gombrich, E. J. 1960. *Art and Illusion: A Study in the Psychology of Pictorial Representation*. Princeton: Princeton University Press.

Goodman, Paul. 1968. Mini-Schools: A Prescription for the Reading Problem. *New York Review of Books* 9: 16–18.

Gowers, Sir Ernest. 1962 (1954). *The Complete Plain Words*. Baltimore: Penguin.

Gusfield, Joseph. 1981. *The Culture of Public Problems: Drinking-Driving and the Symbolic Order*. Chicago: University of Chicago Press.

Gutman, Judith Mara. 1967. *Lewis W. Hine and the American Social Conscience*. New York: Walker and Company.

Haacke, Hans. 1975. *Framing and Being Framed: Seven Works, 1970–75*. Halifax: The Press of the Nova Scotia College of Art and Design.

Haas, Jack. 1972. Binging: Educational Control among High Steel Ironworkers. In *Learning to Work*, ed. Blanche Geer, 31–38. Beverly Hills: Sage Publications.

Hall, Edward T. 1958. *The Silent Language*. New York: Doubleday.

Hall, Oswald. 1948. The Stages of a Medical Career. *American Journal of Sociology* 53: 327–36.

Hansberry, Lorraine. 1964. *The Movement*. New York: Simon and Schuster.

Hardt, Robert H., and George E. Bodine. 1965. *Development of Self-Report Instruments in Delinquency Research*. Syracuse: Youth Development Center, Syracuse University.

Harris, R. 1964. *The Real Voice*. New York: Macmillan.

Henslin, James. 1967. Craps and Magic. *American Journal of Sociology* 73: 316–30.

Herndon, James. 1968. *The Way It Spozed To Be*. New York: Bantam.

Hersey, John. 1980. The Legend on the License. *Yale Review* 70: 1–25.

Hersh, Seymour. 1968. *Chemical and Biological Warfare: America's Hidden Arsenal*. Indianapolis: Bobbs-Merrill.

Hill, Richard J. 1969. On the Relevance of Methodology. *Et. Al.* 2: 26–29.

Hoffman, Theodore. n.d. The Acting Student: Species, Habitat, Behavior. Unpublished.

Holt, John. 1967. *How Children Learn*. New York: Pitman.

Hooker, Evelyn T. 1965. Male Homosexuals and Their "Worlds." In *Sexual Inversion*, ed. Judd Marmor. New York: Basic Books.
————. 1967. The Homosexual Community. In *Sexual Deviance*, ed. John H. Gagnon and William Simon. New York: Harper and Row.
Horan, J. D. 1955. *Mathew Brady, Historian with a Camera*. New York: Bonanza.
————. 1966. *Timothy O'Sullivan: America's Forgotten Photographer*. New York: Bonanza.
Horowitz, David. 1969. Sinews of Empire. *Ramparts* 8 (October): 32–42.
Horowitz, Irving Louis. 1968. *Professing Sociology: Studies in the Life Cycle of a Social Science*. Chicago: Aldine-Atherton.
————, and William H. Friedland. 1970. *The Knowledge Factory: Student Power and Academic Politics in America*. Chicago: Aldine-Atherton.
————, and Martin Leibowitz. 1968. Social Deviance and Political Marginality: Toward a Redefinition of the Relation between Sociology and Politics. *Social Problems* 15: 280–96.
House Government Operations Committee. 1971. Hearings, May 3–5, May 26. Washington: Government Printing Office.
Hughes, Everett C. 1971. *The Sociological Eye*. Chicago: Aldine-Atherton.
Humphreys, R. A. Laud. 1970. *Tearoom Trade*. Chicago: Aldine.
Hunter, Floyd. 1953. *Community Power Structure: A Study of Decision Makers*. Chapel Hill: University of North Carolina Press.
Hurley, F. Jack. 1972. *Portrait of a Decade*. Baton Rouge: Louisiana State University Press.
————. 1973. Russell Lee. *Image* 16 (3): 1–8.
Ivins, William, Jr. 1953. *Prints and Visual Communication*. Cambridge: MIT Press.
Jackson, Bruce. 1977. *Killing Time: Life in the Arkansas Penitentiary*. Ithaca: Cornell University Press.
Jacobs, Philip. 1957. *Changing Values in College: An Exploratory Study of the Impact of College Teaching*. New York: Harper.
Kertész, André. 1972. *Sixty Years of Photography*. New York: Grossman.
Kitsuse, John I. 1962. Societal Reaction to Deviance: Problems of Theory and Method. *Social Problems* 9: 247–56.
————, and Aaron Cicourel. 1963. A Note on the Use of Official Statistics. *Social Problems* 11: 131–39.

Kluckhohn, Clyde. 1945. The Personal Document in Anthropology. In *The Use of Personal Documents in History, Anthropology, and Sociology*, ed. Louis Gottschalk, Clyde Kluckhohn, and Robert C. Angell. New York: Social Science Research Council.

Knowles, John C. 1973. The Rockefeller Financial Group. In *Superconcentration/Supercorporation*, ed. Ralph L. Andreano. Andover: Warner Modular Publications.

Koch-Weser, Jan, et al. 1969. Factors Determining Physician Reporting of Adverse Drug Reactions. *New England Journal of Medicine* 280: 20–26.

Kroeber, Alfred, and Clyde Kluckhohn. 1963. *Culture: A Critical Review of Concepts and Definitions*. New York: Vintage Books.

———, and Talcott Parsons. 1958. The Concepts of Culture and of Social System. *American Sociological Review* 23: 582–83.

Kuhn, Thomas. 1962. *The Structure of Scientific Revolutions*. Chicago: University of Chicago Press.

Latour, Bruno. 1983. Give Me a Laboratory and I Will Raise the World. In *Science Observed*, ed. Karin D. Knorr-Cetina and Michael Mulkay. Beverly Hills: Sage Publications.

———. 1984. *Les microbes: guerre et paix (suive de) Irréductions*. Paris: A.-J. Métaillié.

———. 1985. Visualization and Cognition: Thinking with Eyes and Hands. In *Knowledge and Society*, ed. H. Kuclick. New York: JAI Press.

———, and Françoise Bastide. 1983. Essai de Science-Fabrication: Mise en evidence experimentale du processus de construction de la réalité pour l'application de methodes socio-semiotiques aux textes scientifiques. *Etudes Françaises* 19: 111–33.

———, and Steve Woolgar. 1979. *Laboratory Life: The Social Construction of Scientific Fact*. Beverly Hills: Sage Publications.

Lee, Nancy Howell. 1969. *The Search for an Abortionist*. Chicago: University of Chicago Press.

Lemert, Edwin M. 1951. *Social Pathology*. New York: McGraw-Hill.

———. 1962. Paranoia and the Dynamics of Exclusion. *Sociometry* 26: 1–20.

Lennard, Henry, et al. 1972. *Mystification and Drug Misuse*. New York: Harper and Row.

Lerman, Paul. 1967. Argot, Symbolic Deviance and Subcultural Delinquency. *American Sociological Review* 32: 209–24.

Lesy, Michael. 1973. *Wisconsin Death Trip*. New York: Pantheon.

————. 1976. *Real Life: Louisville in the Twenties.* New York: Pantheon.

Levine, Edward. 1972. Chicago's Art World. *Urban Life and Culture* 1: 292–322.

Lieberson, Stanley. 1985. *Making It Count: The Improvement of Social Theory and Research.* Berkeley: University of California Press.

Lindesmith, Alfred. 1948. *Opiate Addiction.* Bloomington: Principia Press.

————. 1969. *Addiction and Opiates.* Chicago: Aldine.

Lofland, John. 1970. *Analyzing Social Settings.* Belmont: Wadsworth.

Lyon, Danny. 1968. *The Bikeriders.* New York: Macmillan.

————. 1969. *The Destruction of Lower Manhattan.* New York: Macmillan.

————. 1971. *Conversations with the Dead.* New York: Holt, Rinehart and Winston.

Lyons, Nathan, ed. 1966. *Contemporary Photographers: Toward a Social Landscape.* New York: Horizon.

————, ed. 1966. *Photographers on Photography.* Englewood Cliffs: Prentice-Hall.

Mandel, Jerry. 1966. Hashish, Assassins, and the Love of God. *Issues in Criminology* 2: 149–56.

Mandel, Mike, and Larry Sultan. 1977. *Evidence.* Santa Cruz: Clatworthy Colorvues.

Marshall, Hannah Meara. 1972. Structural Constraints on Learning: Butchers' Apprentices. In *Learning to Work,* ed. Blanche Geer, 39–48. Beverly Hills: Sage Publications.

Matthews, Donald R. 1954. *Social Background of the Political Decision Makers.* Garden City: Doubleday.

Maurer, David W. 1968. How to Consort with Con Men. *Psychiatric and Social Science Review* 2: 26–31.

Mayes, Elaine. 1970. Photographs of Haight-Ashbury . . . *Aperture* 15 (2), unpaged.

McCall, Michal. 1985. Life History and Social Change. *Studies in Symbolic Interaction* 6:169–82.

McCloskey, Donald N. 1983. The Rhetoric of Economics. *Journal of Economic Literature* 21: 481–517.

McCullin, Donald. 1973. *Is Anyone Taking Any Notice?* Cambridge: MIT Press.

Mead, Margaret, and Gregory Bateson. 1978. Margaret Mead and Gregory Bateson on the Use of the Camera in Anthropology. *Studies in Visual Communication* 4:78–80.

Mechanic, David. 1962. *Students under Stress*. New York: Free Press.

Meiselas, Susan. 1976. *Carnival Strippers*. New York: Farrar, Straus and Giroux.

Meltzer, Bernard. 1949. The Productivity of Social Scientists. *American Journal of Sociology* 53: 25–29.

Mennerick, Lewis A. 1972. External Control of Recruits: The Country Jail School. In *Learning to Work*, ed. Blanche Geer, 79–88. Beverly Hills: Sage Publications.

Mercer, Jane. 1973. *Labeling the Mentally Retarded*. Berkeley: University of California Press.

Miller, Delbert C. 1958. Decision Making Cliques in Community Power Structures: A Comparative Study of an American and English City. *American Journal of Sociology* 54: 299–309.

Miller, Stephen J. 1970. *Prescription for Excellence*. Chicago: Aldine.

Mills, C. Wright. 1940. Situated Actions and Vocabularies of Motives. *American Sociological Review* 5: 904–13.

———. 1956. *The Power Elite*. New York: Oxford University Press.

Molotch, Harvey, and Marilyn Lester. 1974. News as Purposive Behavior: On the Strategic Use of Routine Events, Accidents, and Scandals. *American Sociological Review* 39: 101–12.

Morganstern, Oskar. 1963. *On the Accuracy of Economic Observations*. Princeton: Princeton University Press.

Moulin, Raymonde. 1967. *Le marché de la peinture en France*. Paris: Les Editions de Minuit.

Museum of Modern Art. 1968. *Brassäi*. Greenwich: New York Graphic Society.

Myers, John Bernard. 1983. The Art Biz. *New York Review of Books* (December 2): 39–42.

Myrdal, Gunnar. 1944. *An American Dilemma*. New York: Harper and Brothers.

NACLA (North American Congress on Latin America). 1968. *Who Rules Columbia?* New York: NACLA.

Natali, Enrico. 1972. *New American People*. Hastings-on-Hudson: Morgan and Morgan.

Newhall, Beaumont. 1964. *The History of Photography*. New York: Museum of Modern Art.

New, Peter Kong-Ming, and Rhea Pendergrass Priest. 1968. Problems of Obtaining a Sample in a Study of Deviancy: A Case of Failure. *Social Science and Medicine* 1: 250–54.

Nicolaus, Martin. 1969. The Professional Organization of Sociology: A View from Below. *Antioch Review* 29 (Fall): 375–87.

Northwestern University Law Review. 1973. Research Study: Public Access to Information. *Northwestern University Law Review* 68 (2): entire issue.

Notkin, Marilyn. 1972. Situational Learning in a School with Clients. In *Learning to Work*, ed. Blanche Geer, 49–58. Beverly Hills: Sage Publications.

Oberschall, Anthony. 1972. The Institutionalization of American Sociology. In *The Establishment of Empirical Sociology*, ed. Anthony Oberschall. New York: Harper and Row.

Ogburn, William F. 1922. *Social Change*. New York: Viking.

Olesen, Virginia, and Elvi W. Whittaker. 1968. *The Silent Dialogue*. San Francisco: Jossey-Bass.

Orth, Charles D., III. 1963. *Social Structure and Learning Climate*. Cambridge: Harvard Graduate School of Business Administration.

Orwell, George. 1954. *A Collection of Essays*. Garden City: Doubleday.

Owens, Bill. 1973. *Suburbia*. San Francisco: Straight Arrow Books.

Palfi, Marion. 1973. *Invisible in America*. Lawrence: University of Kansas Art Museum.

Park, Robert E., and Ernest W. Burgess. 1921. *Introduction to the Science of Sociology*. Chicago: University of Chicago Press.

Penn, Irving. 1974. *Worlds in a Small Room*. New York: Viking.

Peterson, O. L., et al. 1956. An Analytical Study of North Carolina General Practice, 1953–54. *Journal of Medical Education* 31: 1–165.

Platt, Anthony. 1971. *The Politics of Riot Commissions*. New York: Collier.

Polsky, Ned. 1967. *Hustlers, Beats and Others*. Chicago: Aldine.

Ragin, Charles, Susan E. Mayer, and Kriss A. Drass. 1984. Assessing Discrimination: A Boolean Approach. *American Sociological Review* 49: 221–34.

Rainwater, Lee, and William L. Yancey. 1967. *The Moynihan Report and the Politics of Controversy*. Cambridge: MIT Press.

Ransom, David. 1970. The Berkeley Mafia and the Indonesian Massacre. *Ramparts* 9 (October): 27–29, 40–49.

Read, Herbert. 1952. *English Prose Style*. Boston: Beacon Press.

Redfield, Robert. 1941. *The Folk Culture of Yucatan*. Chicago: University of Chicago Press.

Reiss, Albert J. 1961. The Social Integration of Peers and Queers. *Social Problems* 9: 102–19.

Riis, Jacob A. 1971 (1890). *How the Other Half Lives*. New York: Dover.

Rorty, Richard. 1979. *Philosophy and the Mirror of Nature*. Princeton: Princeton University Press.

————. 1982. *Consequences of Pragmatism*. Minneapolis: University of Minnesota Press.

Rose, Arnold. 1967. *The Power Structure: Political Processes in American Society*. New York: Oxford University Press.

Rosenblum, Barbara. 1978. *Photographers at Work*. New York: Holmes and Meiers.

Roth, Julius. 1963. *Timetables*. Indianapolis: Bobbs-Merrill.

Ruby, Jay. 1972. Up the Zambesi with Notebook and Camera or Being an Anthropologist without Doing Anthropology . . . With Pictures. Paper presented at the 71st Annual Meeting of the American Anthropological Association, Toronto.

Ryan, William. 1971. *Blaming the Victim*. New York: Pantheon.

Salomon, Erich. 1967. *Portrait of an Epoch*. New York: Macmillan.

Sampson, Harold, Sheldon L. Messinger, and Robert D. Towne. 1965. *Schizophrenic Women*. New York: Atherton.

Sander, August. 1973. *Men without Masks*. Greenwich: New York Graphic Society.

Schacter, Stanley, and Jerome Singer. 1962. Cognitive, Social and Physiological Determinants of Emotional State. *Psychological Review* 69: 377–99.

Schatzman, Leonard, and Anselm L. Strauss. 1973. *Field Research: Strategies for a Natural Sociology*. Englewood Cliffs: Prentice-Hall.

Scheff, Thomas J. 1966. *Being Mentally Ill*. Chicago: Aldine.

Schelling, Thomas C. 1963. *The Strategy of Conflict*. Cambridge: Harvard University Press.

Scherer, Joanna Cohan. 1975. You Can't Believe Your Eyes: Inaccuracies in Photographs of North American Indians. *Studies in the Anthropology of Visual Communication* 2: 67–86.

Schur, Edwin M. 1969. Reactions to Deviance: A Critical Assessment. *American Journal of Sociology* 75: 309–22.

Schwartz, Richard D., and Jerome H. Skolnick. 1962. Two Studies of Legal Stigma. *Social Problems* 10: 133–42.

Seaman, Barbara. 1969. *The Doctor's Case against the Pill*. New York: Peter H. Wyden.

Sekula, Allan. 1975. The Instrumental Image: Steichen at War. *Artforum* (December): 26–35.

Shils, Edward. 1969. Plenitude and Scarcity. *Encounter* 32 (May): 37–48.

Sibley, Elbridge. 1963. *The Education of Sociologists in the United States*. New York: Russell Sage Foundation.

Siegel, Jeanne. 1971. Interview with Hans Haacke. *Arts Magazine* (May): 18–21.

Skolnick, Jerome. 1966. *Justice without Trial*. New York: John Wiley and Sons.

Slavin, Neil. 1972. *Portugal*. New York: Lustrum Press.

Smith, Roberta. 1982. Schnabel the Vincible. *Village Voice* (November 2).

Smith, W. Eugene. 1969. *His Photographs and Notes*. New York: Aperture.

———, and Aileen M. Smith. 1974. Minamata, Japan. *Camera35* 18(2): 26–51.

———. 1975. *Minamata*. New York: Holt, Rinehart and Winston.

Snyder, Wendy. 1970. *Haymarket*. Cambridge: MIT Press.

Steichen, Edward. 1963. *A Life in Photography*. Garden City: Doubleday.

Stock, Dennis. 1970. *California Trip*. New York: Grossman.

Stott, William. 1973. *Documentary Expression and Thirties America*. New York: Oxford University Press.

Strand, Paul. 1971. *A Retrospective Monograph*. New York: Aperture.

Stryker, Roy, and Nancy Wood. 1973. *In This Proud Land*. Greenwich: New York Graphic Society.

Sumner, William Graham. 1907. *Folkways*. Boston: Ginn and Co.

Sutherland, J. A. 1976. *Victorian Novelists and Publishers*. Chicago: University of Chicago Press.

Tax, Sol. 1941. World View and Social Relations in Guatemala. *American Anthropologist* 43: 27–47.

Tice, George A. 1972. *Paterson*. New Brunswick: Rutgers University Press.

Tomkins, Calvin. 1983. Season's End. *New Yorker* (July 10): 80–83.

Tuchman, Gaye. 1978. *Making News: A Study in the Construction of Reality*. New York: Free Press.

Tumin, Melvin W. 1953. Some Principles of Stratification: A Critical Analysis. *American Sociological Review* 18: 387–93.

Turner, Alwyn Scott. 1970. *Photographs of the Detroit People*. Detroit: Alwyn Scott Turner.

Vidich, Arthur, Joseph Bensman, and Maurice R. Stein. 1964. *Reflections on Community Studies*. New York: Harper and Row.

Vincent, Clark E. 1961. *Unmarried Mothers*. New York: Free Press.

Waller, Willard. 1932. *Sociology of Teaching*. New York: John Wiley and Sons.

Walton, John. 1966. Discipline, Method and Community Power: A Note on the Sociology of Knowledge. *American Sociological Review* 31: 684–89.

Wax, Murray, Rosalie Wax, and Robert Dumont. 1964. Formal Education in an Indian Community. *Social Problems* 11 (Spring, Supplement).

Weber, Max. 1957. *The Theory of Social and Economic Organization*, ed. Talcott Parsons. Glencoe: Free Press.

Weegee. 1945. *Naked City*. New York: Essential Books.

Winningham, Geoff. 1971. *Friday Night in the Coliseum*. Houston: Allison Press.

———. 1972. *Going Texan*. Houston: Mavis P. Kelsey, Jr.

Woods, Clyde. 1972. Students without Teachers: Student Culture at a Barber College. In *Learning to Work*, ed. Blanche Geer, 19–29. Beverly Hills: Sage Publications.

Worth, Sol, and John Adair. 1972. *Through Navajo Eyes*. Bloomington: Indiana University Press.

Yablonsky, Lewis. 1968. On Crime, Violence, LSD, and Legal Immunity for Social Scientists. *American Sociologist* 3: 254.

Zeitlin, Maurice. 1974. Corporate Ownership and Control: The Large Corporation and the Capitalist Class. *American Journal of Sociology* 79: 1073–1119.

Index